Studies in Childhood and Youth

Series Editors: **Allison James**, Professor Emerita, University of Sheffield, UK, and **Adrian James**, Professor Emeritus, University of Sheffield, UK.

Titles include:

Kate Bacon
TWINS IN SOCIETY
Parents, Bodies, Space and Talk

Emma Bond
CHILDHOOD, MOBILE TECHNOLOGIES AND EVERYDAY EXPERIENCES
Changing Technologies = Changing Childhoods?

David Buckingham, Sara Bragg and Mary Jane Kehily
YOUTH CULTURES IN THE AGE OF GLOBAL MEDIA

David Buckingham and Vebjørg Tingstad (*editors*)
CHILDHOOD AND CONSUMER CULTURE

Tom Cockburn
RETHINKING CHILDREN'S CITIZENSHIP

Sam Frankel
CHILDREN, MORALITY AND SOCIETY

Abigail Hackett, Lisa Procter and Julie Seymour (*editors*)
CHILDREN'S SPATIALITIES
Embodiment, Emotion and Agency

Allison James
SOCIALISING CHILDREN

Allison James, Anne Trine Kjørholt and Vebjørg Tingstad (*editors*)
CHILDREN, FOOD AND IDENTITY IN EVERYDAY LIFE

Nicholas Lee
CHILDHOOD AND BIOPOLITICS
Climate Change, Life Processes and Human Futures

Manfred Liebel, Karl Hanson, Iven Saadi and Wouter Vandenhole (*editors*)
CHILDREN'S RIGHTS FROM BELOW
Cross-Cultural Perspectives

Orna Naftali
CHILDREN, RIGHTS AND MODERNITY IN CHINA
Raising Self-Governing Citizens

Helen Stapleton
SURVIVING TEENAGE MOTHERHOOD
Myths and Realities

E. Kay M. Tisdall, Andressa M. Gadda and Udi M. Butler
CHILDREN AND YOUNG PEOPLE'S PARTICIPATION AND ITS
TRANSFORMATIVE POTENTIAL
Learning from across Countries

Afua Twum-Danso Imoh and Robert Ame (*editors*)
CHILDHOODS AT THE INTERSECTION OF THE LOCAL AND THE GLOBAL

Hanne Warming (*editor*)
PARTICIPATION, CITIZENSHIP AND TRUST IN CHILDREN'S LIVES

Karen Wells, Erica Burman, Heather Montgomery and Alison Watson (*editors*)
CHILDHOOD, YOUTH AND VIOLENCE IN GLOBAL CONTEXTS
Research and Practice in Dialogue

Rebekah Willett, Chris Richards, Jackie Marsh, Andrew Burn and Julia
C Bishop (*editors*)
CHILDREN, MEDIA AND PLAYGROUND CULTURES
Ethnographic Studies of School Playtimes

Karen M. Smith
THE GOVERNMENT OF CHILDHOOD
Discourse, Power and Subjectivity

Eve Stirling and Dylan Yamada-Rice
VISUAL METHODS WITH CHILDREN AND YOUNG PEOPLE
Academics and Visual Industries in Dialogue

Spyros Spyrou and Miranda Christou
CHILDREN AND BORDERS

Rannevig Traustadóttir, Borgun Ytterhus, Snæfríður Egilson and Berit Berg
CHILDHOOD AND DISABILITY IN THE NORDIC COUNTRIES
Being, Becoming, Belonging

Studies in Childhood and Youth
Series Standing Order ISBN 978–0–230–21686–0 hardback
(*outside North America only*)

You can receive future titles in this series as they are published by placing a
standing order. Please contact your bookseller or, in case of difficulty, write to
us at the address below with your name and address, the title of the series and
the ISBN quoted above.

Customer Services Department, Macmillan Distribution Ltd, Houndmills,
Basingstoke, Hampshire RG21 6XS, England

Children's Spatialities

Embodiment, Emotion and Agency

Edited by

Abigail Hackett
University of Sheffield, UK

Lisa Procter
University of Sheffield, UK

Julie Seymour
University of Hull, UK

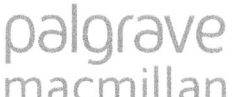

First published 2015 by
PALGRAVE MACMILLAN

Palgrave Macmillan in the UK is an imprint of Macmillan Publishers Limited,
registered in England, company number 785998, of Houndmills, Basingstoke,
Hampshire RG21 6XS.

Palgrave Macmillan in the US is a division of St Martin's Press LLC,
175 Fifth Avenue, New York, NY 10010.

Palgrave Macmillan is the global academic imprint of the above companies
and has companies and representatives throughout the world.

Palgrave® and Macmillan® are registered trademarks in the United States,
the United Kingdom, Europe and other countries.

ISBN 978–1–137–46497–2

This book is printed on paper suitable for recycling and made from fully
managed and sustained forest sources. Logging, pulping and manufacturing
processes are expected to conform to the environmental regulations of the
country of origin.

A catalogue record for this book is available from the British Library.

Library of Congress Cataloging-in-Publication Data
Children's spatialities : embodiment, emotion and agency / Abigail Hackett,
    Lisa Procter, Julie Seymour.
        pages cm. — (Studies in childhood and youth)
    ISBN 978–1–137–46497–2 (hardback)
    1. Space perception in children.   2. Spatial behavior.   3. Child
    development.   4. Child psychology.   I. Hackett, Abigail, 1980–
    editor.   II. Procter, Lisa, 1981– editor.   III. Seymour, Julie, editor.
    BF723.S63C46 2015
    155.4′13752—dc23   2015021833

Contents

Figures and Tables

Figures

Tables

Foreword

This important book takes up Foucault's challenge to examine the critical power of space and place in the being and becoming of children's lives:

> a whole history of spaces – which would be at the same time a history of powers – remains to be written, from the grand strategies of geopolitics to the little tactics of the habitat.
>
> Foucault, 1980, p. 149

Embracing 'the grand strategies of geopolitics to the little tactics of the habitat', this book's distinctive contribution lies in considering children's everyday worlds through the lens of space and place in order to open up new ways of understanding society and human experience. Written from the perspective of a number of different disciplines including geography, philosophy, anthropology, architecture and sociology, the terms space and place are used interchangeably, depending on the disciplinary affiliations of each individual chapter. This range of different disciplinary approaches produces a 'diffractive' reading across the book that operates to unsettle the very disciplinary boundaries within which they are generated and thus opens the possibility of new interdisciplinary conversations (Haraway, 2004).

I have previously explored the critical power of place in relation to researching subjugated knowledges, a category that in many ways applies to children's knowing (Somerville, 2012). I proposed a conceptual framework of place as a concept that bridges the material and symbolic, the local and global, and indigenous and non-indigenous knowledges. In each of these binaries, Western knowledge privileges one side of the binary as dominant or legitimate – the symbolic over the material, the global over the local, and the non-indigenous over the indigenous. I propose that place has critical power because it contains the possibility of reversing the order of privilege so that the material, the local and the indigenous can come to the fore. Place alerts us to the material effects of our discursive relations within the places where we live, work and play. The conceptual framework of place is thus proposed as the basis for a critical qualitative research.

In only one instance was I compelled to use the concept of space rather than place. I had visited a crowded demountable school classroom early in the day and watched the children navigate desks, chairs, boxes, hanging artworks and other objects that made up this decidedly classed school classroom. I thought about Lefebvre's contention that the whole of social space proceeds from the body (Lefebvre, 1991). I could see that the social space of this classroom was produced by these movements, bodies and objects, producing, in turn, the subjectivities of the children there. My attention was especially drawn to Mary, a child with Down's syndrome, moving awkwardly in this crowded space always accompanied by the appendage of an integration aide.

When I returned after school the teacher and the integration aide, still working in the well-worn classroom, invited me to watch a short DVD of the rehearsal for the Christmas concert. There on the interactive screen, larger than lifesize, the children came to life as frogs, dancing their frog dance to music made entirely of frog calls. In their visits to the local wetlands the children get to know the frogs from their specific frog calls. The classroom, cleared of debris, becomes the space of the wetlands. Children dance to frog calls moving frog limbs, fingers splayed, jumping, leap frogging, becoming frog to frog music. Mary, in particular, loves the performance, moving freely in this frog collective, unaccompanied by her integration aide. In one brief sequence towards the end she smiles pure pleasure into the camera, her body liberated in frog dance. I understand the critical power of space in this moment of Mary's becoming, made possible by an alternative imagination of the spaces of learning that includes the wetlands, digital technologies and a reconfigured school classroom.

The authors of the book, like the theorists they draw on, take up notions of space and place differently with some tending to use space or place primarily or exclusively, while others write about both space and place in relation to each other. The book introduces the reader to a rich overview of the theoretical possibilities of space and place ranging from the pioneering critical work of Lefebvre and Soja on how space is experienced in the everyday to Massey's spatio-temporal events and Ingold's wayfaring. While each of these theorists offers important possibilities for thinking through issues of space and place, children were not their primary area of interest. It is the authors in this book who bring children and space/place together to unsettle assumptions about everyday life in both directions. It asks: how does a consideration of children disrupt our taken-for-granted assumptions about space and place and how do the categories of space and place throw light on the formation of children's becomings in the world?

The book reveals that children of all ages have their own views and understandings of their worlds. It is also clear from some of the studies that like many other outsider groups within society, they may have little power, spending much of their time in places that are regulated by adults. Over the past decade and a half there has been increased interest in conducting research with children, as is evident within these pages. Children are understood as cultural producers and social actors in their own right rather than pre-adult becomings, actively involved in shaping their social and environmental transactions at a variety of socio-spatial scales. They articulate and construct their own unique perspective as dynamic members of their communities with different values regarding place and space from those of adults. The book allows us into these worlds of children. Rather than assuming they know less than adults, it becomes clear that they may know something and this 'something else' is of great interest in research with children.

In many parts of the world, it is still not unusual to find major national, regional or local policy agendas that make no specific reference to children and young people (Horton et al., 2013). Where children and young people do figure in policy discourses, their presence is often slight, circumscribed and precarious. Many policy and educational interventions with children and young people tend to be limited in their spatial scope, being overwhelmingly focused upon either learning in the classroom or behaviours in the home. This tendency underestimates the complexity of these places and overlooks the much more complexly distributed everyday ecologies of life courses and lifestyles. Such limitations preclude consideration of complex interconnections between everyday spaces and global processes (Horton et al., 2013, p. 250). It is these interrelationships that bring both 'the grand strategies of geopolitics and the little tactics of the habitat' together in this book.

Some important themes emerge through the critical lens of space and place. Space and children are both seen to be in a state of becoming through the actions of adults as well as children, and the more-than-human world of objects and other life forms. Embodiment and tacit knowing are seen to be important considerations as are identity and emotion. The need for a private space for their becomings emerges as crucial in research about energy use in bathrooms where children engage through their sensing bodies with everyday environments of showering and bathing. This need can be at least partly understood in terms of the over-regulation of children and public spaces/places evident in adult-designed children's playgrounds. At times in the book the quirky energy of children bursts forth, as in the girls who repeatedly visit the large stuffed bear who tickles them in the museum, or the girl who reconfigures time in her photography journey through the hallway of her house. The actions of *sliding, shifting, displaying* and *exceeding* in children's risk-taking play could offer metaphors for contemplating the complexity of children's self-directed playful analysis of their spatial intra-actions.

Through this book I have come to know children through entering into their worlds. I have come to know more about how the critical power of space and place offers a lens that disrupts taken for granted assumptions about how the world is. Most importantly *Children's Spatialities* invites us into the world of the future where different imaginings of children, space and place offer the possibility of shaping that future differently.

Margaret Somerville
Professor of Education
Director of the Centre for Educational Research
University of Western Sydney

References

Foucault, M. (1980) *Power/Knowledge: Selected Interviews and Other Writings 1972–1977*. Gordon, C. (Ed). Translated by Gordon, C. Marshall, L. Mepham, J. & Soper, K. New York: Pantheon Books.

Haraway, D. (2004) *The Haraway Reader*. London: Routledge.

Horton, J., Hadfield-Hill, S., Christensen, P. & Kraftl, P. (2013) Children, Young People and Sustainability. Local Environment: *The International Journal of Justice and Sustainability*, 18(3), 249–254.

Lefebvre, H. (1991) *The Production of Space*. Translated by Nicholson-Smith. Oxford: Basil Blackwell. Originally published 1974.

Somerville, M. (2012) 'The Critical Power of Place', in G. S. Cannella and S. Steinberg (eds) *Critical Qualitative Research Reader*, 67–81. New York: Peter Lang.

Acknowledgements

We would like to thank the following people for their helpful comments and suggestions: Penny Curtis, Kathryn Ecclestone, Allison James, Kate Pahl, Margaret Somerville.

Contributors

Matej Blazek is Lecturer in Human Geography at Loughborough University. He is a social geographer with an interest in the formation of agency, geography of marginalisation and community development, working usually with, for or as a practitioner.

Elizabeth Curtis is Lecturer in Primary Education (Social Studies) at the University of Aberdeen. She has a background in both archaeology and primary school teaching and specialises in teaching and researching how people make sense of time and place. Her current research focuses on what people learn through participation in community history and heritage projects organised through the Heritage Lottery funded All Our Stories project.

Abigail Hackett is a research associate at the Centre for the Study of Childhood and Youth, University of Sheffield. Her ethnographic research mainly focuses on the meaning-making of very young children, and she is also interested in collaborative approaches to research with community participants. Before completing her doctorate, Abi worked in the cultural sector, specialising in learning and community engagement, for a number of years.

Helle Skovbjerg Karoff is an associate professor at Aalborg University Copenhagen, Denmark. Her research examines the relationship between play, children and toys through the perspective of play as practices of moods. Helle also studies technology as a source of inspiration for play. In addition to seeing technology as a source of inspiration, she is interested in the interaction across traditional dichotomies such as technology/non-technology, and particularly how these dichotomies shift in relation to toys, technology, spaces and media.

Natalia Kucirkova graduated in psychology, holds a master's in research methods and a doctorate in education. She worked at the Oxford University Education Department, pursued a pre-doctoral fellowship at the Harvard Graduate School of Education and currently works as Lecturer in Developmental Psychology at the Open University. Her research concerns innovative ways of supporting shared book reading, digital literacy, community engagement and the role of personalisation in early years. Natalia's doctoral research inspired the development of the Our Story tablet/smartphone app. She has been commended for her engagement with teachers and parents at a national and international level.

Kerstin Leder Mackley is a research associate at the Loughborough Design School, UK. She has researched digital media, emerging technologies and everyday life in the context of domestic energy consumption (www.leedr-project.co.uk) and hot water futures (www. hothouse-project.co.uk). Her articles have appeared in a range of peer-reviewed journals, including *Media, Culture & Society*, *Sociological Research Online* and *Transactions on Computer-Human Interaction* (*TOCHI*).

Roxana Moroşanu holds a PhD from Loughborough University. Her doctoral research looked at questions related to everyday temporalities, human agency and domesticity in the context provided by an interdisciplinary project researching domestic energy consumption with British families. She co-edited the collection *Practices, the Built Environment and Sustainability: Responses to the Thinking Note Collection* (2015).

Sarah Pink is Professor of Design and Media Ethnography at RMIT University, Australia. She is a visiting professor at Loughborough University, UK, and Halmstad University, Sweden. Her books include *Doing Sensory Ethnography* (2nd edition, 2015), *Digital Ethnography: Principles and Practices* (co-authored 2015), *Doing Visual Ethnography* (3rd edition, 2013) and *Situating Everyday Life* (2012). In 2014 she launched the Energy and Digital Living website at http://energyanddigitalliving.com/.

Lisa Procter is Lecturer in Early Childhood Education at the School of Education, University of Sheffield. Her research explores the relationships between emotion, place and children's identities and meaning-making. Her work considers children's emotional engagements with place across a range of spaces including schools, green spaces and parks, neighbourhoods, and virtual spaces. Recent publications include 'Emotions, Schooling and Power: The Socialisation of "Angry Boys" ', *Journal of Political Power*, 6 (2013): 495–510; and 'Exploring the Role of Emotional Reflexivity in Research with Children', *Emotion, Space and Society*, 9 (2013): 80–88.

Mona Sakr is Lecturer in Education and Early Childhood at Middlesex University. Her research focuses on digital technologies in childhood, with a particular focus on how the digital re-shapes creative, playful and art-making experiences for young children. Current and previous research projects include a phenomenological analysis of children's experiences of digital augmentation during history learning, observation studies of collective digital art-making in early years educational settings and a case study of parent-child art-making with different technologies in the home.

Caterina Satta holds a PhD in sociology from the University of Padua and is currently a senior fellow at the University of Ferrara. She works in the field of sociology of childhood and everyday life. Her main research interests are children's spatialities and socio-spatial processes of exclusion/inclusion; children's culture and everyday life; play, sport and urban space. Her publications include *Bambini e adulti: La nuova sociologia dell'infanzia* (Carocci 2012); and 'Una città giusta è una città a misura di bambini? Note critiche su un immaginario urbano', *Mondi Migranti* 1 (2014). She is co-editing a special issue for *Modern Italy* on 'Sport and Public Space in Contemporary Italy'.

Julie Seymour is Senior Lecturer in Medical Sociology at the Hull York Medical School, Hull, United Kingdom. Her research interests focus on family and childhood practices in relation to domestic labour, health and illness, emotional labour, work–life balance and body donation. Recent publications include E. Dermott and J. Seymour (eds), *Displaying Families: A New Concept for the Sociology of Family Life* (2011), and J. Seymour, 'The Transgressive Potential of Families in Commercial Homes' in Casey and Taylor (eds) *Intimacies, Critical Consumption and Diverse Economies* (2015).

Helen Woolley is a chartered landscape architect and Reader in Landscape Architecture and Society at the University of Sheffield. Helen's research interests include children's and skateboarders' use of urban areas, playgrounds particularly for disabled children and green and open spaces. Helen also works with government departments, NGOs, national organisations, charities and commercial companies. She was a Commission for Architecture and the Built Environment (CABE) space advisor and is an alumni of the Japan Society for the Promotion of Science.

Introduction: Spatial Perspectives and Childhood Studies

Abigail Hackett, Lisa Procter and Julie Seymour

This book highlights how recognising the role of space can enhance understandings of children's ordinary, everyday experiences. Our aim is to connect spatial theory to the interdisciplinary field of childhood studies. We argue that spatial perspectives are central to understanding how children's practices and trajectories are situated within more-than-social contexts. They move beyond the notion of the individual agent to recognise that agency exists within and between the spaces where children's lives happen. Examining the entanglements between children and the worlds in which they are situated offers new perspectives on how spaces affect and shape children's experiences and frame how they choose to navigate their lives. Soja (1996, 2004) recommends 'putting space first as a critical interpretation perspective' (2004, p. ix), drawing on Lefebvre's (1991) promise that such a 'critical thirding'[1] (Soja, 1996, p. 5) has the possibility to disrupt, leading to new ways of understanding society and human experience. This, we argue, is crucial to rethinking the role of space in supporting childhood diversity and difference, where the multiplicity of childhood experiences and perspectives can be valued. This book is timely because it challenges an established policy context which positions children as 'becomings' rather than 'beings' (James et al., 1998), and thus prioritises interventions intended to direct how they develop and what they will become as adults. A spatial lens, in contrast, recognises the non-linearity of children's lives, by bringing to the fore the complex ways that children's meaning-making unfolds in dynamic exchange with the spaces and places they inhabit. In establishing situated understandings of children's lives, this book raises important questions for policy and practice. The theoretical and empirical work presented connects a wide range of disciplines, many of which do not start with space as the object of study. The contributions have applied resonance in relation to the development of a wide range of spaces used by children, including schools and nurseries, green spaces and play areas, museums and galleries, and streets and public spaces; by drawing on emerging conceptualisations of space and place, which connect with theories of embodiment, emotion and agency, they examine the interdependency between children's experiences and the material and immaterial worlds they inhabit. As such, this is a book about the intersectionality between space and children's everyday lives. In examining this intersection, we ask:

- What new insights and interpretations does a critical spatial perspective of children's everyday lives offer?
- What approaches and strategies are best for connecting (or dissolving the binary between) global and local conceptualisations of space/place in children's lives?
- What are the implications for spatial theory and practice when children's lives become the primary focus of research?

The three editors of this book have each crossed disciplines, from an area with an explicitly spatial focus (archaeology, architecture, geography) to research with children (in sociology, education), where bringing a spatial perspective is beneficial and brings us new insights. Hackett originally trained as an archaeologist, a discipline which is primarily historical, but locates this knowledge about life in the past within a spatial and material context of, for example, excavation and landscape. Her background shaped her attentiveness to the contextuality and subjectivity of human activity in place; for example, in considering phenomenological approaches to landscape archaeology (Tilley, 1994). With a first and second degree in architecture, Procter has a longstanding interest in the diverse ways in which people inhabit space. This background informs her educational research on the spatial dimensions of children's meaning-making. For Seymour, a sociological researcher, a first degree in geography meant intellectual training in which space was to the fore. The spatial epistemologies we adopt within our current research practice do not begin with space as an object of study, but as an analytic lens or interpretative perspective, and this is reflected in the purpose and positioning of this book. Social processes of children's everyday lives are at the heart of the contributions in this collection, and we highlight how these social processes take place in space. Spatiality is thus a lens to exemplify the underlying concepts within the interdisciplinary field of childhood studies. By spatiality we refer to Keith and Pile's (1993, p. 6) term for the ways in which the social and the spatial are 'inextricably realized one in another'.

Within our own work, we recognise the potential of a spatial lens for influencing policy and practice in relation to children's lives. Hackett's work around children's experience of museums reflects the central role of the embodied, engaged and sensory in children's meaning-making. Established theories of how children learn in museums stress the specialness of engaging with museum objects, and the potential of this to open up new possibilities for grasping concepts, asking questions or family conversation (e.g. Leinhardt et al., 2002). However, these theories did not fit well with the young children's physical, movement orientated experience of the museum place in Hackett's study. Spatial theories, particularly Ingold's (2007) work on wayfaring and Pink's (2009) writing on emplaced knowing, offer museum practitioners alternative, non-deficit ways of viewing how the youngest children come to know the museum. Procter's work is framed by a focus upon the opportunities and limits of children's agency in both the design and inhabitation of space. She considers the ways in which childhood emotions are enabled and constrained by spatial contexts. Her work presented in this volume draws on phenomenological orientations towards space and place, which foreground embodied perception in the ways that people inhabit place (see e.g. Trigg, 2012), and connect these spatial perspectives with sociological framings of the social construction of emotion in childhood. Finally, Seymour's work uses spatiality (Keith and Pile, 1993) as a lens to consider the production and impact of social processes within children's lives. Her recent work on children's experiences of family hotels (Seymour, 2007) connects with the recent explicit focus on space in the area of family sociology that has been evident at a range of scales: domestic space (Gabb, 2008; Seymour, 2011), spatially separate relationships (Duncan and Phillips, 2010) and transnational families (Baldasser and Merla, 2013). This work on family spatialities speaks directly to the development of family services, such as support for the 'left-behind' children of migrant parents. Our work, which explores different spaces of childhood – the museum, school and home, is connected through a shared commitment to the 'more than social' (Kraftl, 2013a) study of childhood, which has interrogated the agency of children through spatial illustrations, a number of which contribute to this volume.

Spaces, places and children's experiences

This book is framed by understandings of space as dynamic, political and socially constructed (Lefebvre, 1991; Soja, 1996; Massey, 2005) and an interest in lived space, or place, as imbued with personal meaning (Casey, 1996; Cresswell, 2004). These are understandings of space and place that sit within a wider cross-disciplinary interest in 'the spatial turn', as outlined by Warf and Arias (2009). Space is constantly in a state of becoming, and the actions and imaginations of adults, children and the non-human world play a part in this becoming. An overarching focus throughout this book is on the processes through which children construct space, and through which adults construct places for children (Fog Olwin and Gulløv, 2003; Rasmussen, 2004). The chapters are divided into three themed sections – embodiment, emotion and agency – reflecting the different ways in which they connect to this core understanding. We discuss the scope of each of these sections later in this introduction. Embodiment, emotion and agency each give us a route into the intersection between spatial theories and childhood studies, by foregrounding specific aspects of spatial perspectives, namely, phenomenological anthropology, emotional geographies and inter-generational studies, respectively. As such, the thematic organisation of the book offers three different lenses to enable us to ask distinct questions about the application of spatial theories to childhood studies.

- Embodiment: Are children more spatial and their experiences more embodied than those of adults, as has been famously argued by Tuan (1977)?
- Emotion: If emotions are produced through the relationships between places and bodies (Davidson et al., 2005), what are the implications for supporting children's emotional lives?
- Agency: If space is socially produced, as Lefebvre (1991) suggests, what are the potentials for children's agency, actions or perspectives within this process?

We explore the co-production of space through attending to five interconnected concepts, which weave their way through the three sections. The contributors to the book are interested in the **ongoingness** of space, and, as reflected in Mary Thomas' spatial study of multicultural girlhood (2011), see the unfolding production of space as closely tied to the formation of children's identities. Both space and identity are seen as in a constant process of being made and remade through emplaced social interactions (Procter, 2013a, 2013b), tacit knowledge (Hackett and Yamada Rice, 2015), imagination (Wood and Hall, 2011) and ideology (Hörschelmann and Colls, 2009). We are interested in the ways that children come to understand how their actions are both enabled and constrained within different spaces and places. We consider that these knowledges come from the **betweenness** of spatial experience, where children bring knowledges generated through their familiarity with one setting into those which are unfamiliar. Children's inhabitation of certain kinds of place and the ways in which **symbolic and tacit meanings** are attached to space by children (Christensen and O'Brien, 2003) are also recurring themes. Therefore, we consider children's ways of knowing as going beyond spoken or written knowledge, to include what is remembered or imagined by the body as well as the mind, and to a certain extent, is therefore unshareable and unknowable (Niedderer, 2007; Pink, 2009; Dicks, 2014). We are interested in the way in which spaces, and the meanings they evoke, 'matter' (Kraftl, 2013b) to children, and how these **matterings** and their felt **intensities** may be different in comparison to adult experiences and perceptions of space. We argue that the spaces ascribed to children are both political and ideological (see e.g. Gagen's (2006) exploration of early 20th century playgrounds), and that children's freedom is often constrained through access to space or through the way that spaces shape interactions (Youdell and Armstrong, 2011). However, we also attend to children's **subversion** of these controlling influences, as they create new ways of interacting with and in space. Additionally, if, as Lefebvre (1991) argued, '(social) space is a (social) product' (p. 26), we are interested in recognising the role of children in this social construction of space. We ask how processes of conceiving and perceiving space may work differently for children, and the implications of this for the versions of space and place that children produce or recognise.

While children's geographies has led the way in applying spatial theories to understanding children's lifeworlds and perspectives (e.g. Holloway and Valentine, 2000a; Holt, 2011; Hörschelmann and Colls, 2009; Kraftl, 2013a; Philo, 2000; Skelton and Valentine, 1997; Thomas, 2011), spatial theory has also been employed to support theory, methodology and analysis of childhood studies in diverse disciplines including anthropology (Christensen and O'Brien, 2003; Fog Olwin and Gulløv, 2003), literacy studies (Leander and Sheehy, 2004; Nichols et al., 2011), sociology (Kullman, 2014; Lomax, 2014; Seymour, 2007), gender studies (Thorne, 1993), education (Burke, 2013) and architecture (Parnell and Procter, 2011). Of particular note is the cross-fertilisation of ideas across children's geographies and social studies of childhood (Holloway and Valentine, 2000b). The idea for this edited collection came from our experiences of carrying out research in disciplines which were not necessarily 'spatial' but for which the literature of 'the spatial turn' brought fresh insights and new perspectives about the lives of children we sought to understand. Similarly, for many of the authors in this book, spatial theory was not the starting point for research, but added new insights and perspectives to the study. Thus, the purpose of this book is to make a contribution to the field of children's spatialities by bringing a range of theories on space and place, drawn from an explicitly multidisciplinary base (geography, philosophy, anthropology, architecture, sociology) together with empirical childhood studies. We hope to re-articulate what we mean by children, space and place, widen thinking about children and spatiality and, in doing so, develop new avenues for research.

A note on space and place

Different foundational writers on 'space' and 'place' have used these terms in a range of ways; in a book with an explicitly interdisciplinary focus, in which contributors are drawing on diverse spatial theorists, no single definition of space and place would be adequate. In this section, we draw some distinctions between the ways in which the terms space and place have been differently employed and defined, and how scholars have positioned these terms in relation to concepts including time, sociality and movement.

Space and place have been applied differently by different writers; some tend to use one or the other primarily or exclusively, while others write about them in relation to one another. For example, Lefebvre (1991) uses the word space to refer to the perceived, conceived and lived. Lived or social space, similar to what Soja (1996) in turn phrases 'third space', is closest to how space is experienced in the everyday. However, Casey (1996) (and Christensen, 2003, following Casey, 1996) makes similar distinctions between the abstract and embodied, but uses the term place as a contrast to abstract space. Cresswell (2004, p. 10) admits that while space and place are often treated as dualisms in geography, Lefebvre's concept of social space does confuse this distinction.

Massey (2005) critiques the distinction that Casey (1996), Tuan (1977) and others draw between space and place (in which place is seen to be more local or authentic), problematising what is meant by 'local' in an increasingly globalised world. Rather, Massey suggests that places can be seen as the coming together of spatial and temporal elements as 'spatio-temporal events' (p. 130). Issues of scale then, and particularly the relationship between local and global, embodied and abstract, remain the subject of debate (Holloway and Valentine, 2000b), with micro-scale studies of children's spatialities far outnumbering macro-scale structure-based research in this area (Ansell, 2009). This is reflected in Kjørholt's (2003) argument that both the micro and the macro are enacted in children's acts of place-making, with a distinct focus on children's hut-building practices in Norway. She states that a spatial lens can offer new insights into the ways that different scales intersect within children's lives, thus, she argues, attending to the neglected analysis of the affects of the global within childhood research.

The interrelationship between time, space and sociality remains a subject of debate in the literature. Soja (2004) argues that 19th century social science locked history and sociality together, and therefore space has historically been overlooked by social science. The critical spatial perspective of, for example, Lefebvre (1991) was concerned with re-addressing this balance, and encouraging an equal consideration of the social, historical and spatial. Soja traces the growing recognition of the spatial as an overlooked category of experience to the seminal work of Lefebvre and Foucault. Foucault (1995), for example, in his text 'Discipline and Punishment' recognised spatiality as an important mechanism of power. He showed how institutional spaces work upon the body, both enabling and restricting the body's movements and gestures. This work explored the role of both time and space in shaping individuals' inhabitation of institutional spaces. Drawing on Foucault, De Certeau (2011) also considers power and space in his work 'The Practice of Everyday Life' through a focus on how people inhabit the city. He argues that while structures of power ('strategies') shape the city, through, for example, the abstract production of space through mapping, the ways that people inhabit the city ('tactics') are never fully determined by these structures. His work recognises the transformational potential of time and sociality in resisting prescribed patternings of space, society and culture.

Massey (2005) sets her work as distinct from arguments that prioritise time over space by arguing that the important point is 'the *way* we imagine space' (p. 18, emphasis in original). Within Massey's (2005) concept of 'spatio-temporal events', movement is closely related to space; by taking a journey one is not merely travelling through space but is 'a participant in its continual construction' (p. 118). This perspective resonates with Ingold's (2007) theory of wayfaring, in which movement and perception result in 'placemaking' (p. 101). Massey (2005) connects journeying through time and space at a human level with flux and change of natural landscapes, which are also created through the spatio-temporal movements of, for example, melting glaciers and volcanic activity, albeit on a much slower timescale. At both a human and natural landscape level, fixity, boundedness and the antiquity of place is an illusion.

For many of the great writers on space and place that have inspired us, children were not their primary area of study. Therefore, in applying their theories about the spatiality of human behaviour and experience specifically to research with children, this book interrogates how transferable these theoretical ideas and methodological approaches are to the field of childhood studies.

Embodiment, emotion and agency

The overarching themes and questions of this book are explored in and across three sub-sections, which focus on understanding children's spatialities through different lenses.

Senses and embodiment

Within social science, there has been a recent turn to phenomenological accounts of experience, reflected in the increasing attention given to embodied, sensory and tacit experiences of place. Pink traces this 'sensorial turn' (Howes, in Pink, 2009, p. 7) across anthropology, geography, architecture and arts practice, among others. Drawing on Merleau-Ponty's (1962) work, anthropologists have emphasised the role of subjectivity in how we experience the world and the moment-by-moment nature of our body's sensory entanglement with material place. Key influences on thinking here include Feld and Basso's (1996) edited collection of ethnographic studies of how people encounter places and make them meaningful to themselves, Casey's (1996) philosophical work on embodiment and emplacement and Ingold's (2008) work on the entanglement of people and the material world. Within geography, non-representational theory starts from the view that 'human life is based on and in movement' (Thrift, 2008, p. 5) and recognises the challenge of representing what is present in experience. The application of the work of, for example, Ingold (2007) to studies of children's everyday lives, is very much an emerging field (exceptions include Burnett et al., 2014; Curtis, 2008; Hackett, 2014; Kullman, 2010; Pahl, 2012). The first section of this book makes a significant contribution to this field, by examining the implications of a phenomenological lens for the study of children's spatialities.

Leder-Mackley, Pink and Morosanu open this book by considering what theoretical considerations of place, embodiment and sensory perception can bring to the study of children's experiences in environments that traverse the physical and the digital. A phenomenological lens, they argue, enables scholars to engage with the sensory, (im)material and 'more-than-representational' aspects of children's lived experiences. While mostly a theoretical chapter drawing on Ingold's concept of zones of entanglement, the authors illustrate how children's sensory-embodied knowledge and 'making' of home featured in their own ethnographic video research in the UK about digital media and domestic energy consumption. They stress children do not just have a 'voice' that needs to be activated and listened to but also have other contributions that need to be 'seen' or found, because they are not always visible.

Developing this section on senses and embodiment, Chapter 2 by Curtis introduces a temporal perspective to children's spatialities. It explores ideas of children's spatiality in relation to the temporality of place, the development of children's understanding of such, and the role of family, friends and teachers in shaping their encounters and interpretations. Drawing from two examples of children's experiences of being in historical places in Scotland, an archaeological excavation and stone circles, Curtis shows how children develop an embodied knowledge of the temporality of places. She argues that children experience, understand and create histories in relation to the places they inhabit and draws on Bourdieu's concept of habitus, Ingold's concept of the dwelling perspective and Tilley's phenomenological approaches to archaeological interpretation to theorise how children experience and make sense of the past.

In contrast to these group activities, Kucirkova and Sakr focus in Chapter 3 on a case study of one London child's experience of photography with a digital camera at home with her father. They argue that through art-making, children both interact with and construct the world around them; hence the context of art-making offers the opportunity to engage with children's embodied experiences of place and space. They consider how children's embodied interaction during the process of taking photographs, when analysed using Deleuzian concepts of sense-making and rhizomatic structures of experience (rather than linearity), can challenge modern, developmental approaches to interpreting children's experiences of the world. As a result, children's art-making can be liberated from discourses of deficiency and apprenticeship.

The final chapter in this section is provided by one of the editors, Hackett, and focuses on children's perspectives and ways of making meaning during visits to a museum in the north of England. She uses interdisciplinary theories of space and place to interpret young children's actions in the field, with a particular focus on their embodied experience in the museum and their production of their own version of the museum place. Interrogating their interaction with a stuffed bear, she shows that a specific embodied experience of place was created by the children moving through the space, and their embodied meaning-making was a social practice. Both movement and embodied interactions were central to the production of this shared way of knowing the museum.

Emotion and relationships

Another area of focus is emotion. Within geography, a range of scholars have given particular attention to the role of emotion in peoples' place experiences (see e.g. Pile, 1991; Davidson et al., 2005; Blazek and Windram-Geddes, 2013; Kraftl, 2013a, 2013b). This work has extended theoretical understandings of emotion that focus on the interrelatedness of bodies and place; as Davidson et al. (2005) state, emotions are 'located' in both bodies and places. The field of emotional geographies has sought to 'understand emotion – experientially and conceptually – in terms of its socio-*spatial* mediation and articulation rather than as entirely interiorised subjective mental states' (Davidson et al., 2005, p. 3, emphasis original). In recent years, scholars working with children's geographies have also been increasingly bringing an emotional lens to their work; this is demonstrated in the 2013 special edition of *Emotion, Space and Society* entitled 'Children's Emotional Geographies'. Those working within this area connect interdisciplinary perspectives to examine children's emotional lives, including phenomenological perspectives of being (Procter, 2015 forthcoming), psychoanalytical theories of children's development (Blazek, 2013) and interdisciplinary notions of affect (Windram-Geddes, 2013). This section of the book builds on this work to show how examining the interconnections between place and emotion can develop new ways of viewing children's lived experiences and the implications of these insights more broadly.

Blazek leads on this section with a reflection on, and an overview of, the entanglements of geographical debates regarding children and emotions. The chapter outlines why children's emotional geographies matter. In this theoretical piece, he 'sketches a thread of themes connecting theorisations and practices regarding children's emotions and space'. His ultimate call is for an approach to policy and practice that would be both engaged with the spatial elements of the role of emotions in children's lives and attentive to the ontological, epistemological and political differences between adults and children.

In Chapter 6, Karoff responds to this call by examining the role of emotional moods in children's space-making practices in play areas in Danish schools. Her aim is to present a conceptualisation of play activity as experiencing and through this to examine the relationship between play, space and emotion. Through adopting

a phenomenological approach, this chapter provides a new understanding of the role of emotional moods which Karoff considers
closely related to social relationships, possibilities for the future and
the uncertainty of play practices. Attending to the rhythms of play
through ethnographic methods, the research makes clear that within
children's play practices emotions are not things that children have,
but are moods explored through shared play practices.

Staying with research in schools, Procter focuses in Chapter 7 on
the case study of one 10-year-old boy to ask how children create
places in institutional spaces not of their making. Adult discourses
of childhood shape the design and social organisation of these institutional spaces for children and Procter's chapter asks how children
encounter and navigate these emerging spaces, and in doing so create places at school for themselves and with others. It continues
the theme of this section with an examination of the intersections
between the personal meanings children attach to place and their
emotionally embodied engagements in and with space. This spatial
lens is used to consider the role of emotion in the ways that children
negotiate peer relations and emerging identities within the school
context. Children's emotional responses are central to the ways that
they navigate these places and the types of social relationships they
foster.

Spatial agency

The last section engages with theories of spatial agency. Here, agency
is recognised in terms of children's navigations and negotiations of
their own lives but its operation is placed in the context of the inter-
generational relationships which are part of their everyday experiences. The focus is on areas where children's spatial agency might
be perceived as having greater operation – family life, outdoors space
and play centres – and the extent and limitations of such agency
are explored. This links with Soja's (1996) notion of spatial justice,
which examines the spatial configuration of child–adult inequalities and power operations and thus makes them visible. To apply
this to one discipline discussed in this section, that of architecture
and town planning, much of the work in this area suggests that
spatial justice is achieved through participatory approaches design
(Blundell-Jones et al., 2005; Awan et al., 2011). Increasingly such
work recognises that 'architecture is defined by its very contingency,

by its very uncertainty in the face of... external forces' (Till, 2009, p. 1). In this way, Till argues, architecture *depends*. These perspectives on flexible architecture (Schneider and Till, 2007) have also been linked to the notion of learner autonomy in educational settings (Parnell and Procter, 2011). Within town planning, research has highlighted the complexities through which multiple factors denote place and demarcate space, shaping how people navigate and experience towns and cities. For example, Atkinson (2007) has reflected on the power of music, sound and noise in the social patterning of built environments. This section contributes to debates within architecture and town planning as regards the limitations of attempting to design *for* agency, and examines *how* agency happens within children's everyday lives.

The opening chapter by Seymour in this section reviews the consideration of space as an element of children's agency within the social study of childhood and particularly the sociology of families. The chapter reiterates Mayall's distinction between social actors and agents to distinguish between studies which focus on children in spaces and children's spaces at a variety of scales: domestic, public/local, international and global. The second part of the chapter responds to the call to re-situate children into their family lives and discuss the role and study of space in family sociology; that is, to re-place children in family life.

Drawing on a different discipline, that of landscape architecture, Woolley focuses in Chapter 9 on the planning, design and management of outdoor environments, particularly the landscape of cities. She explores the concepts of constructed and found space, the relationship of these to children and young people's use and responses to such spaces in the activities of play and recreation. She shows how children and young people become actors in their daily lives and often respond by using found spaces for activities such as play and skateboarding, eschewing the constructed spaces and the power they represent. The chapter concludes that the challenge for society is to support and enable rather than suppress and control children and young people in the provision and use of outdoor environments in cities.

The section, and this volume, concludes with an examination of a play centre for 4–6-year-olds in Italy. Satta explores how children's spatiality is constructed within these 'play institutions' and asks to what extent do they meet children's desires and promote their agency? She states that the fact that the mission of these places is to 'make' children play may have implications for the interpretation of the nature of child–adult relationships fostered in society. This is related to Soja's concept of spatial justice, which can highlight social inequalities and patterns of inter-generational injustice between children and adults. Satta's conclusion that children's spatiality is not therefore simply tied to the presence/absence of adults but rather to the way in which the adults themselves perceive their adulthood based on their vision of what constitutes a 'proper adulthood', a 'proper childhood' and a proper 'adult–child relationship' provides a fitting end not only to the section on spatial agency but also to this volume on children's spatialities.

Note

1. In this context, the 'critical thirding' which Soja (1996, p. 5) refers to is Lefebvre's (1991) trialetic of time, space and sociality. Soja (1996) critiques modernism for its tendency to create totalising discourses through the construction of binary categories, including social/historical and real/imagined. 'Putting space first' is suggested as a way of overcoming this binary logic.

References

Ansell, N. (2009) 'Childhood and the Politics of Scale: Descaling Children's Geographies?' *Progress in Human Geography*, 33 (2), 190–209.

Atkinson, R. (2007) 'Ecology of Sound: The Sonic Order of Urban Space', *Urban Studies*, 44 (10), 1905–1917.

Awan, A., Schneider, T. and Till, J. (2011) *Spatial Agency: Other Ways of Doing Architecture*, Oxon: Routledge.

Baldasser, L. and Merla, L. (2013) *Transnational Families, Migration and the Circulation of Care: Understanding Mobility and Absence in Family Life*, London: Taylor & Francis.

Blazek, M. (2013) 'Emotions as Practice: Anna Freud's Child Psychoanalysis and Thinking – Doing Children's Emotional Geographies', *Emotion, Space and Society*, 9, 24–32.

Blundell-Jones, P., Petrescu, D. and Till, J. (2005) *Architecture and Participation*, Oxon: Taylor & Francis.

Burke, C. (2013) *A Life in Education and Architecture*. Mary Beaumont Medd 1907–2005, London: Ashgate.

Burnett, C., Merchant, G., Pahl, K. and Rowsell, J. (2014) 'The (Im)materiality of Literacy: The Significance of Subjectivity to New Literacies Research', *Discourse: Studies in the Cultural Politics of Education*, 135 (1), 90–103.

Casey, E. S. (1996) 'How to Get from Space to Place in a Fairly Short Stretch of Time: Phenomenological Prolegomena', in S. Feld and K. H. Basso (eds) *Sense of Place*, Santa Fe: School of American Research Press, pp. 13–52.

Christensen, P. (2003) 'Place, Space and Knowledge: Children in the Village and the City', in P. Christensen and M. O'Brien (eds) *Children in the City. Home, Neighbourhood and Community*, London: Routledge, pp. 13–28.

Christensen, P. and O'Brien, M. (eds) (2003) *Children in the City. Home, Neighbourhood and Community*, London: Routledge.

Cresswell, T. (2004) *Place: A Short Introduction*, Malden: Blackwell Publishing.

Curtis, E. M. B. (2008) 'Walking Out of the Classroom: Learning on the Streets of Aberdeen', in T. Ingold and J. Vergunst (eds) *Ways of Walking: Ethnography and Practice on Foot*. Anthropological Studies of Creativity and Perception, Ashgate, Aldershot, United Kingdom, pp. 143–154.

Davidson, J. Bondi, L. and Smith, M. (2005) (eds) *Emotional Geographies*. London: Ashgate.

De Certeau, M. (2011). *The Practice of Everyday Life* (3rd Revised Edition), London: University of California Press.

Dicks, B. (2014) 'Action, Experience, Communication: Three Methodological Paradigms for Researching Multimodal and Multisensory Settings', *Qualitative Research*, 14, 656–674.

Duncan, S. and Phillips, M. (2010) 'People Who Live Apart Together (LATS). How Different Are They?' *Sociological Review*, 58 (1), 112–134.

Feld, S. and Basso, K. (1996) (eds) *Senses of Place*. Santa Fe: School of American Research Press.

Fog Olwin, K. and Gulløv, E. (2003) 'Towards an Anthropology of Children and Place', in K. Fog Olwin and E. Gulløv (eds) *Children's Places. Cross-Cultural Perspectives*, New York: Routledge.

Foucault, M. (1995) *Discipline and Punish: The Birth of the Prison*, London: Vintage Books.

Gabb, J. (2008) *Researching Intimacy in Families*, London: Palgrave.

Gagen, E. A. (2006) Measuring the Soul: Muscular Consciousness and Physical Health Testing in Early Twentieth Century Playgrounds', *Environment and Planning D: Society and Space*, 24 (6), 827–849.

Hackett, A. (2014) 'Zigging and Zooming All Over the Place: Young Children's Meaning Making and Movement in the Museum', *Journal of Early Childhood Literacy*, 14 (1), 5–27.

Hackett, A. and Yamada-Rice, D. (2015) 'Producing Visual Records of Movement: Making Meaning of Young Children's Interactions with Place', in E. Stirling and D. Yamada-Rice (eds) *Alternate Visions: Academics and Visual Industries Discuss Children and Images*. In Press.

Holloway, S. and Valentine, G. (2000a) *Children's Geographies: Playing, Living, Learning*, London: Routledge.

Holloway, S. and Valentine, G. (2000b) 'Spatiality and the New Social Studies of Childhood', *Sociology*, 34 (4), 763–783.

Holt, L. (2011) *Geographies of Children, Youth and Families: An International Perspective*, London: Routledge.

Hörschelmann, K. and Colls, R. (2009) *Contested Bodies of Childhood and Youth*.

Ingold, T. (2007) *Lines: A Brief History*, London: Routledge.
Ingold, T. (2008) 'Bindings Against Boundaries: Entanglement of Life in an Open World', *Environment and Planning*, 40, 1796–1810.
James, A., Jenks, C. and Prout, A. (1998) *Theorising Childhood*, Cambridge: Polity Press.
Keith, M. and Pile, S. (eds) (1993) *Place and Politics of Identity*, London: Routledge.
Kjørholt, A. T. (2003) ' "Creating a Place to Belong": Girls' and Boys' Hut-Building as a Site for Understanding Discourses on Childhood and Generational Relations in a Norwegian Community', *Children's Geographies*, 1 (1), 261–279.
Kraftl, P. (2013a) *Geographies of Alternative Spaces of Education: Diverse Learning Spaces for Children and Young People*, Bristol: Policy Press.
Kraftl, P. (2013b) 'Beyond "Voice", Beyond "Agency", Beyond "Politics"? Hybrid Childhoods and Some Critical Reflections on Children's Emotional Geographies', *Emotion, Space and Society*, 9, 13–23.
Kullman, K. (2010) 'Transitional Geographies: Making Mobile Children', *Social and Cultural Geography*, 11 (8), 829–846.
Kullman, K. (2014) 'Children, Urban Care, and Everyday Pavements', *Environment and Planning A*, 46, 2864–2880.
Leander, K. M. and Sheehy, M. (eds) (2004) *Spatializing Literacy Research and Practice*, New York: Peter Lang Publishing.
Lefebvre, H. (1991) *The Production of Space*, trans. D. Nicholson-Smith, Malden: Blackwell Publishing (originally published in 1974).
Leinhardt, G., Crowley, K. and Knutson, K. (2002) *Learning Conversations in Museums*, London: Routledge.
Lomax, H. (2014) ' "It's a Really Nice Place to Live!": The Ethnographic Encounter as a Space of Intergenerational Exchange', in R. Vanderbeck and N. Worth, (eds) *Intergenerational Space*, London: Routledge.
Massey, D. (2005) *For Space*, London: Sage.
Merleau-Ponty, M. (1962) *Phenomenology of Perception: An Introduction*, London: Routledge.
Nichols, S., Nixon, H. and Rowsell, J. (2011) 'Researching Early Childhood Literacy in Place', *Journal of Early Childhood Literacy*, 11, 107.
Niedderer, K. (2007) 'Mapping the Meaning of Knowledge in Design Research', *Design Research Quarterly*, 2 (2), 1–13.
Pahl, K. (2012) ' "A Reason to Write" Exploring Writing Epistemologies in Two Contexts', *Pedagogies: An International Journal*, 7 (3), 209–228.
Parnell, R. and Procter, L. (2011) 'Flexibility and Placemaking for Autonomy in Learning', *Educational and Child Psychology*, 28 (1), 77–88.
Philo, C. (2000). ' "The Corner-Stones of My World": Editorial Introduction to Special Issue on Spaces of Childhood", *Childhood*, 7 (3), 243–256.
Pile, Steve. (1991) 'Practicing Interpretative Geography', *Transaction of the Institute of British Geographers, New Series*, 1 (4), 458–469.
Pink, S. (2009) *Doing Sensory Ethnography*, London: Sage.
Procter, L. (2013a) 'Exploring the Role of Emotional Reflexivity in Research with Children', *Emotion, Space and Society*, 9, 80–88.

Procter, L. (2013b) 'Emotions, Schooling and Power: The Socialisation of "Angry Boys" ', *Journal of Political Power*, 6 (3), 495–510.

Procter, L. (fc 2015) 'Children, Nature and Emotion: Exploring How Children's Emotional Experiences of "Green" Spaces Shape Their Understandings of the Natural World', in M. Blazek and P. Kraftl (eds.) *Children's Emotions in Policy and Practice: Mapping and Making Spaces of Childhood*, London: Palgrave.

Rasmussen, K. (2004) 'Places for Children – Children's Places', *Childhood*, 11, 155–173.

Schneider, T. and Till, J. (2007) *Flexible Housing*, Oxon: Routledge.

Seymour, J. (2007) 'Treating the Hotel Like a Home: The Contribution of Studying the Single Location Home/Workplace', *Sociology*, 41 (6), 1097–1114.

Seymour, J. (2011) ' On Not Going Home at the End of the Day: Spatialized Discourses of Family Life in Single-Location Home/Workplaces', in L. Holt (ed.) *Geographies of Children, Youth and Families: An International Perspective*, London: Routledge, pp. 108–120.

Skelton, T. and Valentine, G. (1997) *Cool Places: Geographies of Youth Cultures*, London: Routledge.

Soja, E. W. (1996) *Thirdspace. Journeys to Los Angeles and Other Real-and-Imagined Places*, Massachusetts: Blackwell Publishers.

Soja, E. W. (2004) 'Preface', in K. M. Leander and M. Sheehy (eds.) *Spatializing Literacy Research and Practice*, New York: Peter Lang Publishing, pp. ix–xv.

Thomas, M. (2011) *Multicultural Girlhood: Racism, Sexuality and the Conflicted Spaces of American Education*, Philadelphia: Temple University Press.

Thorne, B. (1993) *Gender Play: Girls and Boys in School*, London: Open University Press.

Thrift, N. (2008) *Non-Representational Theory: Space, Politics, Affect*, London: Routledge.

Till, J. (2009) *Architecture Depends*, Massachusetts: MIT Press.

Tilley, C. (1994) *A Phenomenology of Landscape: Places, Paths and Monuments*, Oxford: Berg.

Trigg, D. (2012) *The Memory of Place: A Phenomenology of the Uncanny*. Ohio: Ohio University Press.

Tuan, Y. (1977) *Space and Place. The Perspective of Experience*, Minneapolis: University of Minnesota Press.

Warf, B. and Arias, S. (2009). *The Spatial Turn: Interdisciplinary Perspectives*, Oxon: Routledge.

Windram-Geddes, M. (2013) 'Fearing Fatness and Feeling Fat: Encountering Affective Spaces of Physical Activity', *Emotion, Space and Society*, 9, 42–49.

Wood, E. and Hall, E. (2011) 'Drawings as Spaces for Intellectual Play', *International Journal of Early Years Education*, 19, 3–4, 267–281.

Youdell, D. and Armstrong, F. (2011) 'A Politics Beyond Subjects: The Affective Choreographies and Smooth Spaces of Schooling', *Emotion, Space and Society*, 4, 144–150.

Part I

Senses and Embodiment

1

Knowing the World Through Your Body: Children's Sensory Experiences and Making of Place

Kerstin Leder Mackley, Sarah Pink and Roxana Moroşanu

In this chapter, we discuss what theoretical considerations of place, embodiment and sensory perception, drawn from phenomenological anthropology, human geography and media studies, can bring to the study of children's experiences in environments that traverse the physical and the digital. In doing so, we advance a steadily growing area of research that goes beyond mainstream psychological and developmental approaches to childhood studies and instead takes into account sensory and 'more-than-representational' modes of inquiry and lived experience. We propose an understanding of children's environments as composed of material and immaterial – invisible and imagined – entities, and of children as perceivers, makers and 'knowers' of ever-changing configurations of place. This, we will argue, has implications for the kinds of questions we ask of young people's lifeworlds and the methodologies through which we might explore them. Yet, rather than *prescribing* how to research children's sensory experiences of place, our conceptualisations of place, embodiment and sensory perception aim to provide a coherent theoretical framework that might offer new methodological and analytical routes within increasingly interdisciplinary contexts of research. For the purpose of illustration, we will address how children's sensory-embodied knowledge and 'making' of home featured in our own research about digital media and domestic energy consumption. However, our main purpose is to propose a set of theoretical-methodological principles through which to advance discussions around frames of research for scholars and practitioners working with young people.

Researching children's experiences

There have been some important developments over the last decades that have transformed childhood studies both in terms of taking more seriously the experience of children as 'beings', rather than 'becomings' (James et al., 1998, p. 207; cf. Oswell, 2013), and in accounting for children's varied lifeworlds in increasingly interdisciplinary contexts. This has included conceptualisations of children's bodies as socially and culturally constructed and reconstructed, as situated, and as continuously changing in their physical, social and experiential manifestations (cf. James, 1993, 2000; Horton and Kraftl, 2006b). In this context, the concept of 'embodiment' has received increased attention, following interests in breaking down the mind/body dichotomy (cf. Shilling, 2013) and taking bodily sensations and emotions seriously (see also Prout, 2005). For instance, in her 1990s research Allison James drew on Csordas's notion of embodiment 'as a seat of subjectivity' with 'the mind/subject/culture...deployed in parallel' (Csordas, 1994, p. 9, in James, 2000, p. 27) to emphasise 'the situated agency of the body and a view of the body as not divorced from the conscious, thinking and intentional mind' (James, 2000, p. 27). James was chiefly interested in how young people's sense of self develops, and how embodied experience and meanings associated with the body form part of this.

More recently, the non-representational dimensions of embodiment have been emphasised, along with the situatedness of learning in place. The pedagogy scholar Elisabeth Ellsworth describes embodiment as one of the 'human universals', along with movement and sensation (2005, p. 166). 'As living, moving, sensing bodies', she argues, 'we all exist only and always in relation even as our individual experiences of relationality are singular and unsharable' (*ibid.*). Her approach to pedagogy as 'knowledge in the making', rather than 'knowledge as a thing made' (p. 2), seeks to explore this relationality – between people, things, environments – as something outside the realms of language and cognition.

Geographers of childhood, such as Horton and Kraftl (2006a), have also adopted a renewed emphasis on the body and embodied experience, whereby the body is not necessarily 'a bounded thing' (2006a, p. 77). They argue:

> close attention to bodies reveals how 'we are not made up of the black and white signifying symbols of the written page – malleable and easily defined – but of biological flows of energy, matter and stimulating chemical fluids (adrenaline, pheromones, endorphins) which are in excess of such definitions, irradiating, condensing, intersecting, building and rippling our senses of being-in-the-world' (Dewsbury, 2000: 485)... [T]his embodiment – and this being-in-the-world – is always becoming: bodies are always in flux; always ongoing; never still.
>
> (Horton and Kraftl, 2006a, p. 77)

In this chapter, we advance the focus on embodiment, perception/knowing and place/environment emphasised in the literature outlined above by outlining a theoretical-methodological approach to researching the relationship between embodiment, sensory perception and place. In doing so, we draw on our research with families in an interdisciplinary study of energy and digital media use in the home (Low Effort Energy Demand Reduction (LEEDR), 2010–2014). In our research, we have employed a sensory-ethnographic methodology that draws on theories from phenomenological anthropology and human geography in terms of how we understand body/environment relations within the research context, and the kinds of knowledges this produces. Our work focused on the routines and experiences of all members of participating families. However, young people and their experiences formed an important part of our study. Here we highlight the ways we worked with them and the particular methodological challenges involved.

An approach to embodiment, perception and place

Tuan is regularly cited for stating that 'the child knows the world more sensuously than does the adult' (Tuan, 1977, p. 185), and children are often attributed with being particularly 'in touch' with their senses, with adults described as increasingly ' "disembodied" ' or marked through an ' "absent body" ' (Leder, 1990 in Bartos, 2013, p. 91). Above we have outlined how the respective works of James, Ellsworth and Horton and Kraftl have shaped ways of thinking about children's worlds as sensory, embodied and not routinely articulated verbally. Giving a 'voice' (or agency) to children within the research context therefore requires a shift towards studying experiences and sensations that go beyond language and also include what had previously been considered as too ephemeral or mundane, the kinds of tacit embodied knowledges that form part of children's everyday lives but that often remain 'unnoticed...unsaid...[or] unsayable' (Horton and Kraftl, 2006b, p. 259). These elements of life, as Horton and Kraftl argue, are fundamental to what it means to be in the world, as children and adults.

Horton and Kraftl used their reflections on a number of their own embodied childhood experiences, which they revisited as adult researchers, to investigate this theme and to highlight 'how glasses-wearing and clumsiness mattered and matter to us; and how feelings of wearing glasses or being clumsy return to us today in sudden, surprising moments of affective realisation (cf. McCormack, 2005)...[demonstrating] how our childhoods live on (and on) in the ongoing-ness and non-linearity of our everyday lives' (2006b, p. 269). Researchers' own personal experiences offer useful insights into childhood experience, yet they do not solve the problem of how we might go about accessing children's own worlds as they are actually lived. While it is impossible to directly access personal lived experience, there are a number of ways in which we might develop empathetic understandings and/or explore children's role in making 'place', both when engaging them in conversation and going beyond. Researchers who work with visual methods have developed various techniques for working collaboratively with children to explore their worlds in ways that go beyond the verbal. As Pink (2007) outlines, these include the work of Andrea Raggl and Michael Schratz, who used photographs they took of children in school to ask the pupils to 'recall learning situations' and to 'reflect *on* or *about* action' (2004, p. 151, original emphasis). Using photography differently, Phil Mizen asked children who worked to photograph their own worlds in a role he refers to as 'researcher photographers' creating photo-diaries in order to 'illustrate, document and reflect upon their work and employment' (2005, p. 126). Likewise anthropological filmmaker David MacDougall's series of films focuses in on the sensory and embodied experience of the school and its environment as an institution (discussed in MacDougall, 2005). Below we expand on this by building on our earlier work of how working with video can open up new empathetic and embodied routes to understanding (e.g. Pink and Leder Mackley, 2012; Leder Mackley and Pink, 2013). First, in the next section we outline our theoretical-methodological approach. This connects with the ways of thinking about children's lives represented in the above literatures – that is with theories of place, embodiment and perception – but takes the further step of considering how these theoretical principles might be played out through practical techniques for researching children's lives. In the subsequent section, we explore examples of how this theoretical-methodological approach was engaged when working with children in the context of bathrooms, digital media and energy use.

Researching through place, embodiment and perception: Life as unbounded

Within childhood studies and childhood geographies, the concept of place has largely been engaged to consider children's relationships to their physical environments. For instance, Bartos has explored children's sense of place and an 'emotional attachment' to (a) place, that is, an '*affective bond* that develops between people and locations over time' (Relph, 1976, cited in Bartos, 2013, p. 89, original emphasis). Although, in this context, place – as a meaningful association – is increasingly discussed as fluid and changing, we argue for pushing the concept of place in childhood studies further, that is, beyond its association with locations. We are interested in the concept of place as it pertains to how people live out everyday life in environments that are not fixed localities that 'exist' in the world but as 'unbounded...places', as 'evershifting constellations of trajectories' (Massey, 2005, p. 151). For the phenomenological anthropologist Tim Ingold, environments are not localities but 'zones of entanglement' (Ingold, 2008, p. 1807) that '*occur* along the lifepaths of beings' (ibid., p. 1808, our emphasis). People – including children – are likewise part of the environment, we both shape and are shaped by the worlds we live in. In this sense, while, as we have noted above, theories of embodiment sought to bring together the mind and body and acknowledge that they are not separate, theories that take the environment as their starting point extend this relationship. As David Howes has put it, this can be thought of as 'emplacement' (2005) whereby the mind-body-environment relationship becomes that which we need to attend to. This shifts the relationship between environments and people, such that the environment is not a thing separate from us that we do things to, but rather we are part of the environment. Therefore, for Ingold, bodies or organisms are conceived not as bounded but as 'bundles of interwoven lines of growth and movement, together constituting a meshwork in fluid space' (2008, p. 1796). Thus seeing everyday life as such as 'zones of entanglement' we understand environments as social, material and digital, as constituted through 'emergent relations between things and processes' and through different 'intensities of [people and] things of which both localities and socialities are elements' (Postill and Pink, 2012, p. 124).

Following from this, the way in which we experience the environment is precisely from within – that is, as part of it. Such a way of thinking about our relationship to the world brings to the fore the need to consider the hidden processes through which everyday environments are constituted; the sensory, tacit and perhaps never-spoken-about aspects of the ways we live and experience the places we are part of, and the activities we engage in in relation to them. Ellsworth's relational approach to the 'living, moving, sensing [body]' (2005, p. 166) suggests that it is through our embodied relation with others, objects and environments through time that we experience. Moreover, Ingold has described embodiment as a process, and as 'the development of [the human] organism in its environment' (1998, p. 259). Accordingly, notions of embodiment and emplacement can be approached as processual throughout a person's life course; children's bodies and activities ongoingly generate place(s) while their multisensorial engagement with their environments impacts on how place is experienced, imagined and remembered. Following this line of thinking we have therefore paid attention to the relational and contingent aspects of children's embodiment and their activities *as constitutive and part of* environments, through sensory and embodied ways of knowing, which are often tacit and not spoken about.

These ways of knowing, experiencing and making environments are equally applied to the digital and physical elements of place as children engage through their sensing bodies with digital media technologies and platforms. While Ingold does not consider the implications of digital technologies in his work, other scholars (e.g. Moores, 2012; Pink and Leder Mackley, 2013; Hjorth and Pink, 2014) have begun to use his ideas to also situate digital media as part of environments. Understanding digital environments in this way allows us to rethink them not as 'empty' or 'minimal', as in Dudek's conception of cyberspace (2005, p. 174), but as similarly felt, imagined, and negotiated; and moreover not as separate from the material worlds that we are part of. The same principle, as we see below, can also be used to understand how technologies like showers and baths fit into the environment of home.

To be able to research an everyday environment that our child participants both inhabit and are constitutive of – which they might not usually speak about and indeed might not have words for – requires research methods that involve learning from children about how they experience their worlds, from perspectives that allow us to imagine what it is like to be inside those very worlds. To undertake this we adapted a sensory ethnography approach (Pink, 2015) which is informed by the theoretical ideas outlined above and which deliberately seeks such forms of collaboration and routes to empathetically understanding everyday ways of knowing and experiencing. We now introduce our project, methods and the ways in which we worked with participants.

Researching energy demand in homes with children

Between 2011 and 2014, we worked with 20 family households in the Midlands (UK) to explore domestic energy consumption and the opportunities that digital interventions might afford in the context of energy demand reduction. Our ethnographic research formed part of the interdisciplinary LEEDR project and informed the work of engineering and design colleagues in terms of supporting numerical models of energy-use practices and changes, and also the creation of digital design concepts. Our methodology built on that of Pink's previous sensory- and visual-ethnographic research into everyday life in the home (Pink, 2004, 2009) and chiefly employed video within collaborative encounters with participants, allowing us to get a specific embodied and emplaced (Pink, 2015) understanding of people's lifeworlds and experiences. For instance, the home video tour was designed to enable us to experience people's homes with them, learning both empathetically from the ways in which they used their bodies and words to demonstrate how it felt to live in their homes, as well as from our own sensory embodied experiences of being there (Pink and Leder Mackley, 2012). We also visited households at a later stage to explore in detail how energy use was implicated in specific domestic activities, such as doing the laundry, cooking, showering and using digital media. When we could we followed activities as they played out, but also asked participants to re-enact certain tasks as a way in which to prompt them to remember and recount normally unspoken experiences in relation to them (Pink and Leder Mackley, 2014).

Our research focused on owner-occupied family households, and a number of technical and structural considerations relating to the energy monitoring part of our project guided our participant recruitment; for instance, we sought out houses that were powered by gas but incorporated a range of building materials. Working with families gave us the opportunity to approach energy use as part of different life stages. Therefore, we could explore the specificities of energy-related activities with regard to young families, teenage households or those where young people were about to leave for university. Children were thus an integral part of our research, though not its key focus.

While there is a long history of visual research methods being used with child participants, our methods were originally developed with adult participants. Thus the project brought new challenges in terms of making these methods work for and with children. Indeed, the research activities we did with children tended to emerge from the particular research encounters that we were developing with the family as a whole. This does not mean that our research with children was just incidental; we designed specific information sheets and assent forms for them to complete, and they were considered to be full participants in the project. However, we adjusted children's level and type of involvement according to their availability, needs and interests. The home video tour was at times too involved or lasted too long to work for some of the younger participants. In contrast the focus on specific activities lent itself to dipping in and out of what children were already doing, allowing them to demonstrate what they were doing, and how, rather than just talking about it. Below we discuss a number of ethnographic examples and the kinds of sensory and embodied knowledges that emerged through engaging child participants in participatory methods, such as re-enactments.

Bathrooms

Energy demand in relation to hot water use in the home constituted one area of inquiry in our study. As such, ethnographic encounters involved getting an understanding of routines and activities around personal hygiene, specifically the use of bathrooms for showering, bathing, washing hands, brushing teeth and so on. Because emplaced knowledge was important to us, we asked family members to talk and walk us through their routines, showing us what they would do in the bathroom on an everyday basis. We have shared some of our ethnographic videos online and encourage readers to engage with them in relation to our writing (see *Energy & Digital Living*: http://energyanddigitalliving.com/video-archive/). Here we first describe the clips before reflecting on what we learned while creating and revisiting them.

One video (clip 34) shows Serena (aged 11) and Abigail (8) as they demonstrated to Kerstin how they would use the shower in their parents' en-suite bathroom. As they guided Kerstin into the bathroom, they explained their mother's role in creating a particular sensory environment by either turning on the fan or opening the bathroom window as they got in. Towels would be placed on the nearby 'weird-looking' radiator to warm them up although, at the time of the research encounter, only the top half of the radiator heated up as there was air in the system. The girls showed Kerstin how they would turn on the shower to its preferred position, about half-way around the dial. They explained that it usually takes a while for the hot water to come through, meaning they had to wait before getting into the shower. Touching the pipes on each side of the tap, Abigail said that when the shower runs 'right up here it's kind of cold, and then down there it's kind of hot'. The shower head itself could be adjusted but was on a low setting, at the time of the visit, for the girls to reach. After the shower their mother would wrap the girls in their towels to warm up and, sometimes, Serena would dance to music from the iPod docking station in the parents' bedroom, with water getting 'everywhere' (mum's words). As Kerstin learned during this encounter and related visits, showering was a social activity for these girls (although Serena was increasingly keen to shower on her own) and often involved singing and dancing in the shower as well as having to jump out if family members used other parts of the water system in the rest of the house (e.g. when someone flushed the toilet and the water pressure dropped, resulting in cold shower water).

Clips 17 and 18 again show two sisters, Bethan (13) and Rhian (9), who re-enacted their bathing and showering routines during one of Kerstin's visits. Kerstin had already learned from the family that they sometimes shared bath water between them, with mum using the bath first, followed by the older and then the younger daughter and, occasionally, the father thereafter. This kind of sharing tended to involve releasing and adding to bath water to achieve the right temperature. Asked what the bathroom feels like when bathing, Rhian reflected 'it's quite warm the side of the bath, so it makes it a little bit warm in the room' and, stepping away from the bath tub towards the other side of the room, 'cos like the warmth comes off it and goes this way' (clip 17).

During the time of Kerstin's visits, however, the girls were also going through a stage of transition: Bethan was increasingly using the shower and Rhian had also begun to do so with the help of family members (as she was too short to reach the electric shower unit or shower head herself). Bethan described both her bathing and showering experiences, demonstrating how much hot and cold water she would add to the tub and, in the case of showering, how she would negotiate steam in relation to hot water use: 'when I'm having a shower, if it's making the room steam up, cos the window is not open, then I normally turn it off... because when it gets really steamy, I find it hard to breathe' (clip 18). In general, the bathroom window was opened or closed depending on the weather but also other environmental factors; as Rhian pointed out, their father often closes the window when going to bed at night so as to shut out the noise from the motorway.

As these examples show, exploring the environment of the bathroom with participants enabled them to show us how they used the bathroom and, importantly, to reflect on how it felt. For instance, we learned about how the feeling of the room was adjusted in a range of ways, taking into account things that were intangible and would be invisible normally to the researcher – such as steam, air coming in from the window, the water going cold because someone had turned a tap on in another room.

Digital media

One of the core themes of our research into energy use focused on digital media. We were both interested in how digital-media use consumed energy as well as how digital technologies might be used for energy demand reduction interventions (e.g. Wilson et al., 2014). In media studies and anthropology the relationship between the digital and material is firmly established. Miller and Slater, for instance, describe media environments as 'continuous with...other social spaces' (2000, p. 5); Lori Kendall has coined the term digital 'overlay' for cyberspace activities over the real world (2002, p. 8); Postill and Pink (2012) speak of different 'digital socialities' that people engage and are bound up in; and Pink et al. (2015) call for a digital ethnography approach that treats the online and offline as part of the same environment. Digital environments are thus considered part of 'real life', and likewise as places contingent on physical place relations. Media studies researchers however seldom bring together questions about media use with research about showering or other everyday activities that consume energy. In our work these themes converged, and indeed our ethnographic work with children in particular enabled us to see how they were related.

Our research included exploring children's and teenagers' use of audio-visual media to 'make place' and, in the process, construct more or less private or shared environments. Some of this involved focusing on children's uses of media more directly. For example, children's engagements with PlayStations and other gaming devices provided some interesting examples of both the role these devices played in changing configurations of place – through their audio-visual, sensory, social and material presence – and how they 'corresponded' (Ingold, 2013) with children's bodies. By this we mean how bodily movement and sensations were bound up with material and sensory affordances, one continuously shaping the other. However, the ways we learned about media use more indirectly, such as when children were showing us how they used the bath or shower, were particularly important for our research. For instance, one child participant who suffered from a skin condition and needed to have daily oil baths described to us how she would pull her CD player from her bedroom onto the landing in order to be able to listen to audiobooks while bathing. The bathroom door would remain open, and this set-up meant that the whole family inadvertently attended to the girl's bath and story times. As with the iPod example above, children in our study often used their mobile phones or iPods to listen to music while in the bath or shower, sometimes timing their showering according to specific songs. Alternatively the bathroom became a hideaway for other engagements with digital technologies, for instance one teenage girl extended 'bath time' by playing on her DS (her dual-screen handheld game console) – set to quiet so as not to draw attention to it – while wrapped in a towel and lying on the bathroom floor. Accordingly, digital technologies became embedded in domestic routines, were used by children to create particular sensory and social environments (consciously as well as incidentally), and were also part of the material environment of the home, as conspicuous and tactile artefacts.

As the examples in this section have shown, children's sensory and embodied ways of knowing in the home do not simply refer to material, physical environments but are equally ways of knowing the digital and technological elements of place. Children engage through their sensing bodies with everyday environments that are digital and technological. As we have demonstrated through the example of showering and bathing, a range of tangible, material, intangible and digital elements configure the environments of home that children make and experience. Through engaging with children in these worlds, with video, we were able to gain an understanding of how their bathroom environments were crafted and, for the purposes of our particular project, what the implications are for both energy demand and for the ways in which digital interventions might be designed for its reduction.

Methodological implications

The above stories can be situated in specific locations involving particular materialities. We were for instance in environments that were, through their material contents and the activities they encouraged, defined as bathrooms. And as a material environment, these bathrooms provided prompts for discussion. However, as the videos exemplify, these bathrooms were also made up of other less material properties, including flows of sound, water, and hot and cold air, that contributed to their configuration of place. Likewise the children in our research were part of and contributors to these environments.

In our work we try to 'access areas of embodied, emplaced knowing and to use these as a basis from which to understand human perception, experience, action and meaning' (Pink, 2009, p. 47). As readers will see when engaging with the *Energy & Digital Living* website, the videos we have described above have a certain performative element to them. We used video in particular interactive and self-reflective ways, in that the video recordings are used as routes to knowledge rather than records of observed events. For example, asking the girls to talk to us in detail about how they use and experience the bathroom disclosed some of those embodied knowledges that they might not otherwise talk about (e.g. not through interviews alone), like knowing when to step in and out of the water, how to set the dial, which parts of the pipes and radiator get hot and cold, and so on. These are things that are sensed, rather than visible, as we might define them as among the invisible flows of home, in this case flows of heat and cold.

Elsewhere we have described these flows as parts of imagined or 'invisible' architectures of home (Pink and Leder Mackley, 2014). These can be understood as known but usually unspoken material and immaterial constituents of what makes up the domestic environment for participants. One key point, which appears obvious but warrants re-emphasising, is that to fully understand children's experiences of place it helps to find routes to emplaced knowledge by actually exploring subjects within the environments of which they are part. This refers to locality and materiality to an extent; but it also went beyond this, in that what became relevant to the research also seeped outside the bathroom to include the wider hot water system, the weather, the auditory environment in and outside the home, as well as socialities and other socio-cultural dynamics. Indeed the above demonstrates a connection between the bathroom and media use.

The concept of flow is also useful in terms of thinking about how the home is a continuously changing and shifting environment. The invisible flows through it change in their qualities and types – including hot water, cool air, smells, sounds and more. But it is not only the home as an environment that is changing. Embodiment, according to Ingold is also a process, part of 'the development of [the human] organism in its environment' (1998). Accordingly, notions of embodiment and emplacement can be approached as processual throughout a person's life course. This is relevant in general but specifically to children's changing bodies, and also to the fact that the world around them is equally shifting and changing in a number of ways. This, we propose, is the context for our research with children – that is, a world in progress, inhabited by people who are also in progress. The same can be said for adults but, as we have emphasised, when we are seeking to learn about those things that might not usually be spoken about and are not accessible through interviews or language-based methods, the ways in which children move through, learn in and know their environments bring new insights to the question of how they can be known.

Therefore, a focus on the sensory-embodied experience of place enables us to understand children as situated in relation to everyday environments, and indeed (following Ingold) to see bodies as part of, rather than separate from the environment. Children's bodies and activities continuously generate place(s) just as much as adults do. It is not necessarily just children's 'voices' that we need to listen to (Clark, 2007; James, 2007). Rather we need to attend to and recognise the ways in which they ongoingly participate in the making of domestic (and other) environments. At the same time we need to appreciate how their multisensorial engagement with their environments impacts on how place is experienced, imagined and remembered.

If we consider places as open and unbounded, then this gives us the chance to explore the different relations, contingencies and 'entanglements' that contribute to place-making and that are experienced as such. We can think of children in this context as knowers and makers of their environments, and the latter is both something that can be imagined as happening through their very existence and movements, but also as something they can have agency in, in that they might try to create, maintain or challenge specific configurations of place. This applies equally to questions around how children use bathrooms, showers or baths to those concerned with how they use digital media in the home. This approach to understanding everyday life, which draws on the non-representational and considers everyday environments, human activity and experience as mutually constituting and processual, requires research methods that go beyond seeking to understand how children 'represent' themselves in research. Rather it entails developing participatory research methods that involve researchers learning from children about how they experience their worlds. A sensory ethnography approach is informed by the theoretical ideas outlined above and offers methods for such forms of collaboration and routes to understanding everyday ways of knowing and experiencing.

Conclusion

As we have emphasised above, it is widely recognised within childhood studies that children are active, meaning-making agents – 'beings' rather than 'becomings' (James and Prout, 1997) – whose voices should be heard and explored in academic and applied research (Clark, 2007). However, precisely how children should be given a voice in research and how to deal with the pitfalls and complexities that this may encompass is still a matter of debate (cf. James, 2007; see also Horton and Kraftl, 2006a). Traditionally, much emphasis has been given to the communicative properties of young people, as evident, for instance, in the notion that it is only 'when children are talking that we hear their voices' (James, 2007, p. 268). Yet, recognising the limitations of language as chief purveyor of young people's lifeworlds, childhood studies and media studies have also increasingly turned to creative methodologies to facilitate children's multi-modal expression, for instance through drawings, mappings, photography and film-making. We have built on these developments, but we wish to move beyond them by shifting theoretical emphasis away from questions of cognition and representation towards a focus on the non-representational (Thrift, 2007), sensory-embodied experience (cf. Pink, 2009; Wilson et al., 2012) and the idea of children as 'knowers' and makers of their environments. To this end, we invite readers to reflect again on Ingold's conceptualisation of the environment. This time consider its implications for how children weave their ways through the world, contributing to its making – not just having a 'voice' that needs to be activated and listened to but, rather, already being active constituents of the world, whose contributions need to be 'seen' or found, because they are not always visible. Ingold writes:

> The trail, in short, is a 'line of becoming' which, as Keith Ansell Pearson explains, 'is not defined in terms of connectable points,

or by the points which compose it, since it has only a "middle" '
(1999, page 169). Becoming is not a connection between this and
that but follows a 'line of flight' that pulls away from both. As we
have already seen, moreover, in that zone of admixture where the
substances of the earth mingle with the medium this line can
appear at once as a trace on the ground and a thread in the air,
as track or string. Each such line, however, is but one strand in
a tissue of lines that together constitute the texture of the land.
This texture is what I mean when I speak of organisms being constituted within a relational field. It is a field not of connectable
points but of interwoven lines, not a network but a meshwork.

(Ingold, 2008, p. 1805)

If we conceptualise the home as such a 'meshwork' and children
as weaving their lines through its world, as both they and it are
ongoingly changing – in relation to each other and to the other
constituents of home – we can easily begin to imagine how, by
tracing the lines children make through the world, we can start to
appreciate how they also contribute to the ways in which energy is
consumed in that environment. Video, in our work, has offered us
a medium through which to follow the children who participated
in our research, and to seek to imagine and understand how they
feel and how they engage with that environment in which they are
entangled.

Acknowledgements

The interdisciplinary LEEDR project (2010–2014), based at Loughborough University, was jointly funded by the UK Research Councils' Digital Economy and Energy programmes (grant number
EP/I000267/1). For further information about the project, collab-
orating research groups and industrial partners, please visit www
.leedr-project.co.uk. The authors would like to thank all the families
who have generously participated in this research.

References

Bartos, A. E. (2013) 'Children Sensing Place', *Emotion, Space & Society*, 9, 89–98.
Clark, A. (2007) 'Early Childhood Spaces: Involving Young Children and
    Practitioners in the Design Process', *Working Papers in Early Childhood
    Development*, Bernard van Leer Foundation.

Dudek, M. (2005) 'Digital Landscapes: The New Media Playground', in M. Dudek (ed.) *Children's Spaces*, Oxford: Architectural Press, pp. 154–177.

Ellsworth, E. (2005) *Places of Learning: Media, Architecture, Pedagogy*, New York: Routledge.

Hjorth, L. and Pink, S. (2014) 'New Visualities and the Digital Wayfarer: Reconceptualizing Camera Phone Photography and Locative Media', *Mobile Media & Communication*, 2 (1), 40–57.

Horton, J. and Kraftl, P. (2006a) 'What Else? Some More Ways of Thinking and Doing "Children's Geographies"', *Children's Geographies*, 4 (1), 69–95.

Horton, J. and Kraftl, P. (2006b) 'Not Just Growing Up but Going On: Materials, Spacings, Bodies, Situations', *Children's Geographies*, 4 (3), 259–276.

Howes, D. (2005) 'Introduction: Empires of the Senses', in D. Howes (ed.) *Empire of the Senses: The Sensual Culture Reader*, Oxford: Berg, 1–20.

Ingold, T. (1998) 'From Complementary to Obviation: On Dissolving the Boundaries Between Social and Biological Anthropology, Archaeology and Psychology', *Zeitschrift für Ethnologie*, 123, 21–52.

Ingold, T. (2008) 'Bindings Against Boundaries: Entanglements of Life in an Open World', *Environment and Planning A*, 40, 1796–1810.

Ingold, T. (2013) *Making: Anthropology, Archaeology, Art and Architecture*, London: Routledge.

James, A. (1993) *Childhood Identities: Self and Social Relationships in the Experience of the Child*, Edinburgh: Edinburgh University Press.

James, A. (2000) 'Embodied Being(s): Understanding the Self and the Body in Childhood', in A. Prout (ed.) *The Body, Childhood and Society*, Basingstoke: Macmillan, pp. 19–37.

James, A. (2007) 'Giving Voice to Children's Voices: Practices and Problems, Pitfalls and Potentials', *American Anthropologist*, 109 (2), 261–272.

James, A. and Prout, A. (1997) *Constructing and Reconstructing Childhood*, 2nd edition, London: Falmer.

James, A., Jenks, C. and Prout, A. (1998) *Theorizing Childhood*, Oxford: Polity.

Kendall, L. (2002) *Hanging Out in the Virtual Pub: Masculinities and Relationships Online*, Berkeley: University of California Press.

Leder Mackley, K. and Pink, S. (2013) 'From Emplaced Knowing to Ethnographic Knowledge: Sensory Ethnography in Energy Research', *The Senses & Society*, 8 (3), 335–353.

MacDougall, D. (2005) *The Corporeal Image*, Princeton, NJ: Princeton University Press.

Massey, D. (2005) *For Space*, London: Sage.

Miller, D. and Slater, D. (2000) *The Internet: An Ethnographic Approach*, Oxford: Berg.

Mizen, P. (2005) 'A Little "Light Work"? Children's Images of Their Labour', *Visual Studies*, 20 (2), 124–139.

Moores, S. (2012) *Media, Place and Mobility*, London: Palgrave Macmillan.

Oswell, D. (2013) *The Agency of Children: From Family to Global Human Rights*, New York: Cambridge University Press.

Pink, S. (2004) *Home Truths: Gender, Domestic Objects and Everyday Life*, Oxford: Berg.

Pink, S. (2007) *Doing Visual Ethnography*, 2nd edition, London: Sage.

Pink, S. (2009) *Doing Sensory Ethnography*, London: Sage.

Pink, S. (2015) *Doing Sensory Ethnography*, 2nd edition, London: Sage.

Pink, S. and Leder Mackley, K. (2012) 'Video and a Sense of the Invisible: Approaching Domestic Energy Consumption Through the Sensory Home', *Sociological Research Online*, 17 (1), 3: http://www.socresonline.org.uk/17/1/3.html.

Pink, S. and Leder Mackley, K. (2013) 'Saturated and Situated: Expanding the Meaning of Media in Routines Everyday Life', *Media, Culture & Society*, 35 (6), 677–691.

Pink, S. and Leder Mackley, K. (2014) 'Flow and Intervention in Everyday Life: Situating Practices', in Y. Strengers and C. Maller (eds) *Social Practices, Interventions and Sustainability: Beyond Behaviour Change*, London: Routledge, 163–178.

Pink, S., Horst, H., Postill, J., Hjorth, L., Lewis, L. and Tacchi, J. (2015) *Digital Ethnography: Principles and Practices*, London: Sage.

Postill, J. and Pink, S. (2012) 'Social Media Ethnography: The Digital Researcher in a Messy Web', *Media International Australia*, 145, 123–134.

Prout, A. (2005) *The Future of Childhood: Towards the Interdisciplinary Study of Childhood*, Abingdon: RoutledgeFalmer.

Raggl, A. and Schratz, M. (2004) 'Using Visuals to Release Pupils' Voices: Emotional Pathways Into Enhancing Thinking and Reflecting on Learning', in C. Pole (ed.) *Seeing Is Believing? Approaches to Visual Research*, Oxford: Elsevier, 147–162.

Shilling, C. (2013) *The Body and Social Theory*, 3rd edition, London: Sage.

Thrift, N. (2007) *Non-Representational Theory: Space/Politics/Affect*, London: Routledge.

Tuan, Y. (1977) *Space and Place: The Perspective of Experience*, Minneapolis: University of Minnesota Press.

Wilson, G., Leder Mackley, K., Mitchell, V., Bhamra, T. and Pink, S. (2014) 'PORTS: An Interdisciplinary and Systemic Approach to Studying Energy Use in the Home', *Proceedings of UbiComp Adjunct 2014*, 971–978.

Wilson, S., Houmøller, K. and Bernays, S. (2012) ' "Home, and Not Some House": Young People's Sensory Construction of Family Relationships in Domestic Spaces', *Children's Geographies*, 10 (1), 95–107.

2
The Place of Time in Children's Being

Elizabeth Curtis

This chapter approaches children's spatialities from a temporal perspective. It explores how children experience, understand and create histories in relation to the places they inhabit. Following archaeologist Chris Tilley who has argued that, 'places gather together persons, memories, structures, histories, myths and symbols' (Tilley, 2004, p. 25), I will discuss ideas of children's spatiality in relation to the temporality of place, the development of children's understanding of such, and the role of family, friends and teachers in shaping their encounters and interpretations. Drawing from two examples of children's experiences of being in historical places, I will show how children develop an embodied knowledge of the temporality of places. The first example considers the experiences of children in the formal context of a small rural primary school with a community archaeologist, in which children's participation in an archaeological excavation created a particular way of understanding the relationship between places and their history. The second example explores the experiences of children visiting stone circles while participating in everyday family activities such as visiting heritage sites at weekends or on holiday, going for walks, exercising dogs, cycling and picnicking. Through these examples I will discuss how Bourdieu's concept of habitus (Bourdieu, 1977), Ingold's concept of the dwelling perspective (Ingold, 2000) and Tilley's phenomenological approaches to archaeological interpretation (Tilley, 2004) contribute to an understanding of how children experience and make sense of the past.

Time, temporality and place

Within the context of education and formal schooling, Cooper has argued that the past is a dimension of children's social and physical environment and they interact with it from birth, noting that, '[t]hey hear and use the vocabulary of time and change: old, new, yesterday, tomorrow, last year, before you were born, when mummy was little, a long time ago, once upon a time' (Cooper, 1995, p. 2). Embodied learning has come to be considered core to the development of children's understanding of place and time through the curricular areas of history and geography. This is reflected in the emphasis given to 'hands on' learning in history (e.g. Turner-Bisset, 2005; Cooper, 2012) and fieldwork in geography (Catling and Willy, 2009; Scoffham, 2010).

The study of history is one way of exploring time, and my intention is to explore the idea of children's spatialities from a temporal perspective as well as more traditional models of historical understanding in terms of how children make sense of the past in their everyday experiences of life. In his discussion of temporality, Ingold (2000) makes a clear distinction between temporality, in which time is experienced in place, and abstract concepts of time as understood/experienced in relation to history, chronology and time as understood/experienced in terms of historicity. Regarding the former he argues that chronology frames the understanding of time as 'any regular system of dated time intervals' and that history frames time as 'any series of events which may be dated in time' (Ingold, 2000, p. 194). He argues that if history is conceived within a temporal rather than chronological framework then history is created 'through the experiences of those, who in their activities, carry forward the process, social life' (*ibid*.), rather than as a series of isolated events.

Taking this approach, place is key to the development of a deep understanding of time in terms of both personal and collective ideas of history, being the context in which people experience it. In cities and in the countryside, people have built their homes, places of worship and recreation and worked and extracted from the land over thousands of years. Citing the author George Mackay-Brown, Hilary Cooper offers the example of the deep connection between history and place in Orkney:

There are stories in the air here ... These islands are a microcosm of the world. They've been continuously lived in for about 6000 years, and the layers of cultures and races are inescapable and unavoidable wherever you go .... History has not been parcelled up into Heritage in Orkney. The past is the present.

(MacKay-Brown, *The Times*, 25 July 1992, quoted by Cooper, 1995, p. 9)

This resonates with the phenomenological approaches to archaeological fieldwork taken by Tilley. Only by experiencing places, Tilley argues, is it possible to understand the histories of people who previously inhabited those places (Tilley, 2004).

As Mackay-Brown says, the traces of people's lives in the past are not just frozen moments in time but are there to be experienced and understood in the present, and continuously being added to; as Ingold (2000) argues, 'the landscape is always in the nature of work in progress' (p. 199). So it is that children's experiences of being in historic places are just as much about their experiences of being in the present as a means of thinking about the past.

Practice

The ways in which children experience and understand ideas of time and history are complex, situated and socially produced. In their consideration of the future of children's geographies, Horton and Kraftl (2006) identified 'everydayness', 'material things,' 'practices', 'bodies', 'affect' and 'ongoingness and education' as neglected areas of research within the field; this resonates with Cooper's argument highlighted earlier that children's understanding of time in relation to the past is not only spatially but socially developed (Cooper, 1995). Both of these positions can be understood more broadly in relation to Bourdieu's (1977) concept of habitus, which recognises that knowledge is socially produced and embodied in both physical and mental actions and passed on and reworked through time. In the context of the socialisation of children, Allison James has noted that for Bourdieu it is habitus 'that provides the link between social structures, institutions and ways of behaving and what actually goes on inside people's heads' (James, 2013, p. 41). Thus children's temporal experiences and ideas of the past are understood in this chapter in a way which recognises that through living, working and learning together people simultaneously create and are created by the places in which they live.

Ingold builds on the idea of habitus in his discussion of the temporality of landscape (Ingold, 2000) and argues, as noted above, that people are an integral part of the place in which they live and that landscape should be understood from a 'dwelling perspective'. 'Human children', Ingold (2000, p. 186) argues, 'like the young of many species, grow up in environments furnished by the work of previous generations, and as they do so they come literally to carry the forms of dwelling in their bodies – in specific skills and dispositions'. In Ingold's idea of the dwelling perspective, time and landscape/environment go hand in hand; he argues that, 'the landscape is constituted as an enduring record of – and testimony to – the lives and works of past generations' (Ingold, 2000, p. 189). If habitus can be considered from this perspective, it can be understood as fluid and dynamic. A practice-based analysis situates the study and experience of being in an archaeological place in the context of the social world in which the co-existence of the monument in particular places and the practices of groups of people at particular times continually define and redefine how a place and its past is experienced and understood in the present.

Heritage

Contemporary studies of heritage emphasise the role of visitors as active participants in the creation of heritage, rather than as passive consumers of highly mediated historical settings. Indeed, Laurajane Smith has argued that 'there is really no such thing as heritage' (Smith, 2006, p. 11) and that rather than only thinking of heritage as a noun, it should instead be understood in terms of actions or 'cultural practice', in addition to its materiality. She emphasises those practices which are involved in the 'negotiation and regulation of a range of cultural and social values.... [and the] conservation and preservation of social and cultural meanings' (Smith, 2006, p. 12). Children too can be seen to play an active role in the cultural practices related to doing heritage. By being active participants in the investigation of the past, children also become the creators of new histories rather than the recipients of a ready-made, event-driven account of life in the past.

In the example below I will discuss how such concepts aid the understanding of how children have come to understand both their personal ideas of time and their development of wider ideas of history. I will also discuss children's temporal-spatial experiences of different kinds of historical places and in different social and spatial contexts. This example focuses on the experiences of children revealing the temporal context of a local woodland through their participation in an excavation and in carrying out archival work near to their school.

Creating time

As Smith (2006) has shown, heritage should be considered from a practice point of view in that it is actively created, experienced and recreated through a range of activities, including day trips to officially recognised sites of heritage. She argues that ideas of the past are not developed in isolation, but as part of a wider development of a child's place in society with particular reference to the role of the family and the school. The context for this example is a small rural primary school of two classes, (Primary 1–3 and Primary 4–7) in north-eastern Scotland in which the pupils, aged between 5 and 12, their class teachers and a local archaeologist all worked together to plan and carry out archaeological fieldwork including excavations and archival research on an estate next to their school. This culminated in an exhibition of their work, including archaeological finds, for family and friends, which the children led and which I supported alongside the class teacher and archaeologist. This project was also part of an Arts and Humanities Research Council Connected Communities Research for Community Heritage project, 'Sustainable community heritage in Scotland's North East: Bennnachie and beyond', between April and June 2012.

Children, teachers and I took photographs of the excavation and post-excavation work, and the resulting photos were used as a basis for the children to discuss their experiences of carrying out archaeological fieldwork and creating the history of the area next to their school. The photographs included images of the children digging, sorting, interpreting and exhibiting finds from their excavation and, in the case of the younger children, things which they had dug up in their own gardens or collected from the beach. They were all asked to make a selection of images, which they stuck to large sheets of paper, and either independently or with the help of a scribe write what they thought they had learned and how the experiences had made them feel. In choosing photographs to reflect on their experiences, children picked a variety of locations linked to their explorations of time including the excavation site, the classroom where they cleaned, sorted and interpreted their finds, and the replica collector's cabinet which housed their final exhibition.

Planning and conducting an excavation carries with it a particular kind of understanding of the relationship between places and their history. In this case study, the children worked in an area of woodland close to where they frequently went to participate in forest school activities such as den-building and woodworking. Through their partnership with a local archaeologist, their experience and understanding of their familiar woodland transformed as they considered who had buried all the old bits and pieces including glass, pottery, broken shoes and ironwork in the rubbish dump or midden which they excavated weekly over a spring term. As noted above, Hilary Cooper (1995) argues the importance of embodied learning in relation to making sense of time. Throughout this project the participating children learned a particular way of knowing about the past through the practice of archaeology, which encompasses both spatial and temporal practices and understanding (Figure 2.1).

The children's responses to the practical experience of excavation situated the past as lying underground, below the level of the present, and identified key items which were dug up as being particularly useful markers of specific times in the past. This is reflected in the responses by younger children from the Primary 1–3 class (aged 5–7) who made frequent use of generic phrases such as 'digging for pottery' and 'I found a lot of things' to describe images of themselves and others at work outside. Older children from the Primary 4–7 (aged 8–12) class also noted objects as indicators of specific times in the past; one child said that 'John took a lot of pictures of what we were doing in the digging place, the place where John is sitting was where we found the most and unique pieces of pottery', whilst another child said that 'the section we were in was the most popular because there was heaps of pottery found there!'

The site of excavation itself was therefore discussed in relation to the concentration of finds, as the site included the remains of an old rubbish dump in one corner, which the children were allowed

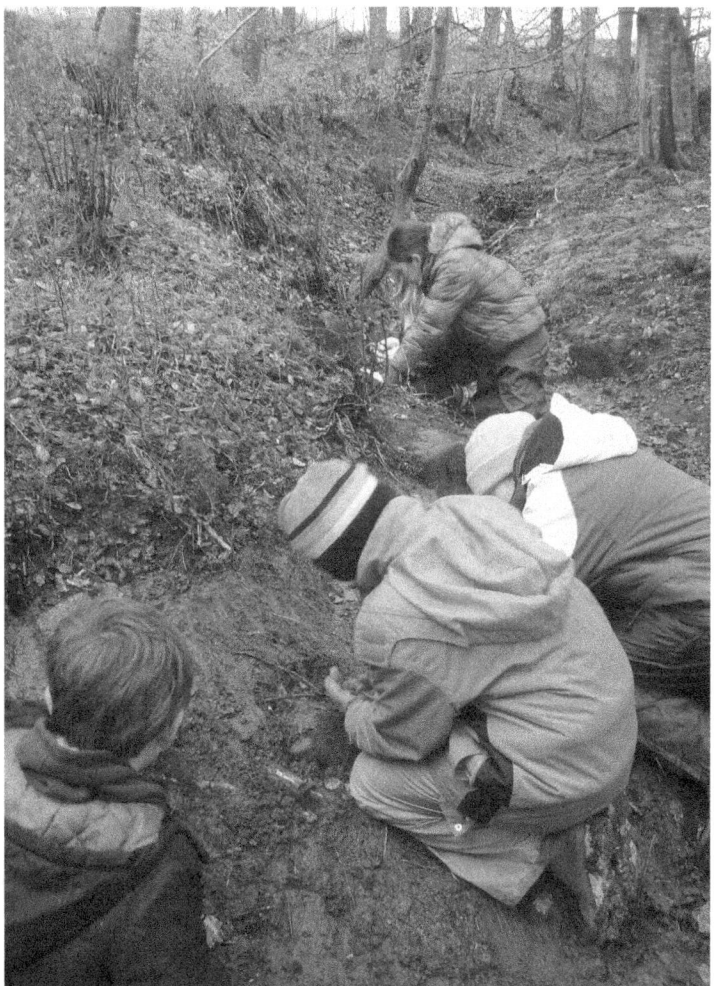

Figure 2.1   'Digging for Pottery'

to excavate. Their experiences of working in different parts of the site reflected the way in which they made connections between what was revealed through digging and their interest in being in particular parts of the site. As well as a midden, the site contained the remains of what was thought to be a water mill, but this was largely ignored by children when they chose photos to talk about. Unlike the midden, this part of the site contained hardly any things to find, instead it was the shaping of the ground itself which indicated its use in the past.

The older Primary 4–7 children were more aware of the importance of the relationship between the actual location or context of an object under the ground and the way in which an archaeologist places the object in time. They wrote more frequently about the way in which they had to learn to work like an archaeologist and acknowledged the role of the community archaeologist in teaching them the skills they needed to develop to understand the way in which time was embedded in the woodland beneath their feet. One boy wrote that 'you don't dig straight down you dig in layers and keep the ground flat as possible.' Reflecting on an image of herself and two friends digging, one of the Primary 7 girls commented that 'This was the last week of digging so we were quite good at digging now! It took me a few weeks to learn how to dig properly!' Likewise one of the younger Primary 1 children acknowledged the social context of their learning to work as an archaeologist: in writing about an image of the archaeologist using a mattock to break the ground, he noted that 'I liked watching Craig pulling down the dirt.'

These children, reflecting on participating in an excavation, focused on the skills which they learned by first watching the archaeologist at work, and then by trying them out for themselves and gradually getting used to the feel of the trowel in their hand and the earth moving beneath it. The older children also recorded the time and patience it takes to carefully 'take the soil away in layers instead of clumps' and understood that the skill of archaeology is the ability to see the strata of earth as different layers of time through which history stretches through the ground, rather than as a series of disconnected small holes in the ground. This is echoed in the reflection of one of the Primary 2 girls who was commenting on an image of a drawing she had made of a sherd of pottery, in which she had taken the tiny remaining pattern on the sherd and had extended it to fill the paper. She said that 'I liked drawing and copying the pottery. I enjoyed digging, cos we found lots of pottery but I didn't like the rain but the next time we did it, it was sunny. I learned how it was for people in the old days.'

The second place that children chose images of was the classroom where they washed, sorted and interpreted the artefacts they had found. This provided a different place in which the children created their understandings of the past. The finds from each day of digging were initially sorted into trays which represented a particular place of excavation and also reflected when they were collected. Fewer children reflected on this process, but those who did highlighted the quantity of finds and the care which was needed to clean them carefully. For example, one of the children from the older class commented that 'In this photo its most of the class cleaning all the pottery. We must have found heaps because we had heaps of buckets of our finds to clean! We used toothbrushes to clean all the finds', whilst a child from the younger class noted the relationship between cleaning and sorting the finds and finding out about life in the past, commenting that 'After the digging we had to clean the finds in order to know what they are.'

The third place chosen by the children to reflect on their experiences was the school's community hall where an exhibition of their work for parents and extended family was held. As part of their preparation for creating the exhibition, the children visited the University of Aberdeen's King's Museum and participated in a workshop which focused on how exhibitions are created by museums. Building on this experience, the children worked as a whole school to plan how they were going to design their own exhibition in a replica Renaissance collector's cabinet so that it would be informative and capture the interest of family and community visitors who came to see their work. The children organised part of their exhibition chronologically and designed a quiz for visitors to find the oldest object and to guess the function of others. On the night of the exhibition, the pupils acted as guides to visitors, encouraging them to open the drawers of the cabinet to discover their archaeological finds. On recognising the pattern on one of the sherds of pottery, one of the children's grandparents told her grandchild her memories of growing up on a nearby farm and how they prepared brose in bowls with similar patterns for their breakfast. This experience resonates with both Bourdieu's idea of habitus and Ingold's contention that 'the practice of archaeology is itself a form of dwelling' (Ingold, 2000, p. 189) and highlights the centrality of rich social culture in supporting how children learn to inhabit the world. Through their experiences of working with the community archaeologist and the museum staff, and engaging their families and wider community in their work, the children learned to experience their local woodland and to dwell in it as archaeologists and historians. Their woodland now had a dimension in time as well as place. With the archaeologist they learned how to use historical maps and estate archives to choose a place of historical interest to excavate and then the practical skills of surveying and digging.

Social construction of the past

In the previous example, the children came to know their local area from a temporal perspective within the context of their school through the practice of archaeological fieldwork. In the following example, I consider the experience of children who physically encounter ancient monuments in the contemporary landscape, mostly in the company of family and friends or in the company of their peers.

This example is drawn from responses by children given as part of a wider remote visitor survey at six stone circle sites in Aberdeenshire between July and October 2006; the survey consisted of a questionnaire and an invitation to visitors to take a photograph on a disposable camera of their visit. Over the three-month period around 700 people responded to the questionnaire and about 300 photographs were taken. Of these returns, 43 were completed by children and 42 by adults accompanied by children. Unlike the children in the previous example, their experiences of being in an ancient place was not part of their formal learning but formed part of everyday activities such as walking the dog, going for a cycle or part of the practice of being on holiday. As Ingold has argued,

> knowledge of the world is gained by moving about in it, exploring it, attending to it, ever alert to the signs by which it is revealed. Learning to see, then, is a matter not of acquiring schemata for mentally constructing the environment but of acquiring the skills for direct perceptual engagement with its constituents, human and non-human, animate and inanimate.
>
> (Ingold, 2000, p. 55)

There are the remains of around 100 stone circles in this part of Scotland and they form an iconic part of the ancient landscape of

Put a ring around any of the words below which you would use when talking about stone circles

archaeology	stewardship	timeless	heritage
sacred	megalithic	solitude	wholeness
nature	peace	geology	ruin
neolithic	energy	people	old
bronze age	government		

Put a ring around any of the words below which describe what you do when you visit a stone circle

look at view   touch   count   excavate   sing
                     listen

perform rites   talk   rest   stand

        play   leave offerings

climb   party   picnic   dowse   sit
                     draw

take photographs   think   walk   eat

        read   write

drink

Figure 2.2   Extracts from visitor survey questionnaire (Curtis, 2011)

north-east Scotland. As part of the questionnaire respondents were asked to comment on why they came to visit and the places which they enjoyed visiting, circling words which they associated with the place and the kinds of things which they do when there (Figure 2.2).

Two of the stone circle sites are situated within walking distance of nearby villages, and this is reflected in the responses from children. For example, a boy from the village of Daviot completed a questionnaire at the stone circle next to his village. He had gone there in the evening with his mum and dogs to 'walk the dog'. The boy circled the words 'timeless, sacred, nature, peace and old' in relation to the stone circle and listed the following things which he did whilst there: 'touch, play, climb, sit, think, walk'.

In contrast a group of 14–18-year-olds from the same village completed a questionnaire at Daviot stone circle on a September evening. They noted that they had come to the circle to 'play on tree swings, banter!'. The only word which they circled in relation to stone circles was 'old'; in terms of what they did, they listed the following: 'touch, sing, play, talk, rest, stand, climb, party, sit, think, walk, eat, read, write, drink, smoke'. A similar response was left by a group of young people who lived near the circle at Tomnaverie, who recorded their visit on a summer night and gave their reason for visiting as 'party'. In relation to talking about stone circles they circled: 'megalithic, ruin, neolithic, people, old'; for things they had done, they circled all of the possible words.

The freedom to play away from the public gaze is also reflected in a set of photographs taken by a group of two men and their four teenage children. They had visited Tomnaverie at night and used the whole of one of the films in a disposable camera to photograph each other dancing and playing on the stones in the dark. Night-time provides a different form of embodied experience in which the sense of vision is diminished and other senses heightened. It also resonates with stories which highlight the role of fire and moonlight in the ancient uses of the circles.

Earlier in this chapter I argued following Smith (2006) that heritage should be considered as a socially constituted practice. The responses from some of the children in the survey demonstrate wider family practices of visiting places associated with particular times in the past and stone circles in particular. A 14-year-old from a village within 15 miles of Easter Aquorthies stone circle noted that she had gone there as 'something to do for the day', with 'my family' and that she had also visited the nearby circle at 'Daviot, places in Ireland, some different places around England', and that she also enjoyed visiting 'National Trust Properties'. She selected 'archaeology, heritage, sacred, nature, old', to describe stone circles and listed 'look at view, talk, sit, climb and think' as things which she did when there.

A 12-year-old boy from Aberdeen noted that he had arrived at Tomnaverie stone circle because he was 'on a bike ride to see around Tarland' with his mum. He listed other local stone circles and ancient monuments which he had visited, and noted that he enjoyed visiting bike trails and rivers. He selected 'archaeology, timeless, sacred, solitude, ruin and energy' in relation to stone circles, and listed 'look at view, touch, walk' as things which he did when there.

Ingold describes how the novice hunter 'travels through the country with his mentors, and as he goes, specific features are pointed out to him. Other things he discovers for himself, in the course of further forays, by watching, listening and feeling. Thus the experienced hunter is the knowledgeable hunter' (Ingold, 2000, p. 190). Like novice hunters, several children stated their reasons for coming to visit a stone circle as related to an existing family interest in places with ancient stones. A nine-year-old girl from Norfolk came to 'visit the stones,' with her 'mummy & dog' and noted that she had visited '8 others'. She selected the following words as associated with stone circles, 'timeless, nature, peace, people, old, bronze age', and listed the following as what she did whilst there: 'look at view, touch, count, play talk, rest, stand, leave offerings, climb, take photographs, think, walk'. A more local ten-year-old boy accompanied by his granddad noted that he had come because he had an 'interest in stone circles and Stonehenge' and that he had visited 'most local ones'. In all these examples, touch is a recurrent action noted in questionnaire returns and recorded in the images of children leaning, climbing, sitting and lying on stones. This resonates with a comment from Mark Paterson, citing Crang, with regard to haptic geographies: 'The recognition of the importance of haptics in everyday embodiment also signals the use of the body "as an instrument of research"...' (Crang, 2003, in Paterson, 2009, p. 771).

Returning to Bourdieu's concept of habitus and Ingold's idea of dwelling it is clear that for the children in this study the experience of visiting a stone circle is part of routines of both their day-to-day routines and their holiday practices. Through visiting them as part of walks, children encounter these places as a suitable destination point which offers a link to an ancient past, a good view and fresh air. Children also learn rules of visiting and expectations of behaviour both in relation to respect for the past and also in terms of links to a spiritual present.

Conclusion

Bourdieu (1977, p. 90) wrote that 'the "book" from which children learn their vision of the world is read with their body, in and through movements and displacements which make the space within which they are enacted as much as they are made by it'. While the social constructivist model promotes the benefits of working in social groups in which the more able help the less able to move beyond their current capacity, it is predominantly driven by the primacy of language. Bourdieu's ideas about the importance of embodied experience underline practice as being fundamental to the ways in which people represent the world.

In this chapter I have discussed different ways in which children have experienced and made sense of temporal aspects of place through examples of children in different social contexts. In each of these, children have played an active part in constructing their ideas about the past through direct experience in particular places and in particular social contexts. They took part in an excavation, designed an exhibition and explored stone circles. Their curiosity has been inspired through physical experience of the temporal aspects of place.

Ingold's idea of the dwelling perspective is particularly enlightening, however, when considering the first case study. While their archaeological work was a new experience, they carried out their archaeological work in an already familiar place where they were used to doing forest school activities as part of their outdoor learning. Through participation in the excavation children came to know this familiar place differently and came to understand it as a place of both the present and the past. Their familiarity can be seen as having offered them a sense of habitus: being pupils of a school with a strong commitment to learning outdoors gave them the confidence to engage with an archaeologist in the social practice of archaeology, and through this opportunity to master new sets of enquiry skills, which then led into producing an exhibition of their finds and archival work.

Through their experiences of visiting stone circles, children were making routes through the landscape, linking places of meaning to other parts of their lives. This combination of spatiality and temporality was particularly clearly seen through the process of excavation, finds processing and creating an exhibition, in which the children developed skills and become active social agents who were able to convey their developed understandings of their local place to other people. Through their participation in family activities and environmental learning organised through schooling, children have constructed their understandings of temporality and spatiality in tandem, entangling these ideas within their own social lives as they themselves contribute to the histories of these places.

References

Bourdieu, P. (1977) *Outline of a Theory of Practice*, trans. Richard Nice, Cambridge: Cambridge University Press.

Catling, S. and Willy, S. (2009) *Teaching Primary Geography (Achieving QTS series)*, Exeter: Learning Matters.

Cooper, H. (1995) *History in the Early Years*, London and New York: Routledge.

Cooper, H. (2012) *History 5–11: A Guide for Teachers*, London: Routledge.

Curtis, E. (2011) *Bringing Stone Circles Being: Practices in the Long 19th Century and Their Influence on Current Understanding of Stone Circles in the North-East of Scotland*, University of Aberdeen, unpublished thesis.

Education Scotland (2010) *Curriculum for Excellence Through Outdoor Learning*: http://www.educationscotland.gov.uk/learningteachingandassessment/approaches/outdoorlearning/about/cfethroughoutdoorlearning.asp.

Horton, J. and Kraftl, P. (2006) 'What Else? Some More Ways of Thinking and Doing "Children's Geographies" ', *Children's Geographies*, 4 (1), 69–95.

Ingold, T. (2000) *The Perception of the Environment: Essays on Livelihood, Dwelling and Skill*, 189. London and New York: Routledge.

James, A. (2013) *Socialising Children*, Basingstoke: Palgrave Macmillan.

Paterson, M. (2009) 'Haptic Geographies: Ethnology, Haptic Knowledges and Sensuous Dispositions', *Progress in Human Geography*, 33 (6), 66–788.

Scoffham, S. (2010) 'Young Geographers', in S. Scoffham (ed.) 2nd edition, *Primary Geography Handbook*, Sheffield: Geographical Association.

Smith, L. (2006) *Uses of Heritage*, London: Routledge, 15–33.

Tilley, C. (2004) *The Materiality of Stone: Explorations in Landscape Phenomenology*, Oxford: Berg.

Turner-Bisset, R. (2005) *Creative Teaching: History in the Primary Classroom*, London: David Fulton.

3
Making the 'Here' and 'Now': Rethinking Children's Digital Photography with Deleuzian Concepts

Mona Sakr and Natalia Kucirkova

The context of art-making offers the opportunity to engage with children's embodied experiences of place and space. Through art-making, children both interact with and construct the world around them. The recent application of Deleuzian frameworks to studies of children's art-making has disrupted the tendency to understand this process in terms of schemata organised into linear narratives (MacRae, 2011; Clark, 2012; Knight, 2013). In particular, Deleuzian notions of sense-making and of the rhizome unsettle modern, developmental approaches to art-making that emphasise the role of schematic representation and mimesis in children's embodied experiences of space. As a contribution to this unsettling process, this chapter focuses on how these concepts can facilitate insights into children's photography and the way photography enables children to engage with and construct the 'here' and 'now'. By examining children's photography from this perspective, we can develop new insights into how children's experiences of and relationships to place unfold. In particular, we consider how children's embodied interaction during the process of taking photographs, when analysed using these Deleuzian concepts, can challenge modern, developmental approaches to interpreting children's experiences of the world.

The chapter opens with an overview of the theoretical framework, which introduces the Deleuzian concepts of sense-making (as contrasted with the notion of 'common sense') and rhizomatic structures of experience (as contrasted with linearity). We then explore how these perspectives relate to a short episode of collaborative child-parent photography in the home and the way in which the child engages with and constructs the physical world around them through this experience. Analysis of this episode focuses on the child's bodily practices as a means for grasping the world anew, and how these come into tension with the father's bodily practices, which construct photography as a means for evenly spaced mimetic representations of the surrounding environment. These tensions are explored further through four dimensions of dissonance in the child's and the parent's bodily practices: proximity, direction, pace and stillness. In the discussion, we argue that using Deleuzian concepts allows greater value to be placed on children's embodied interaction with art-making media, including photography, and the capacity for this interaction to be seen as innovative and a productive challenge to adult-led navigation and negotiation of the physical world.

Sense-making versus common sense

Deleuzian sense-making is seen as a continuous process in which ideas are formed and re-formed through experiences that are in constant flux (Lambert, 2005; Surin, 2005). As a result, the conceptions that we have of the world around us are not static, but continuously evolving. What we might refer to as 'here' is 'becoming-here'; similarly what is 'now' is only ever 'becoming-now'. This understanding of how we think about the world is in tension with the conception of 'common sense', which suggests that thought primarily involves the recognition in the world of objects or events that match pre-existing schemata. For example, using a 'common sense' approach, when encountering a dog, we settle for a sense of 'dogness'; in Deleuzian notions of sense-making, the ideas that arise in an encounter with a dog are specific to that particular situation, and are imbued with the abundant details that make the particular dog different from all others. While a 'common sense' ontology 'domesticate[s] difference' (Poxon and Stivale, 2005, p. 66), sense-making from a Deleuzian perspective emerges directly from experience and fully engages with the endless differences that constitute the world.

While notions of 'common sense' may seem fitting for understanding our commonplace interactions with the everyday world, the more elaborate practice of sense-making may be foregrounded in experiences of active exploration and creative engagement with the world around us. Expressive arts practices for example, have been suggested as a vehicle through which the differences of the world, in all their constant newness and ornateness, can be found and embraced. The practice of 'making strange', for example, as celebrated by the interdisciplinary scholar and professor of dance and philosophy Maxine Sheets-Johnstone, explores the potential of dance to displace and disrupt familiar or habitual movements, and, in doing so, to offer time and space to new sensations and ideas that arise through new experiences (Sheets-Johnstone, 1999; Loke and Robertson, 2008). The practice of 'making strange' can be thought of as a shift away from a 'common sense' perspective towards the notion of sense-making as described by Deleuze (2004). While the language of adult art-making often draws on this form of engagement and exploration (Irwin et al., 2006; Springgay, 2008), children's art-making is typically understood in terms of the representation of schemata (e.g. Coates, 2002; Ahn and Filipenko, 2007; Coates and Coates, 2011; Golomb, 2011). Within this approach, photographs taken by children are understood in relation to the discernible objects that are included in these photographs and how this relates to the wider schemata that the child has knowledge and understanding of.

Through the notion of sense-making, Deleuzian approaches to children's art-making have drawn attention to the multiplicity of influences on meaning-making, as it is shaped through the interrelation of bodies, materials and environments (Springgay, 2008; MacRae, 2011; Clark, 2012; Knight, 2013). Recent observational research on children's art-making has suggested that the meanings children construct through art-making are best understood as fleeting ideas that are 'unstable and contingent' (Sellers, 2013, p. 10), which exist to build the world anew rather than to represent the existing world. According to this perspective, 'the expressed does not exist outside its expression' (Lambert, 2005, p. 33), and as such, children's artwork is not seen as a representation of something else but instead an active grasping and constructing of the 'here' and 'now'. Without the constant search for the 'whole or truthful image' (Knight, 2013, p. 8) that is assumed to underpin art-making, we can engage more readily with the 'unexpected or unexplainable' (*ibid.*, p. 9) and the 'characterising affect' (Sellers, 2008, p. 9) of children's ideas.

Rhizomatic versus linear structures

As well as challenging the schemata that underpin a 'common sense' perspective, Deleuze and Guattari (1987) challenge the linear narratives according to which we often describe and represent our experiences. They invoke the biological structure of the rhizome to suggest an alternative structure for our experiences of the world around us. The rhizome has a continuously growing stem with lateral offshoots. With no beginning or end, rhizomatic structures suggest that all exists within a 'muddle~middle' that is 'ceaselessly establishing connections' (Sellers, 2013, p. xv), to be organised (if at all) through plateaus, rather than linear alignments. Feminist poststructuralist studies have applied the concept of the rhizome as a new way of seeing and understanding children's interactions with the world around them (Sellers, 2013).

Building on the concept of 'lines of flight', MacRae (2011) notes the potential of children's ideas, particularly within art-making, 'to take flight into unforeseen directions, shattering any emerging direction or order' (p. 103). Applied to children's junk modelling, she notes how each item is often an addition in relation to the one added just before, so that there is no single act of composition but instead a constant re-composition which 'disrupts usual ways of thinking about representation and intention' (MacRae, 2011, p. 106). The 'rhizo mo(ve)ment' is a concept developed by Sellers (2013, p. xix) to suggest how children's offshoots in ideas are visible through their physical engagement with the world around them. Moments of creative diversion are also movements of physical diversion; this suggests that a focus on children's bodily engagement would be particularly helpful in engaging with how children construct place and space through art-making practices as understood from a Deleuzian perspective. Adult interventions in children's bodily practices can be read, according to this view, as an attempt to linearise what appears to be randomness and serendipity in the interactions of children (Sellers, 2013).

The present study

Applying the concepts of sense-making and rhizomatic structures to collaborative parent-child photography can help us to rethink children's experiences of taking photographs and their engagement with the practice as a means for constructing the world around them. Concepts that have been foregrounded in studies of photography (both adult and child photography) can be related back to the debates that were introduced in the previous sections of this chapter. The centrality in investigations of photography on 'framing' and chronological ordering can be challenged through these Deleuzian notions.

Framing photographs

Photography as a process has often focused on the act of framing. Framing is understood to be a rhetorical device through which photographers create and distribute particular messages about the world (Edwards, 2006). Understanding framing as a central act within photography highlights the intentionality of the photographer and suggests that, in line with 'common sense' perspectives, experiences of the world around us are organised through schemata that we look for and recognise. The frames we create in photographs are seen as an expression or reaction to our recognition of objects in the world. This aspect of the photographic process, along with the notion of storytelling, is often emphasised within childhood photography where a common follow-up activity is to organise the photographs sequentially, following a chronological order. This approach is also followed by several digital story-making and art-making applications, including the app Our Story, which the child and parent used as part of the study described here.

Rhizomatic photography

Alternative perspectives on photography have suggested that photographs should be understood more as fragments of experience, rather than as part of a coherent whole (Szarkowski, 1973). This relates to Knight's (2013) description of children's drawings as a 'momentary stillness', and suggests that photography could also be conceptualised as specific 'here' and 'now' constructions within the haphazard sense-making process described by Deleuze and Guattari (1987). For Barthes (1977), the complexity and magic of photography arises from its potential to conjoin the 'here' and 'now' with the 'there' and 'then', and in doing so, photography highlights the fleeting nature of current experiences. This echoes the Deleuzian focus on the emergence of ideas directly from experience and a full engagement through sense-making with the singularity of each moment of experience. This type of engagement can be seen to some extent in studies of child photography that initially set out to use photographs as a form of visual elicitation. For example, Richards (2009) used photography as a means for children to 'share their stories' (p. 8) on art-making but documented examples of child engagement in which photography was used as a means for exploring the world, rather than representing it. For example, one child took repeated close-ups of various objects, so that they were no longer discernible, in order to explore the block colour effect that this would create.

While there are various ways of conceptualising photography, and these are more or less related to Deleuzian notions of sense-making and rhizomatic structure, we were keen to engage with children's actual experiences and practices of taking photographs to see whether and how these concepts are made visible through bodily practices in unfolding interactions. In order to explore these ideas further, we analysed a short episode of collaborative child-parent photography which took place in the home. This episode was taken from a case study research project designed to explore parent-child collaborative art-making in the home with four different art-making resources.

Study participants

The study participants were a three-year-old girl and her father. At the time of the study, the girl was the only child of the family. She attended an inner-city London nursery each weekday between 8 am and 5.30 pm, where she was described by the nursery practitioners as making above-average levels of educational progress. Her father was 35 years old at the time of the study and worked as a journalist. The father picked up his daughter most days from the nursery and the pair frequently engaged in shared activities at home, and this sometimes, though not often, included making art together. Prior to this study, the child and father had never taken photographs together, and according to the father, the child had never before taken photographs by herself or in the nursery setting. Observations of the child taking photographs supported the parent's observation, suggesting that this was indeed her first experience of manipulating and using an iPad camera.

Over the course of the entire research study, the child and father engaged in two episodes of photography using an iPad2 with inbuilt camera. In both episodes, they took photographs using the camera tool on the iPad and later collated these images using the iPad application Our Story. Our Story was developed at the Open University and was designed to enable children, members of their family and their friends to work together to produce a multimodal personalised narrative by combining photographs, audio recordings and written text. Users can use their existing pictures saved in the 'camera roll' or they can take new pictures using the iPad camera. There are several stages involved in making a product via Our Story including taking photographs, organising these photographs into a sequence and adding audio and/or written captions to the photographs; in this study, we only focus on the process of taking new photographs.

The primary researcher recorded the episode using a handheld video camera. As the child's aunt, the primary researcher knew the family very well which enabled observations to remain relaxed and sensitive to the context (see Adler and Adler, 1996, for discussion of family-member-as-researcher). The primary researcher was careful to interrupt the parent-child collaborative art-making as little as possible, though she was sometimes drawn into the interaction by the child and responded sensitively to this.

The study was approved by the ethics committee at the Open University, UK, and followed the BERA's Revised Ethical Guidelines for Educational Research (2004), as well as the NCRM's Guidelines for Visual Research.

Data analysis

To engage with the data, we used multimodal interaction analysis. Multimodal approaches focus on the wide range of communicational forms that individuals use when interacting with each other (Jewitt, 2009; Kress, 2010). In the case of multimodal interaction analysis, there is a close focus on various communicational modes (including body position, movement, gaze, body posture, gesture, speech) in order to understand how activity is organised sequentially (Jewitt et al., 2001) and the 'semiotic work' that particular aspects of the interaction are doing in the wider social context of the interaction (Goodwin, 2000; Sakr et al., 2014). 'Rough' multimodal transcripts were created for all of the data collected from the study. This enabled familiarisation with the data and the identification of specific episodes that could support further analyses in relation to particular issues and ideas.

The short episode of interaction presented here, approximately 30 seconds long, focuses on an investigation into the potential of the child's 'rhizo mo(ve)ments' to disrupt linear organisation of the experience of taking photographs around the home. Fine-grained multimodal interaction analysis provided a means for identifying and gaining insights into how the child's and the father's bodily practices reflected (or did not reflect) the Deleuzian concepts of sense-making and rhizomatic structures of the experience.

In order to explore this short episode, and drawing on the approach of Charles Goodwin (2000), the data were re-worked through various types of visual analysis (Rose, 2012). In the findings, these different representations of the data are used to further examine the relevant concepts. For example, by mapping their movement through the hallway space, we could consider the dissonances between the parent's and the child's physical engagement with the space. These dissonances were organised into particular dimensions of dissonance in their bodily practices.

The episode

This episode is taken from video footage of the first time in which the iPad was used by the child and the father. The episode occurred early in the interaction, between 1:52 and 2:15 in a total of 15 minutes of engagement. In the episode (Table 3.1), the child and her father are walking through the hallway of the house. The child is holding the iPad up in front of her and looking at her surroundings through the screen. She points the camera down, so that it is directed towards a bag lying on the hallway floor. The father stands back and asks from behind 'What is it?'; she replies 'Mona's bag'. As she says this, she is already taking a couple of steps to the right and positioning the camera, ready to take another photograph, this time of the telephone handset in the corner of the hallway on the floor. The father asks: 'And what's down there?'. Immediately he says: 'Wait to take it' (suggesting that she should be still before she captures the image); she then takes the photograph and he comments: 'That's it'. The father

62

Table 3.1 The selected episode in detail

Time (mins:secs)	Image	Child	Father
1:52		C: 'Mona's bag.' The child takes a photograph of something on the floor while standing still.	The father stands back. F: 'What is it?'
2:04		Child walks away a couple of steps and positions the camera to take another photograph, this time of the telephone handset on the floor. She takes a series of photographs of the telephone, each time shifting her body orientation and posture slightly.	F: 'And what's down there?' F: 'Wait to take it, that's it.'

2:07	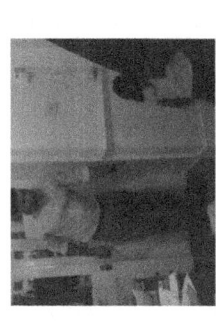	The child stands and re-positions the camera, taking photographs of other objects/same objects that are nearby.	F: 'Shall we go in the front room?' Father laughs. Father begins to open the door to the front room. His gaze is on the child. F: 'Shall we go into the front room and see what we can see?'
2:11	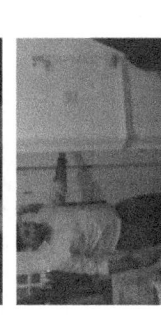	Child is looking at the iPad screen and continuing to take photographs of the objects immediately around her. C (distracted): 'Yeh?' Child is taking more photographs.	Father pushes the door of the front room open. F: '[name of child]?' Father stands still, gaze on the child.
2:14	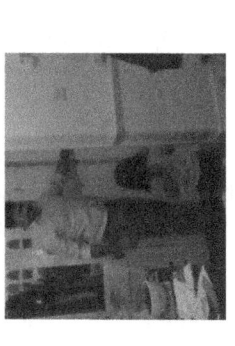	Child walks towards the front room and through the door. C: 'I've finished.'	Father holds the door open.

takes a few steps forward towards the closed door of another room. Holding the door handle, he asks: 'Shall we go in the front room?'. The child does not reply. She re-positions the camera closer to the telephone and takes another photograph. This sequence is repeated two more times. The father laughs and looks briefly at the researcher. He asks 'Shall we go in the front room and see what we can see?'. He begins to open the door to the front room while looking at the child. The child continues to look at the iPad screen and to take photographs of the objects around her. The father calls the child by her name while pushing the door open. The child responds distractedly: 'yeh?'. After a few seconds of silence in which the child is taking more photographs, the child looks up and walks towards the front room saying 'I've finished'.

Organising the verbal and non-verbal interactions of the child and the father via the multimodal transcript suggested some clear dissonances in the child's and the father's bodily practices. For example, the father's verbal engagement is dominant and there is a lack of verbal response on the part of the child. The father appears ready to move on physically, but the child is preoccupied and resists her father's suggestion. We wanted to explore these apparent dissonances further in order to investigate conceptual tensions and debates as they are made visible through the body. The episode analysed in-depth in this chapter was chosen because of its illustrative value in exemplifying these dissonances.

Dimensions of dissonance

Initial analysis of this episode suggested dissonances in the child's and the father's bodily practices, which suggested differences in the way they were constructing the process of taking photographs. To explore these dissonances further, we considered them according to four dimensions of the interaction in which dissonances were particularly visible. These dimensions were developed in dialogue with existing literature on multimodal interactions and sequences (e.g. Hornby, 2010; Sakr et al., 2014), but are not drawn directly from an existing framework; they are:

- proximity – the closeness of the photographer to the object being photographed or explored;

- stillness – whether the individual is still before taking a photograph or whether they take photographs while moving;
- direction – the individual's orientation of physical interest and how this unfolds over time;
- pace – how the individual navigates space over time and the points in time at which shifts in orientation of physical interest occur.

Proximity

Across the entire interaction, the father often suggested to the child that she should stand further away from the object she was photographing. It is likely that this directive stemmed from the value placed by the father on capturing a 'whole and truthful image' (Knight, 2013, p. 8), which he conceived as a complete framing of a physical object. For example, in capturing a photographic image of the phone, it was important to the father that this photograph would include a discernible representation of the whole telephone. Capturing schematic representations in this manner relates to the notion of 'common sense' as well as the perceived need for linear narratives, in which schematic representations are easily organised into a logical sequence; for example, a chronological sequence. This episode demonstrates how the adult prioritised the skill of framing to be central in photography. This may stem from a belief that this is a key skill to be 'passed on' to the child, but it is also likely to be influenced by elements of the context including the use of the application Our Story, which suggests that photographs will be organised into a linear, potentially chronological, narrative.

Despite her father's verbal advice, the child repeatedly held the camera very close to the object she was interested in, often taking photographs while moving closer and closer to the object. The father's repeated instruction to stand further away and to stay still while taking a photograph suggested that he perceived the child's movement in photography as representative of underdeveloped skill on the part of the child. However, there are other ways of perceiving the child's close and increasing proximity to objects that she wanted to photograph. Richards (2009), in her research on children's photography of their art-making experiences, described a particular child who repeatedly took close-up photographs in order to experiment with the creation of blocks of colour. In our study, there were few representations of discernible objects, but other visual effects were

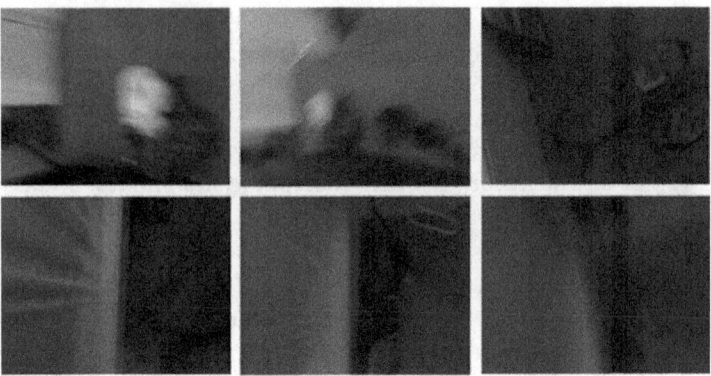

Figure 3.1   A series of six photographs taken by the child

created through the child's close-up photography (see Figure 3.1). The photographs are mostly blurry, conveying a sense of motion and the transient nature of experience. As early as in the 1880s, Cizek emphasised children's ability to 'transcend the ordinary or everyday through imaginative creativity' (Malvern, 1995, p. 262). While adult photography is often characterised by realistic depictions of objects in the space, the child's conceptualisation is clearly different and possesses a distinct creative potential.

Stillness

The child often took multiple photographs while moving towards an object of interest. Photographs taken while the photographer is moving create an interesting tension between the stillness of the resulting image, and the movement that is captured across the sequence of photographs taken one after the other (see Figure 3.1). In taking these photographs, the child is constructing the 'here' and 'now' as a set of moments strung together. According to Barthes' (1977, 1981) understanding of photography, photography provides us with the sense of an immediate presence in the world, the 'there' and 'here' are conjoined and intertwined. In the episode analysed here, the child tracked her own journey through the space through rapid and repeated photography, constructing the 'here' and 'now' while in motion. Knight (2013) suggests that drawings are best understood as a 'momentary stillness' in a sequence or pattern of motion; in the experience here, the child's photographs are multiple 'momentary stillnesses' both capturing motion and created *in* motion.

According to the father, it is important to be still when taking a photograph. He tells the child to 'wait to take it', meaning that she should approach the object, position herself in relation to the object, stand still and then take the photograph. The notion of capturing a discernible image is important again here – the desire to capture a 'whole and truthful image' (Knight, 2013, p. 8), as well as a respect for the principles of 'balanced composition' (Arnheim, 1974/1954; Winner and Gardner, 1981; Golomb and Farmer, 1983). In addition to these principles, the father is drawing on his embodied knowledge of the conventions of taking a photograph. He has an awareness of a conventionalised bodily routine that is often associated with taking photographs; this involves waiting to be still before taking a photograph. This routine, however, may be changing in the age of digital iPad photography, where numerous images can be taken and discarded immediately and can capture motion in the form of motion blur.

Direction

The father plots his movement through space in this episode according to objects of interest that he considers to be 'photograph-worthy'. His attention shifts steadily from one discrete object to another. His interest in these objects as 'photograph-worthy' is suggested by his emphasis on naming the objects that the child is photographing. As she takes a photograph of a bag on the hallway floor, he asks 'What is it?' and the child replies. When the child's direction of attention shifts to other objects including the telephone, telephone cord, shoes and radiator, he asks again: 'And what's down there?'. This time however, the child does not reply. Through this questioning, the father is attempting to narrate the journey through the house according to a series of objects that they encounter. Furthermore, once the child has taken a photograph of one particular physical area, he assumes that she will be ready to move onto another area and the objects it contains. As a result, he moves ahead of her to the next place he expects them to go: 'Shall we go into the front room?'. He is ready to move on before the child, because the direction of his attention shifts as soon as a photograph displaying a discernible representation has been taken.

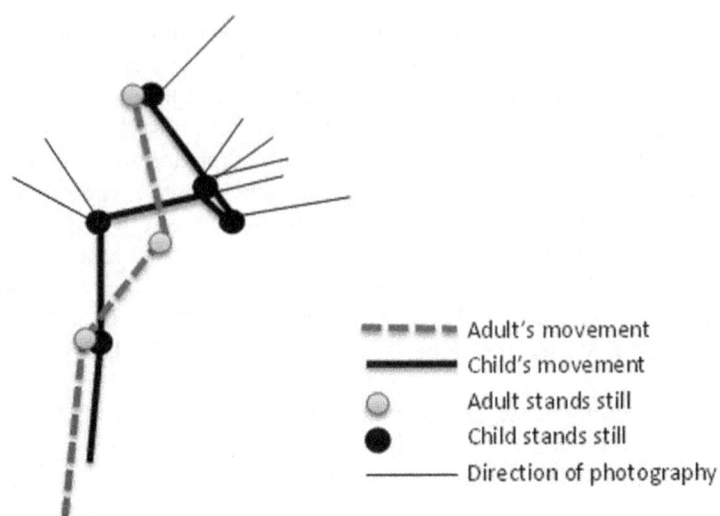

▬ ▬ ▬ ▬	Adult's movement
▬▬▬▬	Child's movement
◯	Adult stands still
●	Child stands still
————	Direction of photography

Figure 3.2   Movements through the space of the hallway

The movement of the child through space is less linear as can be seen in Figure 3.2, which traces the father's and the child's movements through the hallway. The child's movements correspond to the rhizo mo(ve)ments suggested by Sellers (2013) and the 'lines of flight' described by MacRae (2011). One particular way in which this is visible is through the dramatic shifts in the scale of the child's movements. While the father has an expectation that they will move from one object to another, the child's movements shift from this type of exploration to more finely grained movements. For example, when her interest and attention is directed towards the telephone on the hallway carpet, she moves around much more 'on the spot', shifting her upper body and changing the positioning of her hands while taking photographs, but not taking any steps. This sequence of minor re-orientation suggests that the child, in contrast with her father, does not consider this to be a repetitive taking of the same image, but instead an exploration of differences that exist on a small scale. There are parallels here with the principles of professional digital photography, where even small movements with the camera can enable artists to capture a distinct impression of the space.

Pace

As described in the section above, the child's movement during this episode changes scale, from gross movements to finer-grained adjustments in position. This mirrors the changes in pace that the child goes through. She speeds up in certain moments to take multiple photographs of the 'same' object (though the sameness of the object depends on taking a schematic view), and then waits to move through a relatively large area of space before taking another photograph. For example, she takes multiple photographs of the telephone, while changing her position only slightly, and then moves off towards the front room, walking quickly and without taking any photographs. This manner of engagement led to photographs that were not evenly spaced in time or place. Instead, what was created corresponded much more to the Deleuzian notion of lateral offshoots in experience which are each explored to a different extent.

On the other hand, the father's movement through space suggests a prioritisation of a steady pace, in which time and space are evenly 'cut' with the taking of photographs. His rhythm, throughout the activity of taking photographs around the house, involved a repeated sequence of taking a few steps, standing still, framing the photograph and taking the photograph. These regularly spaced moments were also often accompanied by the naming of the object captured in the photograph. The documents that he strived to create represent a steady paced journey through the house, punctuated by the 'collection' through photography of discernible objects that are easily sequenced according to the chronological order in which they were encountered. It could be that the father's movements and behaviours were in this episode influenced by the prospect of using the photographs for a digital narrative with the Our Story app, and by the consideration that the episode was being observed for the purposes of a research project about art-making. Photographs are typically arranged in a sequence to tell a story (e.g. Das and Conway, 1992) and the father may have modelled the behaviour he expected the child to follow. Because he didn't make it explicit to the child, however, she did not focus on taking pictures in a specific sequence but instead, enjoyed the 'here and now' interaction with the space.

Discussion

Knight (2013) has argued that a Deleuzian approach to children's art-making can help us rethink early childhood art-making, and look beyond schematic representations and linear narratives. In this study, we explored the potential for this perspective to elucidate not just children's relationship with art-making, but their embodied engagement with place and space through the practices of photography. More specifically, we focused on two Deleuzian concepts – sense-making and rhizomatic structures of experience – and used these to explore dissonances in the bodily practices of a child and her father while they engaged in photography around the home. In a fine-grained analysis of a short episode of interaction, dissonances between the child and the father were observed in terms of: proximity to the object of interest; the need for stillness when taking photographs; the direction of interest; and the pace of the photographic journey around the house.

Sense-making and the rhizome enabled us to appreciate the potential value in children's rhizo mo(ve)ments and the 'lines of flight' that characterise their movements through space when engaged in an art-making experience. Rather than thinking about children's art, in this case photography, as deficient representations of a 'whole or truthful image' (Knight, 2013, p. 8), we thought differently about its creative intent and outcome. Children's initial experiments with art-making media are often conceptualised in terms of an asymmetrical relationship between adults and children, with the child positioned as an apprentice to an adult, who gradually acquires a set of skills that will allow the child to engage appropriately with a particular media. Drawing on Deleuzian concepts, a child's initial experiments with photography are no longer seen as deficient acts of representation, but active constructions of the 'here' and 'now'. In her study of children's art-making, MacRae (2011) used Foucault's idea of heterotopia along with Deleuze and Guttari's concept of 'smooth space' – space through which rhizomatic movements and 'lines of flight' can occur – to argue that the various artefacts produced by children participating in her research often did not have a representational purpose but were instead actively grappling with the 'here' and 'now'. As MacRae (2011) puts it: 'I now see pieces of work that previously might have appeared as deficient representations of space in terms of their potential to re-create it' (p. 111). From this perspective, not only is children's art-making not deficient, it is informative and inspiring. We can return to the idea of 'making strange', as introduced and practiced by Sheets-Johnstone (1999), to understand the potential of looking carefully at children's engagement with space through photography for rethinking our own embodied interaction with space, particularly when engaged in art-making experiments and experiences. Schematic representations and linear narratives are a 'cultural arbitrary' (Bourdieu and Passeron, 1990), and represent only one potential of many for how to engage with the surrounding space. We can learn from children's syncopated engagement with the world around them, their dramatic shifts in space, their lateral offshoots, their desire to do close-ups with a camera and their experiments with motion and stillness.

In this chapter, we have introduced Deleuzian concepts that have the potential to re-invigorate and challenge modern, developmental approaches to children's art-making. Instead of thinking in terms of schematic representation and linear narrative, we have suggested that the Deleuzian concepts of sense-making and the rhizomatic structure of experience can help to shift our perceptions of children's photography and the way in which children construct the 'here' and 'now' through their photographic practices. To explore this further, we considered a short episode of parent-child collaborative photography around the home, and investigated the dissonances between the child's and the father's embodied interaction with the process of photography. These dissonances were organised according to four dimensions, which enabled insights into the cultural conventions, or 'arbitraries', that were guiding the father's interaction with the space around him, and the space that the child's bodily engagement with photography was challenging. The analysis showed that despite the father's expectations and his directions to his daughter, her photography was not characterised by linear progression through the space or stillness when taking individual pictures.

The findings of this study are particularly relevant for digital photography and children's applications using photography as a means of engaging children in art-making and enabling them to consider and explore their relationships with space. With the advent of portable multimedia technologies such as iPads, children of increasingly young age have begun to engage in photography and photo-sharing. Tablets and iPads allow the possibility of taking photographs with an inbuilt camera. In addition, there are several art-making applications which can be downloaded on the device and which leverage the facility of photography. This study did not focus on a particular photography app, but instead considered the *process* of digital photography by a young child. The portability and ease of use of the device were contributing factors to the observed patterns, as they allowed the child to direct and pace her photography and control the proximity between her and the depicted object. With the rise of wearable technologies, future research might consider how these processes change in response to novel characteristics of the camera (e.g. the Autographer™ camera enables spontaneous, hands-free image capture). It is also worth considering how the parent-child dynamics of the photography process change in relation to specific iPad apps using digital images. The Our Story app used as part of our study comes with a linear design, where pictures can be arranged in a sequence on a filmstrip (Kucirkova et al., 2014). To take a photograph, however, the user is taken outside of the application to the digital camera, thus allowing for free, open-ended photography. We need to examine how the process of arranging captured images in a chronological order on the app filmstrip influences parents' and children's perceptions of the 'here' and 'now' of photography.

In conclusion, we borrowed the concepts of sense-making and rhizomatic structures and applied them to a child's experience of photography with a digital camera at home with her father. By looking at children's photography through the lens of Deleuzian concepts, we argued that children's art-making, particularly their initial experimentation with an art-making medium like photography, can be liberated from discourses of deficiency and apprenticeship. Instead, we can gain much from carefully engaging with children's ways of engaging with the world around them through photography; they can 'make strange' and therefore enrich our own embodied interactions with the world around us.

References

Adler, P. and Adler, P. (1996) 'Parent-as-Researcher: The Politics of Researching in the Personal Life', *Qualitative Sociology*, 19 (1), 35–58.

Ahn, J., & Filipenko, M. (2007) 'Narrative, Imaginary Play, Art, and Self: Intersecting Worlds', *Early Childhood Education Journal*, 34 (4), 279–289.

Arnheim, R. (1954/1974) *Art and Visual Perception*, Berkeley, CA: University of California Press.

Barthes, R. (1977) *Image, Music, Text*, London: HarperCollins.

Barthes, R. (1981) *Camera lucida: Reflections on Photography*, London: Macmillan.

Bourdieu, P. and Passeron, J. C. (1990) *Reproduction in Education, Society and Culture* (Vol. 4), London: Sage.

Clark, V. (2012) 'Art Practice as Possible Worlds', *International Journal of Child, Youth and Family Studies*, 3 (2–3), 198–213.

Coates, E. (2002) ' "I Forgot the Sky!" Children's Stories Contained Within Their Drawings', *International Journal of Early Years Education*, 10 (1), 21–35.

Coates, E. and Coates, A. (2011) 'The Subjects and Meanings of Young Children's Drawings,' in D. Faulkner and E. Coates (eds) *Exploring Children's Creative Narratives*, London: Routledge, pp. 86–110.

Das, J. P. and Conway, R. N. (1992) 'Reflections on Remediation and Transfer: A Vygotskian Perspective', in C. Haywood and D. Tsuriel (eds) *Interactive Assessment*, New York: Springer-Verlag, pp. 94–115.

Deleuze, G. (2004) *Anti-Oedipus*, London: Bloomsbury Publishing.

Deleuze, G. and Guattari, F. (1987) *A Thousand Plateaus: Capitalism and Schizophrenia*, Minneapolis: University of Minnesota Press.

Edwards, S. (2006) *Photography: A Very Short Introduction*, Oxford: Oxford University Press.

Golomb, C. (2011) *The Creation of Imaginary Worlds: The Role of Art, Magic and Dreams in Child Development*, London: Jessica Kingsley Publishers.

Golomb, C. and Farmer, D. (1983) 'Children's Graphic Planning Strategies and Early Principles of Spatial Organization in Drawing', *Studies in Art Education*, 24 (2), 86–100.

Goodwin, C. (2000) 'Action and Embodiment Within Situated Human Interaction', *Journal of Pragmatics*, 32 (10), 1489–1522.

Hornby, L. (2010) 'Stillness and the Anticinematic in the Work of Fiona Tan', *Grey Room*, (41), 48–71.

Irwin, R. L., Beer, R., Springgay, S., Grauer, K., Xiong, G. and Bickel, B. (2006) 'The Rhizomatic Relations of A/r/tography', *Studies in Art Education*, 48 (1), 70–88.

Jewitt, C. (ed.) (2009) *The Routledge Handbook of Multimodal Analysis*, London: Routledge.

Jewitt, C., Kress, G., Ogborn, J. and Tsatsarelis, C. (2001) 'Exploring Learning Through Visual, Actional and Linguistic Communication: The Multimodal Environment of a Science Classroom', *Educational Review*, 53 (1), 5–18.

Knight, L. M. (2013) 'Not as It Seems: Using Deleuzian Concepts of the Imaginary to Rethink Children's Drawings', *Global Studies of Childhood*, 3 (3), 254–264.

Kress, G. (2010) *Multimodality: A Social Semiotic Approach to Contemporary Communication*, London: Routledge.

Kucirkova, N., Sheehy, K. and Messer, D. (2014) 'A Vygotskian Perspective on Parent–Child Talk During iPad Story Sharing', *Journal of Research in Reading*. Article first published online: 3 June 2014, DOI: 10.1111/1467-9817.12030.

Lambert, G. (2005) 'Expression', in C. J. Stivale (ed.) *Gilles Deleuze: Key Concepts*, Chesham: Acumen Publishing, pp. 31–42.

Loke, L. and Robertson, T. (2008) 'Inventing and Devising Movement in the Design of Movement-Based Interactive Systems', Proceedings of the 20th Australian Conference on Human–Computer Interaction (OzCHI'08), New York: ACM, pp. 81–88.

MacRae, C. (2011) 'Making Payton's Rocket: Heterotopia and Lines of Flight', *International Journal of Art & Design Education*, 30 (1), 102–112.

Malvern, S. B. (1995) 'Inventing "Child Art": Franz Cizek and Modernism', *British Journal of Aesthetics*, 35 (3), 262–272.

Poxon, J. L. and Stivale, C. J. (2005) 'Sense, Series', in C. J. Stivale (ed.) *Gilles Deleuze: Key Concepts*, Chesham: Acumen Publishing, pp. 65–77.

Richards, R. D. (2009) 'Young Visual Ethnographers: Children's Use of Digital Photography to Record, Share and Extend Their Art Experiences', *International Art in Early Childhood Research Journal*, 1 (1), 1–16.

Rose, G. (2012) *Visual Methodologies: An Introduction to Researching with Visual Materials*, London: Sage.

Sakr, M., Jewitt, C. and Price, S. (2014) 'The Semiotic Work of the Hands in Scientific Enquiry', *Classroom Discourse*, 5 (1), 51–70.

Sellers, M. (2013) *Young Children Becoming Curriculum: Deleuze, Te Whariki and Curricular Understandings*, Abingdon: Routledge.

Sellers, W. (2008) *Picturing Currere Towards c u r a: Rhizo-Imaginary for Curriculum*. Unpublished PhD thesis, Deakin University.

Sheets-Johnstone, M. (1999) 'Emotion and Movement. A Beginning Empirical-Phenomenological Analysis of Their Relationship', *Journal of Consciousness Studies*, 6 (11–12), 11–12.

Springgay, S. (2008) 'An Ethics of Embodiment, Civic Engagement and A/r/tography: Ways of Becoming Nomadic in Art, Research and Teaching', *Educational Insights*, 12 (2), 1–11.

Surin, K. (2005) 'Force', in C. J. Stivale (ed.) *Gilles Deleuze: Key Concepts*, Chesham: Acumen Publishing, pp. 19–31.

Szarkowski, J. (1973) *From the Picture Press*, New York: Museum of Modern Art.

Winner, E. and Gardner, H. (1981) 'The Art in Children's Drawings', *Review of Research in Visual Arts Education*, 14, 18–31.

4
Children's Embodied Entanglement and Production of Space in a Museum

Abigail Hackett

In this chapter, I draw on a range of interdisciplinary theories of space and place to show how they enabled me to make sense of my research with young children and their families. In particular, during an ethnographic study of young children's meaning-making in museums, I turned to a range of theories of space and place in order to make sense of what I observed in the field. These theories enabled me to recognise and appreciate children's perspectives of the museum and ways of making meaning during the visits. Soja (2004) has identified a cross-disciplinary 'spatial turn' (p. ix) in the last decade, and suggests that, as a result of a 'critical spatial perspective', 'taken for granted ideas are opened up to new forms of critical rethinking' (p. ix):

> we are becoming increasingly aware that we are and always have been spatial beings, active participants in the social construction of our embracing spatialities.
>
> (Soja, 1996, p. 1)

In this chapter, I argue that theories of space and place opened up new possibilities for me to interpret young children's actions in the field, with a particular focus on their embodied experience in the museum and their production of their own version of the museum place.

My research on the meaning-making of children and their families in museums was guided by an interest in recognising children's own perspectives. Drawing on social studies of childhood (James and Prout, 1997; Prout, 2005) I wanted to find ways to move away from paradigms of socialisation and developmentalism, which have dominated research on children within the social sciences. As James and Prout (1997) have argued, assumptions about the rationality of human behaviour and the assumed naturalness of staged, linear development of children have resulted in narrow constructions of childhood which leave little room for children's agency, individuality or the variability of their everyday lives. While in some areas these arguments may be well established and long won (Prout, 2005), the majority of studies of families' learning in museums are grounded in developmental psychology perspectives of learning (Leinhardt et al., 2002; Ellenbogen et al., 2004), particularly Vygotsky's zone of proximal development (Crowley et al., 2001; Ash and Wells, 2006). Therefore, grounding my research in the social studies of childhood meant trying to move away from these dominant models and finding new ways to foreground the perspectives and experiences of the children in the study.

As Soja (2004) points out, the spatial turn itself seeks to rebalance an intellectual privileging of history in academic thought since the 19th century. Soja's (1996) critique of modernism points out the tendency for modernist research to become locked into 'totalizing discourses' (p. 4) which limit the scope of knowledge itself. Specific conceptions of history as a linear, rational and measurable process, which Soja argues have been over-emphasised in transdisciplinary intellectual thinking in general, can also be seen to have dominated research on children, for example through the paradigm of developmentalism (James and Prout, 1997). Social studies of childhood aims to move away from these historically dominating paradigms, and I wondered if a 'critical spatial perspective' could support the 'critical rethinking' (Soja, 2004, p. ix) required for this endeavour in the context of family learning in museums.

My understanding of meaning-making is grounded in multimodality. That is, the understanding that communication is composed of multiple modes, which are combined by the signmaker (or communicator) to make communicative signs (Kress, 2010). As research has shown, children's use of modes depends on the context, and non-verbal modes may be particular significant for children (Flewitt, 2005). Within my own study of children in the museum, the children's movement around the place, through walking, running and other methods, was a significant aspect of their multimodal meaning making, as I have argued elsewhere (Hackett, 2014). When the parameters of what counts as communication are widened beyond spoken or written words to consider embodied modes such as gesture and movement (as is the case in multimodality), space seems to become increasingly significant to a consideration of literacy. In my own fieldwork, the prevalence of the children's movement around the spaces of the museum seemed to make this argument even more pertinent. For Lefebvre space provides a counterbalance to the dominance of written communication in power relationships within societies:

> To under estimate, ignore and diminish space amounts to the over estimation of texts, written matter and writing systems, along with the readable and the visible to the point of assigning to these a monopoly of intelligibility.
>
> (Lefebvre, 1991, p. 62)

Therefore, he argues for a greater emphasis on the lived, the embodied and the unspoken. This perspective fits with my interest in the importance of the non-verbal communicative modes employed by young children. And so for this reason also, I turned to spatial perspectives as a route to reconceptualising and reimagining the competencies with which young children make meaning multimodally in places such as museums.

The purpose of this chapter is to consider what theories of space and place bring to my understanding of children's meaning-making in the museum. First, I will give some context for my wider study of children's meaning-making in museums, and introduce one specific example of this process: two children's interactions with a large stuffed bear. Then, I will draw on the literature of space and place to consider how these bring new ways of understanding and making sense of what the children did when they saw the stuffed bear.

Marco the bear: A socially produced space for a developing friendship

The data in this chapter is drawn from a one-year ethnographic study, during which I made monthly unstructured visits to two local museums with a group of families with children aged between two

Table 4.1 Summary of the families participating in the study

Adults	Children
Teresa	Anna, 48 months
Janice and Barry	Natasha, 52 months and Miriam, 16 months
Myself	Izzy, 36 months

Note: All ages are given for December 2011, when the fieldwork ended.

and four years old. The examples from field data I focus on in this chapter were drawn from the visits to one of the two museums, House Museum. I recruited families for this part of the study through a local children's centre, situated in an area of economic deprivation. The children's centre organised a series of weekly walks through the local park to the nearby House Museum, and some of the families from these trips went on to participate in my study.[1] The number and constitution of the families who participated are summarised in Table 4.1.

My role during this fieldwork was as a participant observer, usually with my own two-year-old daughter with me. I used a FLIP video camera to record the action during these visits, and wrote field notes following the visits. I also carried out interviews with the parents and children involved in the study, and shared extracts from the data with parents in order to explore their interpretations. The study was guided by a broad research question: how do families with young children make meaning in a museum?

The data I will discuss in this chapter focuses on the experiences of two girls, Anna, aged three, and Izzy, who is my daughter, aged two. Anna and Izzy made visits to House Museum, a free entry local authority museum in northern England, as part of a larger group. None of the families had visited the museum before. Anna and Izzy met and became close friends during the course of the fieldwork. This friendship began with a shared fascination with a large stuffed bear in the museum, and a series of shared interactions around the bear. The vignette below, taken from the second visit to the museum, typifies what Anna and Izzy did during each visit to the museum.

Vignette of Anna and Izzy interacting with Marco the bear: Anna and Izzy were shouting 'find the bear!', so we went to look for the bear.

Anna ran ahead through the museum confidently, and I pointed her towards the room with the bear. Anna ran into the room, followed closely by Izzy, and both girls ran straight up to the bear. Anna ran to the bear's right hand side, and reached up to stroke his fur. She cried 'oh, he's tickling me!', and leapt away from him. Izzy ran to the far side of the bear, to his left hand side, and also reached up to touch his fur. Izzy's actions closely mirrored Anna's, including reaching to touch the bear, leaning around to touch his tree stump, and leaping away in pretend horror at his tickling! They ran backwards and forwards between the bear and the space where the parents were standing, laughing and making lots of eye contact with each other. Anna and Izzy continued this episode for several minutes, Anna leading the action, which was very much a performance for the adults as well as Izzy. She frequently looked at her mum and the other grownups when she exclaimed that the bear was tickling her.

Marco the bear (as named by the museum), a large stuffed bear, became a favourite exhibit for the children visiting the museum (Figure 4.1). The main downstairs rooms in this museum are all similarly grand and traditional, painted pale green with ornate coving, large fireplaces and big shuttered windows covered with blinds to shade the objects from the sun. Marco was positioned in the corner of one of the large downstairs rooms, mouth open showing his teeth, arms outstretched holding a tree trunk. Unprotected by glass, the children could walk straight up to him, touch him, hug him and even try to climb on him.

Marco the bear was popular with many of the children in the study. However, he became particularly significant to Anna and Izzy. Interacting together with Marco the bear became the foundation for their friendship, and a focus for them during the visits to House Museum. Each time Anna and Izzy visited House Museum, the girls asked verbally to find Marco the bear, ran along a remembered route through the museum to get to him and then engaged in almost identical behaviour each time, running backwards and forwards to touch him and peep at each other from either side of the bear. The repetition of this behaviour was striking. In total the girls visited Marco on seven different trips to the museum over the course of six months, and engaged in this behaviour together each time.

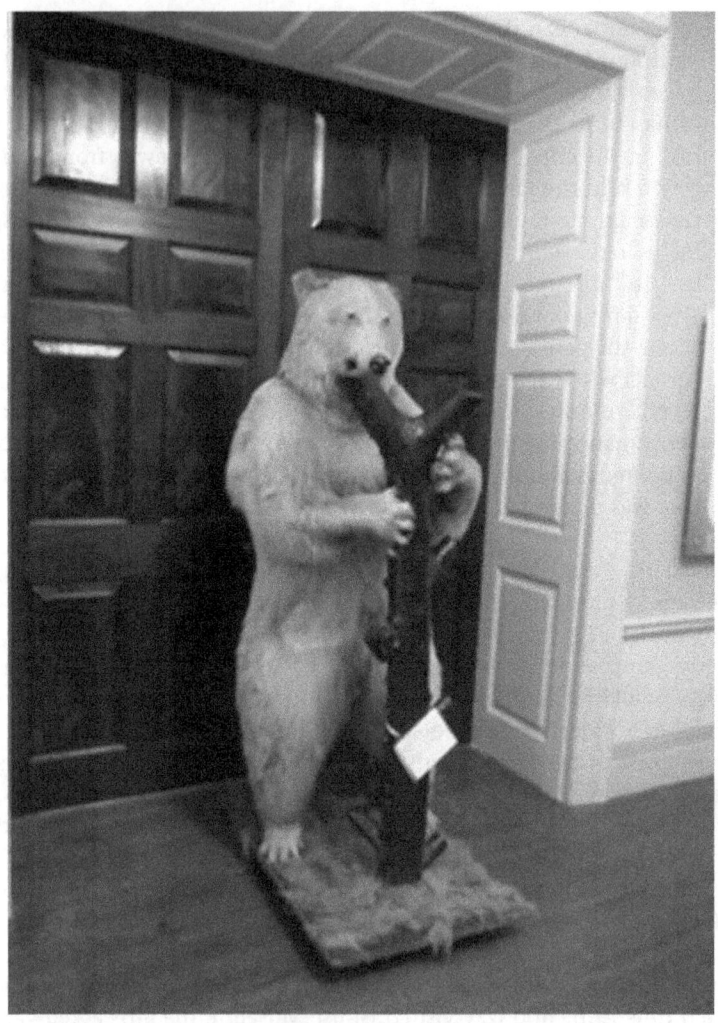

Figure 4.1   Marco the bear

Anna and Izzy's behaviour around Marco the bear was striking not only for its repetition, but also for its intentionality. By this I mean during the museum visits, Anna and Izzy would deliberately look for and request Marco the bear, and they put effort and energy into learning the route through the museum which would lead to Marco. When they reached Marco the bear, they spent an extended period of time interacting around him. They also clearly remembered these interactions from previous visits, building on and repeating the same actions each time. These actions were not modelled by or instigated by adults, and in this way, do not fit with the traditional Vygotskian models of how children learn to communicate (Vygotsky, 1978) and to behave in a museum (Leinhardt et al., 2002). The adults had a role to play in these interactions, as they were an intended audience. They were also frequently an appreciative audience, commented that the girls' behaviour was sweet or funny, and watching them for long periods of time. However, the embodied narrative of Marco tickling the children was a creative response devised by Anna and Izzy, to the surprise of their parents. In the next part of the chapter, I turn to theories of embodied experience of place, to help me further analyse Anna and Izzy's behaviour.

The emplaced knowing of Anna, Izzy and Marco the bear

Pink (2009) stresses the role of the body and place in experience, arguing that firstly the world is experienced through the body, and secondly this body 'is inextricable from our sensorial and material engagement with the environment' (p. 35). Pink refers to the body experiencing in place as 'emplaced knowledge' and argues that researchers need to seek ways of becoming 'similarly emplaced' (p. 40) in order to understand the lifeworlds of others.

Within childhood studies, scholars have similarly stressed the importance of children's embodied experience to their understanding of place. In her study of children's movement around their local area, Christensen (2003) describes the importance of 'the understanding that emerges from embodied movement through place' (p. 16). In their study of children's perceptions of their local neighbourhoods, Rasmussen and Smidt (2003) point out that 'It is, after all, through the child's body that the neighbourhood is perceived' (p. 87). Taking a phenomenological perspective, they argue for a vision of knowledge about place that is not cognitive but embodied, related to physical 'know-how' about the bodily sensations created by moving around a place on different routes and in different ways.

The creation of meaning is basically a physical manifestation (Skantze, 1990). Knowledge about the neighbourhood is therefore not always expressed in verbal language, but is rather expressed through a physical 'know-how', for instance about how to scale a tall fence or the specific manner of climbing a certain tree, or a sense of which shortcut to choose between two locations when in a hurry.

(Rasmussen and Smidt, 2003, p. 88)

Similarly to the studies of Christensen (2003) and Rasmussen and Smidt (2003), Anna and Izzy can be understood as creating emplaced ways of knowing about the museum by moving through it and experiencing it with their bodies. Walking through the museum, with its grand rooms, high ceilings and traditional décor produced particular kinds of bodily experience. In addition, Marco the bear himself is a sensorially engaging object. Particularly from a child's height, Marco seems to tower over visitors, glue glistening on his jaw to evoke spittle. He can be readily touched by visitors, his teeth hard, fur soft and scratchy, and patches of smooth skin where the fur has been worn away by many hands touching him. Moving changed their experience of the bear; being up close to him, the bear towered over the children and they could reach and touch the rough fur and soft skin. Moving between being close to the bear and further away from him was also central to the playful narrative the children created about the bear trying to tickle them, and them trying to escape his reach. Therefore, for Anna, Izzy and the other participants in the study, encountering Marco was a sensory and affective phenomena that evoked specific feelings of being emplaced in this museum location.

Pagis (2010) argues that intersubjectivity – that is, the sense that others understand our lived experience – can be produced through bodily interactions as well as verbal communication. Gaze, gesture or, as in Pagis' (2010) ethnography of a meditation centre, the experience of non-movement, lead to 'a community of space and time' in which 'a feeling of togetherness is produced' (p. 314). From this perspective, the emplaced experiences of Anna and Izzy in the presence of Marco the bear are not only individual but intersubjective. Interacting around Marco the bear was an emplaced way of knowing about the museum which Anna and Izzy shared repeatedly, over a number of months, as their friendship grew. Sheets-Johnstone (1999) argues for a focus on the experience of movement, and an appreciation of the close connection between the kinetic and the affective, that is movement and emotion.

> Movement is not behaviour; experience is not physiological activity, and a brain is not a body. What emerges and evolves – ontogenetically and phylogenetically – is not behaviour but movement, movement that is neatly partitioned and classified as behaviour by observers, but that is in its own right the basic phenomena to be profitably studied.
>
> (Sheets-Johnstone, 1999, p. 274)

From this perspective, the role moving together played in the emerging relationship between Anna and Izzy is not surprising. Facets of this moving together included Izzy's frequent copying of Anna's interactions with Marco, the girls' playing with their fear and excitement at moving close to and away from the large bear, and the repetition of this shared behaviour over time. These aspects of movement lead to Anna and Izzy's 'community of time and space' (Pagis, 2010, p. 314) in which they developed an emotional and affectionate bond.

Movement through the museum together was also an important aspect of how place was experienced bodily by Anna and Izzy. The girls moved through the museum, following discovered and learnt routes, to encounter Marco the bear. As time went on, the girls began to learn the route through the museum to Marco the bear, which enabled them to run and find him without having to negotiate with the adults first. Moving through the museum was therefore part of the ethnographic study. In the next section I turn to the work of Ingold (2007) to consider what spatial theories focused on movement can add to my interpretation of the children's meaning-making in the museum.

Entanglement: Two children, a stuffed bear and lines of moving and knowing

Ingold's (2007) term 'wayfaring', by which he refers to a bringing together of moving and perceiving, was fruitful for me in thinking about movement within the meaning-making of Anna, Izzy and

Marco the bear. Ingold's focus on movement, and the lines with which people move across the place, has led him to emphasise the 'place-making' nature of wayfaring. In this sense, Ingold (2008) argues, we 'make our way through a world-in-formation rather than across its preformed surface' (p. 1802). This sense that space is produced or continually remade through the actions of people adds to Lefebvre's (1991) seminal argument for the social production of space. I consider how space may be socially produced, through words, bodies and interactions, in the next section. In this section, I want to focus on what Ingold proposes about human movement across places, and consider what this adds to my interpretation of Anna and Izzy's experiences in the museum.

The consequence of Ingold's (2007, 2008) focus on lines of movement is a proposal that place is not bounded or fixed, but in a state of continual flux. This is due to the fact that place is made up of the lines of movement, as people come together, in what Ingold terms 'meshwork' (2008, p. 1805).

> A world that is occupied, I argue, is furnished with already-existing things. But one that is inhabited is woven from the strands of their continual coming-into-being.
>
> (Ingold, 2008, p. 1797)

For this reason, Ingold proposes a zone of entanglement, between people and place. The concept of a zone of entanglement was useful for my thinking about Anna and Izzy in the museum. There were physical ways in which the children became 'entangled' with the museum during our visits: footsteps wear down stone floors over time, sticky fingerprints are left on glass cases. Marco the bear himself bore many signs of the entanglement between visitors and object, in the form of patches of skin worn bare by years of being touched. However, there are also important non-material ways in which I think the museum and the children visiting it became entangled. The museum changed when the children were in it, from a quiet environment to a busy and noisy one. Over time, and with repeated visits, the presence of children changed the nature of the place, and the behaviour that was expected in it. For the children themselves, aspects of the museum became entangled in their consciousness, as they took memories and meanings from their visit out into their wider lives. Therefore, I was interested in entanglement as a route into thinking about material and immaterial ways in which, as children made their way through a 'world-in-formation' (p. 1802), they produced and remade it anew.

Marco the bear and the social production of space

So far, I have considered theories of space which have focused on the local, the sensory and the individual's experience of place. However, the work of Lefebvre (1991) and Soja (1996) considers space as socially constructed at the level of societies. Lefebvre stresses the specificity and multiplicity of space, arguing that 'every society... produces a space, its own space' (1991, p. 31). Drawing on Lefebvre, Leander stresses the need to 'move outward from focal data to practices stretched over broader expanses of space and time' (2004, p. 117), by considering how the actions of participants in the production of space both organise social space and transform it through their interactions. In this section, I consider how Lefebvre's theory of social production of space can add further layers of interpretation to Anna and Izzy's meaning-making in the museum.

For Lefebvre, space 'takes on a reality of its own' (p. 26), therefore it is not possible for the existence of space to be separated from its production. Lefebvre's thesis that space is multiple and remade through individual social practices and representations, particularly the embodied and non-verbal, is useful when considering the implications of Anna and Izzy's actions in the museum for the production of the museum space. Through their actions around Marco the bear, Anna and Izzy constructed our (my own and the families in the museum visits) understanding of that space. The actions of Anna and Izzy consisted of both embodied spatial practices (such as touching Marco's fur and leaping away from him) and representations of space, in that the repeated actions around Marco the bear on subsequent visits drew on memories and previous meanings attached to this particular location. Anna and Izzy's interactions, therefore, were central to this community of families producing a space of their own in the museum.

With regard to the processes through which space is produced, Lefebvre stressed the importance of considering the non-verbal, particularly lived social practices, and also art, music and sculpture, in efforts to bridge the 'yawning gap' (1991, p. 5) between language about space and lived everyday practices. To this effect, Lefebvre identifies three kinds of space: perceived, conceived and lived. Perceived space is a form of space produced through daily routines and what people actually do in spaces, while conceived space refers to representations of space, often in written documents, made by planners and urbanists. Lived space is the coming together of how space is described and used and the symbolic meaning attached to it.

I was interested in using Lefebvre's trialectic of perceived, conceived and lived space to understand the way Anna and Izzy used and represented the space around Marco the bear. Lefebvre wrote 'Like all social practice, spatial practice is lived before it is conceptualized' (1991, p. 34); thinking about the girls' use of the space across time, both perceptions and conceptions of space seemed to come into play. The girls put a great deal of emphasis on Marco the bear within this part of the museum, so that he grew in significance, and specific embodied traditions were attached to Marco the bear, namely running to the bear and jumping away as he 'tickled' them. Therefore, Marco was perceived in a sensory and emotional way, an object of meaning, fascination and sensory experience with which the girls wanted to interact. However, the repetition of the actions around Marco the bear across subsequent visits gives an insight into the way in which the bear, and the museum in which the bear was located, was conceived by the girls. Perhaps the first time the girls came across Marco, their behavior and the narrative of 'tickling' was a spontaneous reaction to an engaging object. However, the second, third, fourth, fifth and sixth times the girls visited Marco and repeated the same behavior with him demonstrate that the actions were based on imagination and memory. As the girls performed a narrative of being tickled and running away from Marco for the seventh time, the meaning of the actions was largely in their repetition, and the memories the girls had of visiting Marco previously. Repeating the same actions each time demonstrated to the girls and their audience of adults that they remembered the bear, that they remembered what they did last time they saw the bear and that they remembered their previous collaborative meaning-making around the bear. By spontaneously repeating the same embodied actions, the girls indicated their membership of an exclusive group who conceived Marco the bear in this very specific way. In this way, observing Anna and Izzy's meaning-making around Marco the bear gives an insight into the lived space of the museum for Anna and Izzy. Within this lived space, specific symbolic meanings were attached to Marco the bear through movement and embodied interactions.

Social production of space at a micro-level

Applying Lefebvre's categories of conceived, perceived and lived space to the actions of Anna and Izzy helped me to think about the way in which the girls experienced and imagined this particular part of the museum. Their strikingly repeated behaviour in moving near to Marco the bear and then jumping further away from him affected how both they and their audience of adults felt about and imagined this place. This movement between two specific conceptualised locations and the meaning attached to these two locations, began to produce a specific version of social space. While Lefebvre has argued that '(social) space is a (social) product', the examples he gives are largely on a macro-scale, such as the rhythm of life in an ancient city or the meaning attached to the Mediterranean coast in industrialised Europe (1991, pp. 26, 31, 59). I am interested in thinking about how this production of space might work at an individual level.

The lived space produced by Anna and Izzy around Marco the bear during these museum visits can be conceptualised as containing a set of binary categories, which are summarised in Table 4.2. The children's production of the space according to these categories is also shown visually in Figure 4.2. The most significant of these binary categories was close to Marco the bear/away from Marco the bear. Away from Marco the bear could mean only a step away, and close to Marco the bear was the space within which it was possible to reach over and touch him. The girls created these spatial categories by moving between the two spaces (Ingold, 2008), through use of body movements specific to the two areas (e.g. jumping could only happen away from Marco, and leaning over to touch and be tickled could only happen next to Marco) and also through the narrative they produced about being tickling and then running away. Hallden (2003) showed how, in children's accounts of future lives, the meaning attached to places affected the activities that children imagined could take place there. In the example of Marco the bear, the way in which the space was socially produced affected both the embodied

Table 4.2 Spatial categories the children create through their embodied movements around Marco the bear

Social production of space around Marco the bear	
Close to Marco the bear	Away from Marco the bear
My side of the bear	Your side of the bear

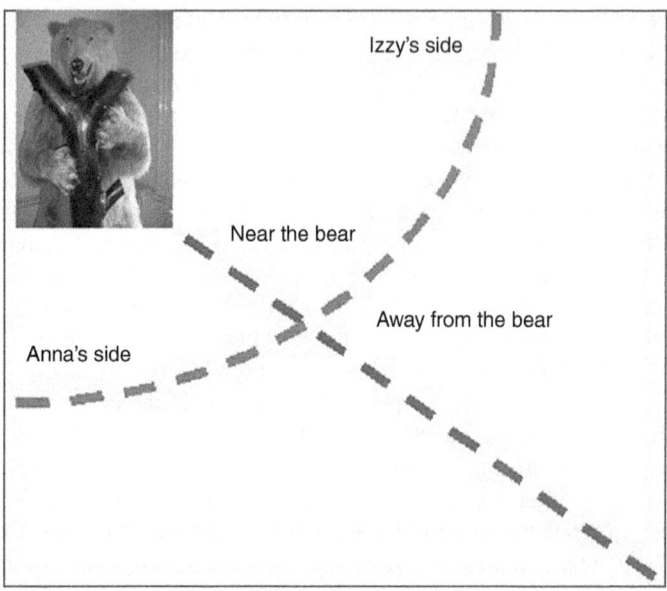

Figure 4.2 Visual representation of the social production of space around Marco the bear

and narrated stories that could be told. For example, Marco the bear could not possibly scare or tickle the girls if they were a step away from him, because this space was categorised as 'away from the bear', even though in physical terms they would still have been within grabbing distance of a live bear!

In addition, a second binary was vital to the production of social interactions between Anna and Izzy: Anna's space/Izzy's space. Each girl has a 'side' of the bear to occupy (Anna on the bear's right, Izzy on the bear's left), and they maintained these 'sides' during the subsequent visits to the museum. They also had a corresponding 'side' of the tree. The corner of the room meant that it was not possible to move in a full circle around the bear. This meant that for Anna, moving to the right took her close to Izzy, moving to the left took her further away. For Izzy, the opposite was true. The girls then put this construction of ownership of space around the bear to work in a number of ways. The girls could see each other and make eye contact with each other at key moments. It meant they could perform the same activities at the same time, creating a mirror image of each other. They each had equal access to the bear, did not have to contest each other for access, and could carry out actions simultaneously, in a flowing sequence one after the other, or independently from each other.

Therefore, the embodied practices of Anna and Izzy both produced space and were a product of spatiality (Leander and Sheehy, 2004). Their meaning-making was situated, in that the meaning was specific to this particular room in this particular museum, while also drawing on wider social meanings. Leander and Sheehy (2004) have argued that words are productive of social space. In the example of Marco the bear, non-verbal communicative practices are also productive of social space, in that space came to be understood through the medium of embodied and emplaced knowing.

Discussion

The aim of this chapter has been to consider how different theories of space and place can aid and widen the possibilities for interpreting the meaning-making of young children. Throughout the chapter, I have drawn on a specific example of children's meaning-making: Anna and Izzy's actions on encountering Marco the stuffed bear. The children's experience of Marco the bear was embodied and emplaced (Pink, 2009), and the knowledge they produced by interacting with him is difficult to express in words. Rather, it was experiential knowing, similar to the 'physical "know-how"' described by Rasmussen and Smidt (2003, p. 88) in their study of children's experiences of their neighbourhoods. Movement was essential to this emplaced experience in the museum, and drawing on the work of Ingold (2007; 2008) enabled me to think about the concept of entanglement in terms of the ongoing production of place; Anna, Izzy and Marco the bear in a 'world in formation' (Ingold, 2008, p. 1802).

A specific embodied experience of place was created by the children moving through the space, and their embodied meaning-making was a social practice. In addition, Anna and Izzy's use of the space affected how the adults involved in the visit (including me) came to imagine and understand the space. The categories created by the children's non-verbal communicative practices produced a specific understanding of or version of space (see Figure 4.2), which had sensory and affective meaning. For example, the category of 'near to Marco the bear' was associated with sensory sensations of soft tickly fur and affective sensations of fear and excitement that the bear evoked. I relate this to Pink's work on the concept of emplaced knowledge, which she describes as,

> An embodied and multisensorial way of knowing that is inextricable from our sensorial and material engagement with the environment and is as such an emplaced knowing.
>
> (Pink, 2009, p. 35)

Pink argues that ethnographers can, by attending to the sensory categories of people's lived experiences, become 'similarly emplaced' (2009, p. 40) as part of the research process. I find this view useful not only for thinking about my own coming to know the museum through the perspectives of the children, but for thinking about the children's emerging and collective embodied and emplaced ways of knowing the museum. Movement and embodied interactions were central to the production of this shared way of knowing. In the example I presented in this chapter, of two girls' interactions in a museum around a stuffed bear, a particular set of spatial practices and representations of space (Lefebvre, 1991) gained power and potency with the families in my research over time, as it was repeated almost identically over subsequent museum visits.

Note

1. The study received ethical approval from the University of Sheffield. Families gave a staged consent to being involved in the original participant observation, and later to the FLIP video footage and field notes being shared at conferences and in publication. The children gave their ongoing

assent to being involved in the study, and museum visits ended when the children were tired, bored or ready for a change.

References

Ash, D. and Wells, G. (2006) 'Dialogic Inquiry in Classroom and Museum: Actions, Tools and Talk', in Z. Berkerman, N. C. Burbles and D. Silerman-Keller (eds) *Learning in Places: The Informal Education Reader*, New York: Peter Lang Publishing, pp. 35–54.

Christensen, P. (2003) 'Place, Space and Knowledge: Children in the Village and the City', in P. Christensen and M. O'Brien (eds) *Children in the City. Home, Neighborhood and Community*, London: Routledge, pp. 13–28.

Crowley, K., Callanan, M. A., Jipson, J. L., Galco, J., Topping, K. and Shrager, J. (2001) 'Shared Scientific Thinking in Everyday Parent–Child Interaction', *Science Education*, 85 (6), 712–732.

Ellenbogen, K. M., Luke, J. L. and Dierking, L. D. (2004) 'Family Learning Research in Museums: An Emerging Disciplinary Matrix?' *Science Education*, 88 (1), 48–58.

Flewitt, R. (2005) 'Is Every Child's Voice Heard? Researching the Different Ways 3-Year-Old Children Communicate and Make Meaning at Home and in a Pre-School Playgroup', *Early Years*, 25 (3), 207–222.

Hackett, A. (2014) 'Zigging and Zooming All Over the Place: Young Children's Meaning Making and Movement in the Museum', *Journal of Early Childhood Literacy*, 14 (1), 5–27.

Hallden, G. (2003) 'Children's Views of Family, Home and House', in P. Christensen and M. O'Brien (eds) *Children in the City. Home, Neighborhood and Community*, London: Routledge, pp. 29–45.

Ingold, T. (2007) *Lines. A Brief History*, London: Routledge.

Ingold, T. (2008) 'Bindings Against Boundaries: Entanglement of Life in an Open World', *Environment and Planning*, 40, 1796–1810.

James, A. and Prout, A. (eds) (1997) *Constructing and Reconstructing Childhood: Contemporary Issues in the Sociological Study of Childhood*, 2nd edition, London: RoutledgeFalmer.

Kress, G. (2010) *Multimodality. Exploring Contemporary Methods of Communication*, London: Routledge.

Leander, K. M. (2004) 'Reading the Spatial Histories in a Classroom Literacy Event', in K. M. Leander and M. Sheehy (eds) *Spatializing Literacy Research and Practice*, New York: Peter Lang Publishing, pp. 115–142.

Leander, K. M. and Sheehy, M. (eds) (2004) *Spatializing Literacy Research and Practice*, New York: Peter Lang Publishing.

Lefebvre, H. (1991) *The Production of Space*, trans. D. Nicholson-Smith, Malden: Blackwell Publishing (originally published in 1974).

Leinhardt, G., Crowley, K. and Knutson, K. (2002) *Learning Conversations in Museums*, London: Routledge.

Pagis, M. (2010) 'Producing Intersubjectivity in Silence: An Ethnographic Study of Meditation Practice', *Ethnography*, 11 (2), 309–328.

Pink, S. (2009) *Doing Sensory Ethnography*, London: Sage.

Prout, A. (2005) *The Future of Childhood*, London: Routledge.

Rasmussen, K. and Smidt, S. (2003) 'Children in the Neighbourhood: The Neighbourhood in the Children', in P. Christensen and M. O'Brien (eds) *Children in the City. Home, Neighbourhood and Community*, London: Routledge, pp. 82–100.

Sheets-Johnstone, M. (1999) 'Emotion and Movement: A Beginning Empirical-Phenomenological Analysis of Their Relationship', *Journal of Consciousness Studies*, 11–12, 259–277.

Soja, E. W. (1996) *Thirdspace: Journeys to Los Angeles and Other Real-and-Imagined Places*, Massachusetts: Blackwell Publishers.

Soja, E. W. (2004) 'Preface', in K. M. Leander and M. Sheehy (eds) *Spatializing Literacy Research and Practice*, New York: Peter Lang Publishing, pp. ix–xv.

Vygotsky, L. (1978) *Mind in Society: Development of Higher Psychological Processes*, Harvard: Harvard University Press.

Part II
Emotion and Relationships

5
Children's Emotional Geographies: Politics of Difference and Practices of Engagement

Matej Blazek

Introduction

Geography is a discipline with much to say about space but, until relatively recently, more reluctance to talk about children and emotions. Over the last 20 years, however, both these areas have become established sub-disciplinary fields within geography with successful dedicated journals (*Children's Geographies* was established in 2003 and *Emotion, Space and Society* in 2008), a flourishing tradition of international conferences (the 5th International and Interdisciplinary Conference on Emotional Geographies and the 4th International Conference on the Geographies of Children, Youth and Families took place in 2015) and a number of journal articles and book publications with impact across the field of geography and far beyond.

The purpose of this chapter is to reflect on the entanglements of geographical debates regarding children and emotions and to present an overview particularly for readers from outside the discipline. The histories of children's and emotional geographies have been reflected and re-reflected in much detail on various occasions, and more comprehensive and accessible invitations to broader debates are available elsewhere (e.g. McKendrick, 2000; Holloway and Valentine, 2000a; Bondi, 2005; Bondi et al., 2005; Smith et al., 2009; Pile, 2010; Holloway and Pimlott-Wilson, 2011; Holloway, 2014; Kraftl et al., 2014; Skelton, 2017 forthcoming). My aim is to focus rather on the points where the two meet and to sketch one of many possible (and fragmented) reflections of why considering children's emotional geographies matters.

The sub-field of children's emotional geographies has not evolved in a disciplinary vacuum and, indeed, many references in the chapter encapsulate an interdisciplinary scholarship. Yet, geographical approaches to children's emotions build on a long-term and sustained focus on spatial concepts, which are then deployed as tools for advanced understanding of social life. In this chapter, I outline this tradition and draw on some of these tools to offer one possible route for engaging with children's emotions, where spatial perspectives on children's lives fuse diverse questions of epistemology, politics and methodology into an account of policy and practice.

The chapter begins by discussing how the two key terms implied in the title of the chapter – childhood and emotions – are viewed in the (sub-)disciplinary scholarship. I briefly look at their intellectual trajectories and trace the emerging debates on the role of emotions and space in children's lives. After that, while being aware of the limited space this chapter offers, I sketch a thread of themes connecting theorisations and practices regarding children's emotions and space, drawing on some recent discussions in the field of children's emotional geographies.

Children's emotional geographies: Trajectories and intersections

Human geography: Space, place spatiality and scale

Since the 1970s, human geography has been refining its conceptual vocabulary and augmenting the theoretical deployment of its key terms (see Clifford et al., 2009). Engagements with social theory, particularly the idea of space as produced in multiple forms (Lefebvre, 1991; Harvey, 2006) extended the traditional view of the three-dimensional Cartesian space as an absolute container in which social life is simply located. Instead, the concept of *spatiality*, the indivisible linkage between the social and the spatial, appropriated a position at the heart of the discipline. Understandings of *place* also burgeoned, extending from a delineated locality on a (Cartesian) map to encompass interconnections and openness beyond physical borders (Massey, 1994) and as carriers of cultural associations producing ways of understanding the world both near and far (Cresswell, 2004). Finally, the idea of *scale* shifted from a mathematical expression of the relationship between space and its cartographic representation to theorisations of global, local and intimate processes; their relations; and the wider political implications of the construction and perpetuation of scalar categories (Marston et al., 2005).

The fields of children's and emotional geographies have developed in such a context of theoretical proliferation, with a particularly prosperous period starting in the mid-1990s. The intellectual trajectories that shaped the two sub-disciplinary fields reveal similarities but also differences and an outline of the genealogy of children's emotional geographies emerges at the junction of the two.

Children's geographies

Holloway and Pimlott-Wilson (2011) recognise three roots of the current sub-discipline of children's geographies. The first is the focus on children's spatial cognition unfolding at the juncture between social geography and developmental psychology (Blaut, 1997; Blaut et al., 2003), the second is feminist interest in geographies of family life and caring (Holloway, 1999), and the third is concern about spatialities of children's lived experiences shaped through engagements with the new social studies of childhood (Holloway and Valentine, 2000b). Of the three, the latter inspired the largest share of interest by putting children's lives into the spotlight and considering children as relevant social actors in their own right instead of subsuming their experiences and practices within broader views of adults.

Bringing children's agency to light has also transformed children into relevant actors in, rather than just objects of, geographical research. The decade following the establishment of children's geographies in the mid and late 1990s saw flourishing in the breadth and depth of methodological developments labelled as participatory, child-centred or child-friendly research approaches (van Blerk and Kesby, 2008).

Elevating the status of children and their agency in the production of geographical knowledge has not remained without a critique; such analysis has implicitly questioned the character of how children are viewed. Most importantly, children's agency has been shown to still have its limits. It remains entrenched in structural constraints which marginalise children in relation to adults but also some children against others, depending on their socio-spatial positionalities (Holt, 2011). As Kesby (2007) argues, it is important to attend to children's individual existences but this does not take away from their need for protection or from their structural vulnerability given by the socio-spatial positionality of childhood (Philo and Smith, 2013; Hörschelmann, 2015). In addition, and like adults, children are not all-knowing actors but their intellectual, embodied and social capacities are limited by a range of factors, material and immaterial (Holt, 2006; Gallacher and Gallagher, 2008; Philo and Smith, 2013). The view of childhood carried forward by sub-disciplinary scholars has thus emerged as one where children and their lives are important in their own right but children's agency is inevitably limited by social, environmental, biological and psychological causes.

Emotional geographies

In the introduction to their book *Emotional Geographies*, Bondi et al., (2005) discuss location (illustrated by geographies of health and embodiment), production (discussing geographies of social relations and identity) and representation (drawing on a wider body of writings that problematise the representing of emotions) as conceptual areas elucidating how emotions matter in geography. Elsewhere, Bondi (2005) traces geography's 'emotional turn' and the emergence of geographers' interest in emotions in three relatively independent theoretical traditions: the humanistic geography of the 1970s and early 1980s and its interest in individual subjective experience, particularly of place, shaped by ideas from phenomenology (Ley and Samuels, 1978); the feminist critique of the body/mind, nature/culture and emotional/rational dualisms and their impacts upon the oppressive gendered production of space and subjectivity (Rose, 1993); and the prospects of non-representational theory critiquing the scholarly fixation on cognitive and representable areas of the human experience (Thrift, 1996). Commenting upon the often clashing views of the importance of the individual versus trans-/pre-individual constitution of emotions, Bondi adds another perspective by drawing from psychotherapy and building a relational understanding of emotions framed within the intersubjective dynamics between embodied individuals.

This brief overview suggests a theoretical diversity to the point of fragmentation and contradiction. Indeed, in a discussion in the journal *Transactions of the Institute of British Geographers*, the prevalent opinion was that theoretical purity eradicates the richness, complexity and elusiveness of emotions and their mattering in space (Bondi and Davidson, 2011; Curti et al., 2011). Emotions have become established at the heart of geographical inquiry but this happened through the proliferation of (often contradicting) theories and practices (Davidson et al., 2014) rather than the constitution of a unique, distinctive framework. What the majority of such works have in common, though, is the recognition that emotions matter, they are shaping and shaped by geographical elements such as places, environments and mobilities, and that their presence, location and effects require attentiveness to relational dimensions of social and 'more-than-social' interactions so they should not be seen as 'possessed' by individuals.

Children's and emotional geographies

These overviews suggest that there were diverse intellectual trajectories that led to the repositioning of the two sub-disciplinary fields from the disciplinary periphery towards its core. Even where the theoretical influences suggest parallels, the particular concepts approached by geographers interested in childhood and emotions often varied, such as when the feminist critique of care and the caring economy informed the development of children's geographies whereas emotional geographies drew primarily (though not exclusively) on the insights of power and subjectivity. This does not mean that geographers interested in childhood have not attended to the relevance of emotions (and, to a much lesser degree, vice versa). Horton and Kraftl's (2006) call to consider emotions, if for no other reason than that they clearly *matter* in children's lives, was echoed in a number of projects important in their own right: Nayak (2003) and Pain et al. (2010) explored children's fear in relation to the local and the global respectively; den Besten (2010) debated the relations between emotional belonging to a place and mobile identities of migrants; Harker (2005), Hemming (2007) and Horton and Kraftl (2009) looked at emotions in the institutional contexts of education and care; and Jones's (2000) interest has been in children's emotional autonomy in the spaces of their own becoming. However, a focused theorisation of the importance of emotions in understanding childhood, and of childhood in approaching emotions, has remained rather fragmented.

In the guest editorial to a special issue of *Emotion, Space and Society*, on children's emotional geographies, Blazek and Windram-Geddes (2013, pp. 1–2) identified eight emerging threads and suggested these themes as a starting (yet incomplete) agenda for an engagement between geographers and scholars from other disciplines interested in the spatialities of emotions in children's lives. First, they assert that 'children's emotions [are] firmly situated within the wider contexts of children's lives', and highlight 'the need to view children's emotional geographies as inseparable from the social, cultural, economic and political landscapes of childhood'. Second, they stress 'the complexity of the media through which children's emotions emerge, are channelled, and come to matter', pointing to the crucial yet insufficient-on-its-own relevance of factors such as embodiment, voice and representation, introspection or memory. Third, they reflect on the importance of 'the spatialities of power in child–adult relationships that co-constitute emotional geographies', re-invoking the construction of childhood in relation to adults as a category of otherness. Fourth, they call for attentiveness to the details of children's everyday social relationships and 'the collective dimension' of the relevance of emotions in children's lives. Fifth, sixth and seventh, they argue for continuous *theoretical* and *methodological* innovation and openness as a channel to contest and re-invent *policies* and *practices* targeting children's emotions. Finally – and consequently – they make a point about the necessity for geographers to engage with other scholars and also practitioners; even to cross the line between different professional identities, retaining the awareness of similar yet often different agendas, but approaching each other's concepts and practices.

The rest of the chapter debates four topics suggested by some of these discussions. They do not present a comprehensive picture of the field but this is neither possible nor necessarily desirable. Instead, I wish to outline an intra-connected sketch indicating how geographical approaches to children's emotions might span through theoretical, methodological and practical areas, and to highlight the relevance of emotions and spatialities in children's lives.

Engaging with children's emotional geographies

Children's emotions, space and politics of difference

In 1990–1991, an early debate on the absence of children in geography turned towards a range of substantial differences between childhood and adulthood (James, 1990; Sibley, 1991; Winchester, 1991) and triggered a series of interventions over the next decade that helped establish the foundations of the sub-discipline (Philo, 1992; Matthews and Limb, 1999; Valentine, 1999). A theme raised by James was the extent to which childhood is a universal experience shared by all adults, and what this implies for the ways in which adults might approach children and childhoods. Responses from Sibley and Winchester problematised the notion of universality, pointing to the different structural circumstances of children's lives that set up not just social and political but also epistemological *gaps* between children and adults. Philo's (1992) contention that children's worlds are 'structured "from without"' but 'experienced "from within"' (198) reinforced the view that the settings which embed children's experiences are fundamentally different from those of adults, and adults' universal experiences of being a child do not mean that understanding children is in any way straightforward.

The debate on differences between adults and children and the approachability of children's experiences from the standpoint of adults remained prominent in both theoretical and methodological terms over the next decade (Jones, 2000; 2003; Philo, 2003). The question of how to understand children was extended to how to understand adult understandings of children and, particularly in the writings of Jones, it evolved from an epistemological problem to a political one. Jones argues that childhood is constructed through lopsided power dynamics with adults, and he labels the structural process of 'reduc[ing] the child's opportunities to control his or her own relationship with time and space' (2008, p. 196) as the 'colonisation' of childhood. Jones argues that disregarding the differences between adults and children and claiming a comprehensive understanding of children are efforts to further colonise children's lives by denying them their cultural and symbolic subjectivity, which is distinctively unequal to adults. Jones views childhood constructed as an unbridgeable (although approachable, see Philo (2003)) otherness to adulthood and proposes to 'strive to imagine children as "other" [as] an attempt to resist colonising them' (Jones, 2013, p. 7). Children's otherness is to be acknowledged and celebrated as one of few means that warrant children's autonomy without subtracting the necessary love and protection.

Jones further argues that such autonomy requires space (Jones, 2000) and encompasses emotional dynamics (Jones, 2013), both of which might surface in a form that would appear strange, imprudent, deeply discomforting or even dangerous to adults. As an illustration, Blazek and Hricová (2015) discuss the street as a kind of space that has a fundamentally different value for adults, protecting its ordering, and children, exploring its opportunistic resources (see Lees, 1998). They recognise detached youth work as a form of practice that supports the links between spatial and emotional autonomy, so instead of seeking to diagnose or govern children's emotions, it is focused on how to accompany those emotions through the provision of relationships which are supportive yet allowed and handled by children themselves. Elsewhere, Dickens and Lonie (2013) show the power of social and spatial arrangements of music studios in youth work practice where young people accept the tangible resources and mentoring from adult practitioners but engage emotionally with their experiences on their own terms through rap lyrics and music. Both these examples mainly illustrate the importance and effects of relationships based on adults supporting young people and accompanying them in a mutually accepted manner, while retaining respect for their need for spatial and emotional autonomy (and their interconnectedness – the space where young people can 'feel' without being regulated, manipulated or condescended to) and recognising the uneven power dynamics inherent in the socio-spatial relations between adults and children.

Articulating emotions

Child-centred programmes of research placed children's participation and voices at the forefront of the geographical inquiry. One line of enquiry critical of this tendency addressed the notion of participation: its instigations and constellations, formulations of the participatory agenda and the relations of participatory modes of work to other forms of practice (Percy-Smith, 2010), but also the emotional dynamics of the underlying power relations between adults and children in participatory processes (Jupp Kina, 2012). Another line, more explicitly concerned with emotions, focused more on the topic of voice and its deployment in the constructions of the politics of childhood (Mitchell and Elwood, 2012; Kraftl, 2013), doing so in two distinctive ways.

First, geographers inspired by non-representational theory argued that the world is too messy and excessive for our cognitive competences to fully comprehend and articulate the human experience, particularly its emotional dynamics, and this applies to both adults and children (Horton and Kraftl, 2006). Horton (2010) illustrates this argument by showing how a focus on children's views often translates to requesting children to articulate 'meanings' from their experiences and how it overlooks children's difficulties to grasp the meanings of certain elements (such as popular culture), even if it is certain that they do 'matter' for them. Horton and Kraftl (2006) then argue that by overlooking the unspeakable facets of children's emotional experience, geographers not only miss an important portion of what matters in children's lives (Harker, 2005), but they also fail to pay attention to the role of emotions in the governance of childhood (Gagen, 2015). Extending the critique, Kallio asserts that many participatory 'projects that aim explicitly at children's empowerment through voice-giving may unintentionally mask, bury or silence their experiences and views' (2012, p. 82) by failing to approach other modalities of children's experience and reflexivity.

Second, a number of geographers, writing from diverse perspectives, critiqued the voice-centred approaches as marginalising those children who are, in various ways, 'voiceless'. The use of participatory video with children (Waite and Conn, 2011; Blazek and Hraňová, 2012; Haynes and Tanner, 2015) is one example of attending to the subaltern emotional registers that children are not ordinarily expected to display and might wish to express in formats less intelligible to adults, and which they struggle to express with words. Psychoanalytical approaches to children's emotions (Blazek, 2013; Holt, 2013; Preece, 2015) are also more focused on interpreting the importance of some children not speaking or of the meanings of their words not necessarily 'matching' their emotions.

The problem of engaging with children's emotions through the channel of their voiced articulations is one of translation: between the unconscious and the conscious, between embodiment and representation, between children's and adults' spatialities, and between the research participants and researchers. Social researchers to some degree know each of these couplets, but in the case of children's emotions, they amalgamate into an extraordinary intersection that highlights the elusiveness of the *meanings* behind children's words because of the messiness of the *mattering* behind their emotions. Geographers have shown that emotions are important in and through the diverse spaces of children's lives, but there are limits to how this importance can be articulated, raising a challenge for methodology.

Method

The socio-political and epistemological distance between children's emotions and adult accounts of them has profound implications for the methodology of researching spatialities of emotions in children's lives. Rather than data collection and analysis, the key problems are those of approaching, conceptualising and (re)presenting. Given the importance of relational intersubjectivity in approaching emotions (Bondi, 2005), taking seriously the spatialities of researching children's emotions is becoming integral and equally important to the very spatialities of those emotions. The idea of the passive field and the active researcher is entirely devastated (Nast, 1994).

Geographers have paid a lot of attention to their own positionalities in fieldwork with children and to the dynamics of their mutual relationships. For lack of space, I will mention just four topics from this area. First, the question of positionality in relation to temporality has been highlighted. Focusing on how positionality exceeds the space and time of fieldwork, Procter (2013) writes about the interpretational shifts between experiential moments of emotional encounters and associations logged and surfacing from adult memory. In contrast, Hadfield-Hill and Horton (2014) ponder upon the temporality of fieldwork itself, highlighting the necessity (rather than need) for dedicating enough time during research to reflect on emotions as they are present in instant moments but generate aftermaths and continuations. Second, the researcher's body and the cultural associations of corporeality are instrumental in setting the dynamics in and through which children's emotions can be encountered. Windram-Geddes (2013), for instance, writes about how her body shape created a powerful social scenery next to which girls in her research talked about their fear and repulsion of fatness. Elsewhere,

Barker and Smith (2001) as well as Horton (2001) explore the impact of the researcher's gender and gendered body on their reception in spaces occupied by children, on the creation of their status as an insider/outside and on the management of children's expectations. Third, discussing the role of relationships with children, Blazek (2013) draws on Anna Freud's psychoanalysis, suggesting that continuous relationships with children are channels that both convey emotions in the events of the fieldwork and also enable further developments and alternative approaches to children in which emotions can surface in different ways. Finally, work within children's emotional geographies reflects Law's ascertainment that '[m]ethod is not... a more or less successful set of procedures for reporting on a given reality. Rather it is performative. It helps to produce realities' (2004, p. 143). The limits of representation in particular have been challenged and geographers have focused on more elusive outcomes of doing emotional geographies, rather than knowledge intended for presentation and circulation, including everyday practices, personal learning and embodied experience (Woodyer, 2008; Blazek and Hraňová, 2012; Pyyry, 2015). In all these four topics, the recognition of emotions as ultimately 'unstable subjects' (Bondi and Davidson, 2011, p. 595) with a lot of importance has been sustained.

Minor policy

One remaining aim of this chapter is to establish (and problematise) links between the theory and methodology of approaching children's emotions and the dynamics of policy-making and professional practice. Blazek and Kraftl's (2015) recent effort to analyse the 'mattering' of emotions in policy and professional practice with children identifies emotions as an important device in the constantly evolving forms of childhood's institutionalisation in the contested spaces of (predominantly) adult governance. It is beyond the scope of these paragraphs to scrutinise this question in full, but the following sketch serves as a conclusion to this debate by linking together the previous themes of theory and method and by articulating a mobile approach to childhood and children through a lens that is attentive to the spatialities of emotions in children's lives.

Blazek and Kraftl (2015) give a prompt to upscale the mattering of children's emotions into policies and practices regarding childhood and at the same time downscale policy and practice to come into tangible terms with the presence and effects of emotions, connecting the 'micro' and 'macro' in children's spatialities (Philo and Smith, 2003). As Collins and Tymko (2015) show, discourses on social policy and professional practice are framed by narratives of rational organisation which conceal the powerful impact of emotions on the construction of public policy. It is important to reflect on the localisation of emotions and on the spacing of their formation in the context of the governance of childhood, and at the same time to consider policy and practice as fields embedding and converging with emotions at various points. Children's emotions should not be viewed simply as objects or targets of policy and practical efforts, but rather as their elements and media.

This in turn requires reflecting on adult positions towards children in order to appraise the intersubjective relationality of the emotional geographies of childhood. Age has been theorised as a relational category (Pain and Hopkins, 2007) and thinking about emotions in and through space gives an opportunity to rethink wider ideas of childhood and how adults position themselves in relation to children. Adults might wish to consider mobile practices diverging from policies or the spatial and emotional autonomy of children as a policy target itself (Blazek and Hricová, 2015), or they might need to succumb to the necessity of nourishing and protecting children by intervening in the spaces of childhood and in children's emotional experiences (Hörschelmann, 2015).

This chapter's narrative linked a number of epistemological, political and methodological dilemmas as they stem from the different positionalities of adults and children, including different ways in which adults and children appropriate, shape, move through and experience space and individual places. My ultimate call is thus for a policy and practical approach that would be engaged with the inevitable elusiveness of children's emotional geographies (the spatial elements of the role of emotions in children's lives), attentive to the ontological, epistemological and political differences between adults and children, and – at the very moral level – sensitive to the difficulties of being a child (Jones, 2013).

References

Barker, J. and Smith, F. (2001) 'Power, Positionality and Practicality: Carrying Out Fieldwork with Children', *Ethics, Place and Environment*, 4 (2), 142–146.

Blaut, J. M. (1997) 'The Mapping Abilities of Young Children: Children Can', *Annals of the Association of American Geographers*, 87 (1), 152–158.

Blaut, J. M., Stea, D., Spencer, C. and Blades, M. (2003) 'Mapping as a Cultural and Cognitive Universal', *Annals of the Association of American Geographers*, 93 (1), 165–185.

Blazek, M. (2013) 'Emotions as Practice: Anna Freud's Child Psychoanalysis and Thinking-Doing Children's Emotional Geographies', *Emotion, Space and Society*, 9 (1), 24–32.

Blazek, M. and Hraňová, P. (2012) 'Emerging Relationships and Diverse Motivations and Benefits in Participatory Video with Young People', *Children's Geographies*, 10 (2), 151–168.

Blazek, M. and Hricová, P. (2015) 'Understanding (How to Be with) Children's Emotions: Relationships, Spaces and Politics of Reconnection in Reflections from Detached Youth Work', in M. Blazek and P. Kraftl (eds) *Children's Emotions in Policy and Practice: Mapping and Making Spaces of Childhood*, Basingstoke: Palgrave, 204–218.

Blazek, M. and Kraftl, P. (eds) (2015) *Children's Emotions in Policy and Practice: Mapping and Making Spaces of Childhood*, Basingstoke: Palgrave.

Blazek, M. and Windram-Geddes, M. (2013) 'Editorial: Thinking and Doing Children's Emotional Geographies', *Emotion, Space and Society*, 9 (1), 1–3.

Bondi, L. (2005) 'Making Connections and Thinking Through Emotions: Between Geography and Psychotherapy', *Transactions of the Institute of British Geographers*, 30 (4), 433–448.

Bondi, L. and Davidson, J. (2011) 'Lost in Translation', *Transactions of the Institute of British Geographers*, 36 (4), 595–598.

Bondi, L., Davidson, J. and Smith, M. (2005) 'Introduction: Geography's "Emotional Turn" ', in J. Davidson, M. Smith and L. Bondi (eds) *Emotional Geographies*, London: Ashgate, 1–16

Clifford, N., Holloway, S. L., Rice, S. P. and Valentine, G. (eds) (2009) *Key Concepts in Geography*, 2nd edition, London: Sage.

Collins, D. and Tymko, M. (2015) 'Smoke-Free Cars: Placing Children's Emotions', in M. Blazek and P. Kraftl (eds) *Children's Emotions in Policy and Practice: Mapping and Making Spaces of Childhood*, Basingstoke: Palgrave, 68–84.

Cresswell, T. (2004) *Place: A Short Introduction*, Oxford: Blackwell.

Curti, G. H., Aitken, S. C., Bosco, F. J. and Goerisch, D. D. (2011) 'For Not Limiting Emotional and Affectual Geographies: A Collective Critique of Steve Pile's "Emotions and Affect in Recent Human Geography" ', *Transactions of the Institute of British Geographers*, 36 (4), 590–594.

Davidson, J., Bondi, L. and Smith, M. (2014) 'An Emotional Contradiction', *Emotion, Space and Society*, 10 (1), 1–3.

den Besten, O. (2010) 'Local Belonging and "Geographies of Emotions": Immigrant Children's Experience of Their Neighbourhoods in Paris and Berlin', *Childhood*, 17 (2), 181–195.

Dickens, L. and Lonie, D. (2013) 'Rap, Rhythm and Recognition: Lyrical Practices and the Politics of Voice on a Community Music Project for Young People Experiencing Challenging Circumstances', *Emotion, Space and Society*, 9 (1), 59–71.

Gagen, E. A. (2015) 'Governing Emotions: Citizenship, Neuroscience and the Education of Youth', *Transactions of the Institute of British Geographers*, 41 (1), 140–152.

Gallacher, L. and Gallagher, M. (2008) 'Methodological Immaturity in Childhood Research?: Thinking Through "Participatory Methods"', *Childhood*, 15 (4), 499–516.

Hadfield-Hill, S. and Horton, J. (2014) 'Children's Experiences of Participating in Research: Emotional Moments Together?' *Children's Geographies*, 12 (2), 135–153.

Harker, C. (2005) 'Playing and Affective Time-Spaces', *Children's Geographies*, 3 (1), 47–62.

Harvey, D. (2006) 'Space as a Key Word', in D. Harvey (ed.) *Spaces of Global Capitalism: Towards a Theory of Uneven Geographical Development*, London: Verso Press, 117–148.

Haynes, K. and Tanner, T. M. (2013) 'Empowering Young People and Strengthening Resilience: Youth-Centred Participatory Video as a Tool for Climate Change Adaptation and Disaster Risk Reduction', *Children's Geographies*, 13 (4), 357–371.

Hemming, P. J. (2007) 'Renegotiating the Primary School: Children's Emotional Geographies of Sport, Exercise and Active Play', *Children's Geographies*, 5 (4), 353–371.

Holloway, S. L. (1999) 'Mother and Worker? The Negotiation of Motherhood and Paid Employment in Two Urban Neighborhoods', *Urban Geography*, 20 (5), 438–460.

Holloway, S. L. (2014) 'Changing Children's Geographies', *Children's Geographies*, 12 (4), 377–392.

Holloway, S. L. and Pimlott-Wilson, H. (2011) 'Geographies of Children, Youth and Families: Defining Achievements, Debating the Agenda', in L. Holt (ed.) *Geographies of Children, Youth and Families: International Perspectives*, London: Routledge, 9–24.

Holloway, S. L. and Valentine, G. (2000a) 'Children's Geographies and the New Social Studies of Childhood', in S. Holloway and G. Valentine (eds) *Children's Geographies: Playing, Living, Learning*, London: Routledge, 1–21.

Holloway, S. L. and Valentine, G. (2000b) 'Spatiality and the New Social Studies of Childhood', *Sociology*, 34 (4), 763–783.

Holt, L. (2006) 'Exploring "Other" Childhoods Through Quantitative Secondary Analyses of Large Scale Surveys: Opportunities and Challenges for Children's Geographers', *Children's Geographies*, 4 (2), 143–155.

Holt, L. (2011) 'Introduction: Geographies of Children, Youth and Families: Disentangling the Socio-Spatial Contexts of Young People Across the Globalizing World', in L. Holt (ed.) *Geographies of Children, Youth and Families: International Perspectives*, London: Routledge, 1–8.

Holt, L. (2013) 'Exploring the Emergence of the Subject in Power: Infant Geographies', *Environment and Planning D: Society and Space*, 31 (4), 645–663.

Hörschelmann, K. (2015) 'Childhood, War and Divided Emotions', in M. Blazek and P. Kraftl (eds) *Children's Emotions in Policy and Practice: Mapping and Making Spaces of Childhood*, Basingstoke: Palgrave, 274–290.

Horton, J. (2001) 'Do You Get Some Funny Looks When You Tell People What You Do? Muddling Through Some Angsts and Ethics of (Being a Male) Researching with Children', *Ethics, Place and Environment*, 4 (2), 159–166.

Horton, J. (2010) ' "The Best Thing Ever": How Children's Popular Culture Matters', *Social and Cultural Geography*, 11 (4), 377–398.

Horton, J. and Kraftl, P. (2006) 'What Else? Some More Ways of Thinking and Doing "Children's Geographies" ', *Children's Geographies*, 4 (1), 69–95.

Horton, J. and Kraftl, P. (2009) 'Small Acts, Kind Words and "Not Too Much Fuss": Implicit Activisms', *Emotion, Space and Society*, 2 (1), 14–23.

James, S. (1990) 'Is There a "Place" for Children in Geography?" *Area*, 22(3), 278–283.

Jones, O. (2000) 'Melting Geography: Purity, Disorder, Childhood and Space', in S. Holloway and G. Valentine (eds) *Children's Geographies: Playing, Living, Learning*, London: Routledge, 28–47.

Jones, O. (2003) ' "Endlessly Revisited and Forever Gone": On Memory, Reverie and Emotional Imagination in Doing Children's Geographies. An "Addendum" to "To Go Back Up the Side Hill": Memories, Imaginations and Reveries of Childhood by Chris Philo', *Children's Geographies*, 1 (1), 25–36.

Jones, O. (2008) ' "True geography []Quickly Forgotten, Giving Away to an Adult-Imagined Universe". Approaching the Otherness of Childhood', *Children's Geographies*, 6 (2), 195–212.

Jones, O. (2013) ' " I Was Born but . . . ": Children as Other/Nonrepresentational Subjects in Emotional and Affective Registers as Depicted in Film', *Emotion, Space and Society*, 9 (1), 4–12.

Jupp Kina, V. (2012) 'What We Say and What We Do: Reflexivity, Emotions and Power in Children and Young People's Participation', *Children's Geographies*, 10 (2), 201–218.

Kallio, K. P. (2012) 'Desubjugating Childhoods by Listening to the Child's Voice and Childhoods at Play', *Acme*, 11 (1), 81–109.

Kesby, M. (2007) 'Methodological Insights on and from Children's Geographies', *Children's Geographies*, 5 (3), 193–205.

Kraftl, P. (2013) 'Beyond "Voice", Beyond "Agency", Beyond "Politics"? Hybrid Childhoods and Some Critical Reflections on Children's Emotional Geographies', *Emotion, Space and Society*, 9 (1), 13–23.

Kraftl, P., Horton, J. and Tucker, F. (2014) *Children's Geographies*, Oxford Bibliographies Online: Childhood Studies.

Law, J. (2004) *After Method: Mess in Social Science Research*, London: Routledge.

Lees, L. (1998) 'Urban Renaissance and the Street: Spaces of Control and Contestation', in N. Fyfe (ed.) *Images of the Street: Representation, Experience and Control in Public Space*, London: Routledge, 236–253.

Lefebvre, H. (1991) *Production of Space*, Oxford: Blackwell.

Ley, D. and Samuels, M. (eds) (1978) *Humanistic Geography: Prospects and Problems*, London: Groom Helm.

Marston, S. A., Jones III, J. P. and Woodward, K. (2005) 'Human Geography Without Scale', *Transactions of the Institute of British Geographers*, 30 (4), 416–432.

Massey, D. (1994) *Space, Place and Gender*, Cambridge: Polity Press.

Matthews, H. and Limb, M. (1999) 'Defining an Agenda for the Geography of Children: Review and Prospect', *Progress in Human Geography*, 23 (1), 61–90.

McKendrick, J. (2000) 'The Geography of Children: An Annotated Bibliography', *Childhood: A Global Journal of Child Research*, 7 (3), 359–387.

Mitchell, K. and Elwood, S. (2012) 'Mapping Children's Politics: The Promise of Articulation and the Limits of Nonrepresentational Theory', *Environment and Planning D: Society and Space*, 30 (5), 788–804.

Nast, H. J. (1994) 'Women in the Field – Opening Remarks', *Professional Geographer*, 46 (1), 54–66.

Nayak, A. (2003) ' "Through Children's Eyes": Childhood, Place and the Fear of Crime', *Geoforum*, 34 (3), 303–315.

Pain, R. and Hopkins, P. (2007) 'Geographies of Age: Thinking Relationally', *Area*, 39 (3), 287–294.

Pain, R., Panelli, R., Kindon, S. and Little, J. (2010) 'Moments in Everyday/Distant Geopolitics: Young People's Fears and Hopes', *Geoforum*, 41 (6), 972–982.

Percy-Smith, B. (2010) 'Councils, Consultations and Community: Rethinking the Spaces for Children and Young People's Participation', *Children's Geographies*, 8 (2), 107–122.

Philo, C. (1992) 'Neglected Rural Geographies: A Review', *Journal of Rural Studies*, 8 (2), 193–207.

Philo, C. (2003) ' "To Go Back Up the Side Hill": Memories, Imaginations and Reveries of Childhood', *Children's Geographies*, 1 (1), 7–23.

Philo, C. and Smith, F. M. (2003) 'Political Geographies of Children and Young People', *Space and Polity*, 7 (1), 99–115.

Philo, C. and Smith, F. M. (2013) 'The Child-Body-Politic: Afterword on "Children and Young People's Politics in Everyday Life" ', *Space and Polity*, 17 (1), 137–144.

Pile, S. (2010) 'Emotions and Affect in Recent Human Geography', *Transactions of the Institute of British Geographers*, 35 (1), 5–20.

Preece, T. (2015) 'Social Suicide: A Digital Context for Self-Harm and Suicidal Ideation', in M. Blazek and P. Kraftl (eds) *Children's Emotions in Policy and Practice: Mapping and Making Spaces of Childhood*, Basingstoke: Palgrave, 138–155.

Procter, L. (2013) 'Exploring the Role of Emotional Reflexivity in Research with Children', *Emotion, Space and Society*, 9 (1), 80–88.

Pyyry, N. (2015) 'Re-cognizing the City by Mapping the Geographies of Hanging out', in M. Blazek and P. Kraftl (eds) *Children's Emotions in Policy and Practice: Mapping and Making Spaces of Childhood*, Basingstoke: Palgrave, 107–121.

Rose, G. (1993) *Feminism and Geography: The Limits of Geographical Knowledge*, Minneapolis: University of Minnesota Press.

Sibley, D. (1991) 'Children's Geographies: Some Problems of Representation', *Area*, 23 (2), 269–270.

Skelton, T. (2017) *Geographies of Children and Young People*, Volumes 1–17, New York: Springer.

Smith, M., Davidson, J. and Bondi, L. (eds) (2009) *Emotion, Place and Culture*, London: Ashgate.

Thrift, N. (1996) *Spatial Formations*, London: Sage.

Valentine, G. (1999) 'Being Seen and Heard? The Ethical Complexities of Working with Children and Young People at Home and at School', *Ethics, Place and Environment*, 2 (2), 151–155.

van Blerk, L. and Kesby, M. (eds) (2008) *Doing Children's Geographies: Methodological Issues in Research with Young People*, London: Routledge.

Waite, L. and Conn, C. (2011) 'Creating a Space for Young Women's Voices: Using Participatory Video Drama in Uganda', *Gender, Place and Culture*, 18 (1), 115–135.

Winchester, H. P. M. (1991) 'The Geography of Children', *Area*, 23 (4), 357–360.

Windram-Geddes, M. (2013) *Everyday Geographies of Girls' Experiences of Physical Activity: Gender, Health and Bodies*, unpublished PhD thesis. University of Dundee, Dundee.

Woodyer, T. (2008) 'The Body as Research Tool: Embodied Practice and Children's Geographies', *Children's Geographies*, 6 (4), 349–362.

6
Reconceptualising Children's Play: Exploring the Connections Between Spaces, Practices and Emotional Moods

Helle Skovbjerg Karoff

Introduction

Children play in all sorts of spaces and a close relationship exists between their emotions, the play spaces they inhabit and their play practices. In recent years descriptions of this relationship have been coloured by learning discourse. A large body of literature primarily sees children's emotions, use of space and play practices as a source of learning and development (Valentine et al., 2004). Playgrounds have become learning spaces where children's abilities are often viewed against a notion of the 'normal' child. Gagen (1998) describes the playground as a way of 'getting hold of the children', where they function as an ideal within a site of social control. This idea of play, drawing on a particular perception of what 'play' means, is chiefly based on a notion of 'function', which is to say that play is understood for its usefulness. As Sutton-Smith points out in *The Ambiguity of Play* (2001), this can dilute and trivialise understandings of the play activity. Rasmussen (2007) polemically asks whether spaces for children are defined as being orchestrated by adults or as organised by the children's relationship to them and their emotional experiences of them. Focusing predominantly on a functional conceptualisation of play neglects the fact that children perform an essential role in making play happen, succeed and unfold. In other words, focusing solely on the function of play disregards the experiences of children (James et al., 1998).

The aim of this chapter, based on a phenomenological study of children's everyday lives, is to present a conceptualisation of play activity focusing upon the relationship between play, emotion and space. Drawing upon a phenomenological approach, which places the playing child in their environment (Jackson, 1996; Merleau-Ponty, 1996; Lefebvre, 2013), I position the child in relation to other people, materialities and practices (Miller, 2009; Karoff & Johansen, 2009), and the immediacy of their experience in regards to what is happening here and now. These are the areas of interest in the fieldwork upon which this chapter draws, which was inspired by Vergunst's (2010) notion of 'rhythms'. By emphasising a phenomenological perspective it is possible to take the participants' actions in play activities seriously and to evaluate the quality of their play. Their experiences of these activities are defined in this chapter as the 'quality of play'. Through an understanding of play as experiencing, I aim to examine the relationship between play, space and emotion.

Drawing on the works of Heidegger (1996) and Schmidt (2011), this chapter suggests that an emphasis on emotional moods offers a way of understanding and framing the relationship between space, emotion and play practices. Moods are first and foremost related to social relations but also to an openness towards a possible future; they are not bound to specific events or experiences, but link to possible ways that the future of the play activities might unfold. Understanding children's emotional moods reveals how emotion in children's play is not only related to a specific moment, but is also closely related to social relationships, possibilities for the future and the uncertainty of play practices. Through adopting a phenomenological approach this chapter provides a new understanding of the role of emotional moods in children's space-making practices. I emphasise the emotional moods of the child, thus allowing an exploration of some of the ways in which qualities of space may arise through children's shared participation. By framing emotion through the lens of moods it becomes clear that within children's play practices emotions are not things that children have, but instead are explored through their play practices.

Initially, this chapter introduces the various theoretical points of departure which frame my understanding of play practices and emotional moods. I draw on these theories to consider how play spaces are created through 'rhythms' of emotional moods. Drawing upon a phenomenological study of children's play, I show how these theoretical lenses have informed four new concepts to expand current understandings of play practices: *sliding, shifting, displaying* and *exceeding*. I then relate these play practices to Heidegger's (1996) notion of moods to consider play as undefined, uncertain and exploratory. Building on this I present four emotional moods: *devotion, intensity, tension* and *euphoria*, which connect back to the concepts of play practice. To sum up I show how these two sets of concepts indicate how children's spaces are produced, used and provide amusement through play practice. My analysis contributes to a richer understanding of the development of children's play spaces and is an attempt to qualitatively demonstrate the connection between space and emotional mood.

Theoretical points of departure: Play spaces and emotional moods

According to Schmidt (1999) practices are an everyday type of bodily behaviour. They are always social and related to others, in addition to constantly being performed through the body. Practices are always social practices (Reckwitz, 2002), underlining the relationship between practice, sociality and body. This perspective is reflected in de Certeau's definition of space, where he suggests that users produce and transform space through practice. De Certeau writes that: 'Space occurs as the effect produced by the operations that orient it, situate it, temporalise it, and make it function in a polyvalent unity of conflictual programs or contractual proximities.' He argues that: 'to practice space is thus to repeat the joyful and silent experience of childhood; it is, in a place, to be other and to move toward the other' (de Certeau, 1984, p. 117). De Certeau underlines the close relationship between space and practice. My emphasis, however, is upon understanding play activity as play practice (Karoff, 2013). Combined, an understanding of play and space is embedded in an understanding of practices.

Murray and Mand define emotions as 'embodied, sensorial, intensely felt and…constructed and reconstructed in mobile space' (2013, p. 73). For Heidegger (1996) moods are closely connected to our existence as human beings; they are an embodied state of being in the world and are embedded in our practices. Drawing on Lefebvre's concept of rhythm, explored in *The Production of Space* (1974) and further developed in *Rhythmanalysis* (2013), it is possible to understand space as enacted through the body. A conceptualisation of play as rhythms enacted through emotional moods emphasises the relationship between practice, space and emotion and can be viewed broken down as follows:

Practice: *a bodily and social practice*
Space: *where bodily and social practice takes place*
Emotional moods: *conceptualisation of being in the world during play practices*
Rhythms: *types and modulation of practices and emotional moods in space*

Research context

This chapter draws upon a large field-based study based in Odense, Demark. The study, supported by the Carlsberg Foundation,[1] examined children's experiences and practices of dangerous full-body play. In Denmark and worldwide a great deal of attention has been given to safety and danger on the playground (Sandseter, 2009; Karoff, 2013). The field study grew out of an interest in the importance of danger as an element of physical play that allows play to continue to be interesting. By exploring the importance of danger in children's play and by examining strategies for managing dangerous events by drawing on the perspectives of children, the study found that children have multiple ways of managing danger in their physical play. Most importantly, they repeat play events over and over again, allowing them to practice, to be prepared for and to discover the limits of their own physical capacities.

The fieldwork draws upon principles from Pink (2007) and Gulløv (2013), who also orientate their work within a phenomenological perspective, to focus on the perspectives of children and their experiences using visual methods as a fieldwork strategy. Six months of empirical work were conducted in a primary and middle school (grades 3–4, ages 7–9) in Odense, Denmark. The school had several large play areas within its grounds, one of which was a small forest with trees, hills and water, while another contained slides, small houses and swings. The fieldwork consisted of participatory observation of a wide range of physical play activities, primarily in these areas. I used a photography-based method to obtain information about the places the children inhabited and what they did within them. This method consisted of distributing cameras periodically to the children and inviting them to take photos. I conducted semiformal interviews with the children based on the photos they had taken, combined with walk-and-talk interviews where they showed me the spaces where they played and explained what and how they liked to play. I quickly realised that a close relationship existed between the modulation and management of different play practices, spaces and the children's emotional moods. For example, one student, Anna, liked to go to the forest and climb the highest tree. I asked her why she had chosen this tree and she said she liked feeling scared. The examples analysed and highlighted in the remainder of this chapter demonstrate how children engage in space-making by considering the relationship between play practices and emotional moods.

Play practices as rhythms of play

Schmidt defines practices as 'a doing and a making, done in a repetitive rhythm' (1999, p. 37). In relation to play, practices are the doing part of the play activities; these include all types of behaviours, such as physical and mental activities, the use of toys, ways of relating to feelings and motives for behaviour. The following extract from my field notes of a play event is used as a starting point for exploring the rhythms of children's play practices:

> *Emily and Diana are standing at the bottom of a hill in the playground at their school. Emily is holding a long thin branch on a tree close to the fence surrounding the playground. The hands of many children who have held on to the branch have worn the leaves on the branch away. I ask them what they are doing and they tell me they are playing on the hill. They want to show me what they do. Emily keeps holding onto the branch as she walks up the hill. At the top she turns around, leans back and then runs downhill. When she is at full tilt, she releases her feet from the ground, leaping away from the hill. Hovering for a moment,*

she stretches out her legs and hits the fence with her feet. The fence gives a little and Emily swings backwards a bit. She then falls on her bottom, laughing, and Diana is laughing too. Now it is Diana's turn to take the downhill ride.

(Field notes)

De Certeau (1984) states that the feel of spaces is shaped by the practices that take place within them. In the play event presented above, Emily and Diana are practising together. They have certain ways of holding and swinging from the branches and of using the hill and the fence that create a shared understanding of practices in this play event and in turn create a shared play space. The girls have ways of laughing, just as others have ways of playing war, play fighting, playing with dolls or climbing trees (Mouritsen, 1998; Jessen and Karoff, 2008). Practices unfold as they are shared with others in the doing of play. In the play event Diana and Emily were able to practice each part of their playing: holding the branch, going uphill, leaning back, running, swinging, stretching their legs and bouncing off the fence with their feet. To be part of this play event, they both have to learn all of these practices. They repeat the play activity because they are both familiar with how this play event has to be performed. The play practices have a rhythm in which one practice follows another, each with its own specific time span. Diana and Emily's play practices have a meaningful relationship to one another; they represent a premise by which they make sense to them. Their play follows a trajectory of rhythms that makes possible a circular set of practices. Whenever one of the girls takes the branch, the play proceeds to the next step, which in this case is going to the hill, leaning back and running. Each of these practices relates to the materiality of the space; the material shapes the play event. As Lefebvre (2004) suggest, the following and exploring of rhythms of practice is an inherently creative activity.

Even though the rhythms of the girls' play are not well defined from the beginning, they share a sense of what the play will involve. However, they do not have to agree in advance what the play practices should or could be. Swinging on the hill, for example, is a play activity that is constantly under development through their 'doings' together; it does not exist as a well-defined or fixed set of practices. Rather than understanding the rhythms of this play as linearly constituted solely through repetitive routines, they can be considered as a field of potential. Lefebvre's *Rhythmanalysis* underlines the importance the impermanence of rhythms suggesting that they are modified through practice. For Lefebvre, a rhythm 'preserves both the measures that initiate process and the re-commencements of this process with modifications' (2004, p. 79).

Four rhythms of play: Sliding, shifting, displaying and exceeding

Based on the empirical study, four rhythms of play were identified: sliding, shifting, displaying and exceeding. In developing these categories it was assumed that such rhythms are bodily and social doings and are related to the surrounding space. The relationship between body, sociality and space is reflected in a conceptualisation, which attempts to reflect how these rhythms unfold. The four categories of play practices are described in the following.

The first rhythm of play is *sliding*, which has a strong repetitive rhythm. The children taking part in this play are orientated towards repetition, primarily in order to continue what is already going on and to make small changes. As soon as Emily and Diana are at the bottom of the hill on their school's playground, they start to move slowly uphill, they use their feet to make their way along a dirt path up the hill, their footprints (and those of other children) have made and continue to produce this path on the grassed embankment. There is little variation in their repetitions of following the path. The same actions recur time and time again, and the two girls continue the trajectory of their play, devoted to the repetition of the rhythm of play with as little change as possible. This recurring rhythm is in focus at the beginning of their play. Sliding is characterised by fluidity and continuity; there is very little conflict or discussion regarding the play practice. The girls' practices do not expand the possibilities of the space, but instead they follow the same rhythmic trajectory.

The second rhythm of play practice is *shifting*. Like sliding this has a strong repetitive rhythm, but over time the rhythm shifts as the girls take chances and create surprises for other players. When Emily is standing at the top of the hill, she starts running and leaps off the ground. Thus, shifting involves the physical movement of her whole body. Her speed changes, as does her direction of movement, often suddenly and surprisingly. Her swinging movement creates dizziness and butterflies in her stomach. When Emily hits the fence her body jolts and swings backwards. A wild trip on a roller coaster could also constitute a shifting practice, or jumping on a trampoline, because on the one hand, there is a strong repetition of movement, but on the other there is a succession of rapid changes in speed, direction and height. The shift between fast and slow, high and low characterises this shifting rhythm of play. A strong repetitive rhythm takes place at the beginning of the play event, for instance when Emily is preparing her swing by walking up the path. The speed and/or change in height make shifting an unpredictable stage of play, which continues until the player has returned to a strong, predictable and repetitive rhythm. The rapid shift from a strong predictable rhythm, such as walking up the dirt path on the hill, to a fast and changing pace when leaving the dirt path, is characteristic of a shifting rhythm of play.

The third rhythm of play is *displaying*, which is characterised by constant changes in the children's play practices over time. Displaying refers to play events involving any kind of informal performance, where skills are demonstrated through activities such as dancing, singing, taking photographs of others or dramatic role play. It involves the children being 'on stage' and letting other players look at them, learn from them and criticise or comment on their performance. When Emily is about to start running downhill in order to swing, for a moment, displaying is at the centre of her play. She waits for Diana to look at her and in this moment the hill becomes a stage for her to perform. In comparison to the two already presented rhythms, sliding and shifting, displaying has a weaker beat and the play practice is actively changed over time. As with shifting there is an element of unpredictability, but displaying also includes an expectation of change. In this sense displaying is not unpredictable; if change does not happen then the players will become disappointed and the play activity, in the longer term, would not continue. When it is Diana's turn, she must also come up with new ways of changing the play practice to prevent the play event from becoming boring and eventually ceasing.

The creative transformation of the play practice is central to the fourth and last rhythm of play practice, *exceeding*. This sits in stark contrast to sliding, as the children are expected to transform the play practice. The expectation is that the play activity must be 'off-rhythm'. While creative interpretation is an important dimension of displaying, it becomes even more important in the exceeding rhythm of play. When children are exceeding, repetition is not the focus and therefore the crazier the play the better. For example, on one occasion, two girls were playing with their dolls during a lunch break at school. They bent the dolls into all sorts of shapes and competed to see who could create the most bizarre shape. They turned the dolls' heads so they looked like they had been put on backwards and they bent the dolls' legs up towards their shoulders. Their doll play contrasts starkly with the loving, caring practices of doll play, as it is often typically perceived. Their peculiar play includes tricks and stories about faeces, dirty words and utter frivolity. These are all representative of the characteristics of an exceeding rhythm of play (Karoff, 2013).

Emotional mood as being in play spaces

As mentioned at the start of this chapter, play rhythms are formed through the practice of play. In contrast, emotional moods are the ways in which children experience play. Emotional experiences can be understood as the relationship between bodily sensations and material objects. Bartos (2013), drawing on Ahmed (2013), argues that we feel a certain way towards something because we are in contact with that specific thing. As Ahmed suggests: 'If the contact generates feeling, then emotion and sensation cannot be easily separated' (2013, p. 6). She adds that 'feelings may stick to some objects, and slide over others' (p. 8). By connecting this conceptualisation of emotion with the notion of moods, I emphasise the social dimensions of being in play spaces. Moods have been linked to sociability, for example Hammershøj states that: 'Moods are social, whereas emotions are individual. Emotions are about the relationship to [one]self, and tell us something about how we feel about this or that specific relationship, whereas moods reveal how we are in this world overall or how we are in the sociality as a whole' (2012, p. 3).

Building on this, I apply Heidegger's (1996) notion of moods to explore how emotional moods facilitate ways of being within children's play events. According to Heidegger, moods are not just something that come and go but are an essential part of human existence. Humans are always in some kind of mood, or, rephrased, moods are a constant human condition. Even if our state of being appears to be completely without a mood, we are nevertheless in a mood. We will never merely observe the world, because things only make sense from the point at which they are viewed in our lives. We also relate these observations to what has previously made sense to us and how we feel they should be included in our imminent futures. In this way, the production of meaning is not just something we do from time to time but in fact constitutes our existence. Heidegger captures this in his conceptualisation of the human being as *Dasein* – a being that is always in space – *da* – and does not exist apart from the world, but always exists in relation to the world. To be in a mood is *Dasein*, that is, being there.

According to Heidegger, a mood is an indeterminate or undefined state revealed to you before any kind of specific feeling can be created. Mood tells you something about your relationship to the space you are in, which is also in keeping with de Certeau (1984), or how you are tuned into the world and the people around you. But moods and our understanding of them are not fully articulated or completely unarticulated. They are placed in an intermediate position where not all is said, but neither does this mean that nothing is said. Heidegger's notion of mood is characterised as a way of 'being there' that is not confined to a specific feeling, but open and ready to be articulated as something specific, even though the specification has yet to happen. In *Time & Being*, Heidegger writes, 'In having a mood, *Dasein* is always disclosed moodwise as that entity to which it has been delivered over in its Being; and in this way it has been delivered over to the Being which, in existing, it has to be' (Heidegger, 1996, p. 39).

Mood is this non-specific way of being, where you are open to experiencing the world. The key point here is that we cannot understand mood only as an inner psychological state of mind (Csikszentmihalyi, 1989) that comes from within, but rather as something that takes place in our engagement as beings, as *Dasein*, in the world of things and in our doings. As Harker (2005) points out, these 'affective' ways of being in spaces of play are not related to an individual body; instead ways of being are characterised through a shared ownership within a specific space at a particular time. Harker writes, 'None of us "owned" this feeling, nor was it located "in" any of us. Yet it was crucial to our enactment of that particular moment' (2005, p. 23). This emerging moment of being, as exemplified by Diana and

Emily's shared play practices, is poetically captured by Heidegger: 'A mood assails us. It comes neither from the "outside" nor from the "inside", but arises out of Being-in-the-world, as a way of such Being' (1996, p. 136).

Significant to this understanding of emotional moods is that the mood state comes before a feeling can be articulated as something specific. It is a state of being where one is distinctly open to new ways of playing and where the possibilities exist for that to happen. It is not something that comes from either within the players or externally, but instead happens through children's engagement in the doings of play, the space they are in and the relationships they have with one another. In other words, mood is about more than the children's play practices. In play practices, emotional mood, like engagement with place, is expressed through that engagement. Schmidt explains:

> The individual is minded one way or another, which is to say that sensibility is shared in a direction attuned to some balancing of the elements and that the individual is positioned to find himself in a particular event. But once that is said, in the same way that you are inclined toward certain senses – even though the other possibilities remain – you can also be more minded toward one mode than another and be more or less in agreement with one register or another. You can be minded 'cool' or 'hot' – aesthetically expressed as more passive than active.
>
> (Schmidt, 2011, p. 286)

Based on these theoretical ideas I have identified four types of emotional moods, which can be related to the four play practices already presented. These emotional moods can be characterised as ways of understanding how the children were tuned into the play space through their play practices. The point here is that play practices create emotional moods.

Four types of emotional moods expressed through four play practices

The first type of emotional mood is *devotion*, which is characterised as the feeling of being in-flow, continuously being in the moment, which is accompanied by a sense of lightness. There is no sense of hardness when in this state, merely concentration and focus. The body is often quiet or feels as if it is moving in slow motion. The rhythm is quiet and continuous, without surprise. When Diana and Emily are about to begin playing together, their bodies slowly follow the dirt path up the hill. They do not confront it or destroy it. Often when children play with Lego or dolls, or draw alone in their rooms, devotion will be the emotional mood in focus, but all sorts of play can often start with devotion. During my field study I played doll with a child named Anna. We totally let ourselves go and immersed ourselves in a state of being where we abandoned ourselves to 'our doings' and were open to seeing where they would lead us – the emotional mood was one of devotion. Our openness towards new practices was first and foremost a wish for continuity and confirmed what was already meaningful to us. This point is also clear in Diana and Emily's use and production of space in the play event on the hill. They looked for a recurring rhythm as they walked up the path. A strong rhythm is a characteristic of sliding, where a repetitive beat is in focus. The use of space changes minimally, and practices are repeated as similarly as possible.

The second type of emotional mood is *intensity*. A rush to the head or butterflies in the stomach can characterise this mood, where one might have an intense bodily experience of being as ready as possible and excited for more. When Diana and Emily are swinging from the tree and bouncing off the fence, their emotional mood can be characterised as intensity, where an openness towards the active production of space is characterised by an expectation of a fast change in rhythm and a feeling that something unpredictable is going to happen (such as rebounding off the fence). In contrast to the mood of devotion, which initiated Diana and Emily's play, change is expected when the mood is intensity. The change occurs when they hit the fence and in this way they use the fence to enhance their play. This emotional mood relates to the ways that practice can shift unexpectedly.

The third type of emotional mood is *tension*, which is characterised by being ready to show yourself and also by being aware of others showing themselves to you. When the girls swing on the hill using tree branches, they are sharing an emotional mood of tension. They constantly show off through the style of their swing, knowing that they are only watched if they display good style. They also look for ways to express their own style when they are in the audience. The girls produce space by performing to an audience and becoming the audience themselves; the space on the top of the hill becomes their stage. There is openness in this emotional mood, observed as an expectation of change in their play practice. This relates not only to a practice of the expected, but also to something unpredictable relating to one's own style. It might be that Diana gets a new idea about how to bounce off the fence, or Emily might come up with an alternative way of swinging. Their staging of space makes that unpredictability possible. The emotional mood of tension relates to the active display of play practices. As demonstrated, this involves the children putting themselves on a stage and letting others judge their play activity.

The last type of emotional mood is called *euphoria* and is characterised by an intense expectation of silliness, where children are ready to experience their own silliness and that of others. This mood is characterised by frequent and unpredictable changes in rhythm. There is an expectation for the players to come up with new acts of silliness in order to maintain the euphoric mood. Children laugh frequently and unrestrainedly; once they start, they find it difficult to stop, and they do not want to stop either. From the point of view of uninvolved parties, this emotional mood often seems manic and space is produced in the most unpredictable of ways. In the play event on the hill, euphoria was not an element; but when children pull faces, have water fights or tease grownups over and over again, the mood can be characterised as euphoric and is most commonly related to the practice of exceeding. Euphoria is the most open-minded of the moods presented here; the children constantly find new ways to express themselves and produce new spaces. The players have to maintain a great openness towards moving beyond earlier practices in order to produce a play space to maintain exceeding play practices. In other words, the players must be tuned into the act of changing space. The emotional mood can be compared to a wild piece of rock music. Euphoria is the opposite of devotion and the corresponding common practice of sliding. Devotion is characterised by quietness, repetition and fulfilling expectations safely, whereas euphoria is characterised by an expectation of being surprised by what will follow. Table 6.1 provides a summary of the types of practices and emotional moods combined with the characterisation of space in the specific moods.

Table 6.1 Overview of practices and emotional moods

Practices	*Sliding*	*Shifting*	*Displaying*	*Exceeding*
Emotional moods	*Devotion*	*Intensity*	*Tension*	*Euphoria*
Space	Following space	Expanding space	Staging space	Exploring space
Rhythm	Following each other	Changing now and then	Swinging according to one's own style	Changing constantly and hard to find

Conclusion

This chapter has presented a phenomenological perspective on children's play practices by considering the relationship between emotional mood and the social production of play spaces. Emphasis on a phenomenological perspective makes it possible to take the experiences of participants in play activities seriously and to evaluate the quality of their play. Their experiences and practices frame the quality of their play and are always valued and evaluated based on how the play activity happens and unfolds. This chapter drew on the work of Schmidt, de Carteau, Lefebvre and Heidegger as a means to examine rhythms of play in relation to emotional mood. This allowed for an examination of the social production of play spaces through shared play practices. Emotional moods have been shown to be essential to play, but are also dependent upon the ways in which players inhabit space and interact with the people they are with. This chapter presented four types of emotional moods that relate to four types of practices; the types of emotional moods and practices indicate different types of play rhythms and at the same time reveal the different ways in which children produce play spaces through enacting these rhythms. In attending to the rhythms of play, it becomes clear that emotions are not something that children have but are explored through shared play practices.

Note

1. The brewer J. C. Jacobsen established the Carlsberg Foundation in 1876. The initial task of the foundation was to provide support for Danish research. The Carlsberg Foundation awards grants for basic research in natural science, humanities and social sciences.

References

Ahmed, S. (2013) *The Cultural Politics of Emotion*, New York: Routledge.
Bartos, A. E. (2013) 'Children Sensing Place', *Emotion, Space and Society*, 9, 89–98.
Csikszentmihalyi, M. (1989) *Flow: The Psychology of Optimal Experience*, New York: HaperCollins Publishers.
De Certeau, M. (1984) *The Practice of Everyday Life*, Berkeley: University of California Press.
Harker, C. (2005) 'Playing and Affective Time-Space', *Children's Geographies*, 3 (1). London: Roudledge.
Gagen, E. (1998) 'Playing the Part: Performing Gender in America's Playgrounds', in S. Holloway and G. Valentine (eds) *Children's Geographies. Playing. Living. Learning*, New York: Routledge.
Gulløv, E. (2013) 'Creating a Natural Place for Children', *Children's Places: Cross-Cultural Perspectives*, 23.
Hammershøj, L. G. (2012) *Kreativitet: et spørgsmål om dannelse*, Copenhagen: Hans Reitzels Forlag.
Heidegger, M. (1996) *Being and Time*, Oxford: Wiley-Blackwell.
Jackson, M. (ed.) (1996) *Things as They Are: New Directions in Phenomenological Anthropology*, Bloomington: Indiana University Press.
James, A., Jenks, C. and Prout, A. (1998) *Theorizing Childhood*. Teachers College Press.
Jessen, C. and Karoff, H. (2008) *Playware and New Play Culture*, Proceedings for BIN Conference: Æstetik og kultur, Island.
Karoff, H. (2013) 'Play Moods and Play Practices', *International Journal of Play*, 2 (2), 76–86.
Karoff, H. and Johansen, S. (2009) Materiality, Practice and Body. Proceedings for IDC2009, Italy.
Lefebvre, H. (1974) *The Production of Space* (Vol. 142), Oxford: Blackwell.
Lefebvre, H. (2013) *Rhythmanalysis: Space, Time and Everyday Life*, London: Bloomsbury Academic.
Merleau-Ponty, M. (1996) *Phenomenology of Perception* (Vol. 1), Motilal Banarsidass Publisher.
Miller, D. (2009) *Stuff*, London: Polity Press.
Mouritsen, F. (1998) *Child Culture – Play Culture*, Working Paper 2. Department of Contemporary Cultural Studies. Syddansk Universitet.
Murray, L. and Mand, K. (2013) 'Travelling Near and Far: Placing Children's Mobile Emotions', *Emotion, Space and Society*, 9, 72–79.
Pink, S. (2007) *Doing Visual Ethnography: Images, Media and Representation in Research*, London: Sage.
Rasmussen, K. (2007) 'Places for Children – Children's Places', *Childhood*, 11.
Reckwitz, A. (2002) 'Toward a Theory of Social Practices. A Development in Culturalist Theorizing', *European Journal of Social Theory*, 2 (5), 245–265.
Sandseter, E. B. H. (2009) 'Affordances for Risky Play in Preschool: The Importance of Features in the Play Environment', *Early Childhood Education Journal*, 36 (5), 439–446.

Schmidt, L.-H. (1999) *Diagnosis I – Filosoferende eksperimenter*, København: Danmarks Pædagogiske Universitet Forlag.

Schmidt, L.-H. (2011) *On Respect*, Copenhagen: Danish School of Education University Press.

Sutton-Smith, B. (2009) *The Ambiguity of Play*, New York: Harvard University Press.

Valentine, G Holloway, S. L., Bingham, N. (2004) 'Transforming cyperspace: children's intervention in new public sphere', in Holloway, S. L. and Valentine, G. (eds) (2004) *Children's Geographies: Playing, Living, Learning*, London: Routledge.

Vergunst, J. (2010) 'Rhythms of Walking: History and Presence in a City Street', *Space and Culture*, 13 (4), 376–388.

7
'No, You've Done It Once!': Children's Expression of Emotion and Their School-Based Place-Making Practices

Lisa Procter

Introduction

In recent years the field of childhood studies has seen scholars drawing upon a spatial lens to understand children's lifeworlds (Christensen and O'Brien, 2003; Fog Olwin and Gulløv, 2003). This anthropological work draws on the concept of place as both 'social position and physical location' (Fog Olwin and Gulløv, 2003, p. 1) in order to examine the social and cultural construction of childhood. These studies pay particular attention to the way that children are *placed* within society. This chapter contributes to this work by considering how children create places in spaces not of their making. It is widely recognised that children's spaces are set aside, reflected for example within playgrounds or skateparks (see Chapter 9). This demarcation of children and childhood within specific spaces of society reflects, as Fog Olwin and Gulløv (2003) argue, 'the increased social marginalisation of children' (p. 2). These spaces of childhood can be understood as 'socially produced' (Lefebvre, 1991), shaped by discourses of childhood that circulate within particular times and cultures. Attending to the social production of spaces for children recognises the interconnections between the physical, social and cultural in the structuring of children's lives. Institutional spaces of childhood are often conceived in terms of children as future citizens, where childhood is viewed as a 'preparatory stage in the life course' and children as a 'future resource' (James et al., 1998, p. 133). The adult discourses of childhood shape the design and social organisation of these institutional spaces for children. This chapter seeks to ask how children encounter and navigate these spaces, and in doing so create places at school for themselves and with others.

I aim to illuminate the relevance of theories of place and emotion in researching children's negotiations of institutional spaces. I draw on the conceptualisation of emplacement to consider how children inhabit, navigate and attribute meaning to the material and immaterial spaces they encounter within their school lives. Emplacement reflects the way that our relationships in and with spaces and places become patterned over time. The key focus of the chapter is the examination of the intersections between children's dynamic meaning-making and their emotional engagements in and with school spaces. In this chapter, children's constructions of emotion and their own feeling bodies are positioned as central to the unfolding social constitution of relationships and identities. However, these 'constructed meanings' (the socially constituted feeling rules which shape how people perform emotion) and 'embodied practices' (the ways in which children's feeling bodies come to tacitly navigate socio-spatial encounters) of emotion (Procter, 2015 forthcoming), are, I suggest, always entangled within space and place. Therefore, to understand children's emotional experiences we also need to attend to the ways that these are 'entangled' (Ingold, 2007) within place. Building on these perspectives, I show how the dynamic interplay between emotion and place is central to the production, reproduction and potential transformation of patterns of relationships and identities between people and within groups. This chapter aims to contribute to childhood studies by exploring how new theories of emotion from geography and sociology can enhance our understandings of children's experiences within institutional spaces. These theoretical orientations attend to the ways that children's emotional experiences are at once rooted within past histories as well as being in flight and orientated towards what is possible. This emotional landscapes perspective disrupts notions of linear time and can enhance understandings of children's relationships and identities. I argue that bringing this theoretical lens to the analysis of children's experiences of schooling renders visible the role of constructed and embodied emotion in children's relationships and identities within institutional spaces.

This chapter draws upon ethnographic fieldwork in a primary school, focused on a class of year 5 children (ages 9–10). The school applied a curriculum that specifically emphasised children's development of 'emotion skills'. Within this context many teachers viewed children's emotions as a key site for educational intervention in order to support their academic success. I draw specifically on the experiences of a boy (aged 10) and his navigation of peer relationships at the school. I examine the ways in which he expressed emotion across a range of interactions with his peers across different school spaces. I look at three examples to consider the ways that children create place at school through enacting emotionalised identities in their interactions with others. The first example is from a lunchtime encounter between Justin and his friend Troy in the 'field', a grassed area in the school playground. The second is a conversation between Justin and Troy while washing pots in the kitchen during a school-organised residential visit to an outdoor pursuits centre. The third is a discussion between Justin and his friends Katie and Cheryl in the school dining hall while they are eating their lunch. These moments are located outside of the 'formal' spaces of schooling; I suggest that within these alternative spaces children seek to *place* themselves through their purposeful subversion and at times transformation of their afforded classroom subjectivities. My analysis considers how children's inner feelings and their expression of emotion within their relational encounters signal, communicate and ultimately create their lived sense of place. However, I also demonstrate how these acts of place-making are positioned in relation to the ways that children come to understand adult constructions of emotions within the school setting.

Emplacement and childhood emotion in school contexts

Emplacement, 'the relationships between bodies, minds and the materiality and sensoriality of the environment', has been viewed as central to the way that people experience the world (Pink, 2009, p. 25). It offers a lens for examining the ways in which people, over time, create place within spaces that were once unfamiliar to them (Hammond, 2003). Through the inhabitation of space people engage personal meanings and the feeling body in the production of relationships and identities. As Hammond states, 'place is the arena for social meaning, and forms the basis for social action and identity formation' (2013, p. 78). Hammond's research, looking at the experiences of child refugees who return to their places of origin, represents children as 'independent and purposive actors in their own emplacement' (2013, p. 79) who actively shape the meanings they attach to the spaces they return to. This accumulation of meaning is shaped by the ways in which spaces work upon and are constituted with and through the body; bodies are entangled within the 'affective choreographies' that are produced within space and place (Youdell and Armstrong, 2011). Research looking at young children's emplacement has shown how the moving and feeling body can also transform such choreographies and bring into being new ways of inhabiting space (Hackett, 2014). While this research focuses on museum spaces, it also reflects the central role that – it is argued – embodied emotion plays in the ways that children encounter and engage with the spatialities of schooling (Procter, 2013). Whether receiving praise from the headteacher in her/his office or playing with peers in the playground, the felt dimensions of experience shape how children engage with and respond to the site they are in, the people they are with and the activity they are doing (Procter, 2014). Such research on children's emotionalities connects felt experience with embodiment, where embodiment is positioned as the 'active engagement with the world' (Trigg, 2012, p. 13). It is through the feeling body that we become aware of our place within social relationships (Clark, 1990), thus shaping our sense of, to use Cresswell's (1996) terminology, being 'in-place' or 'out-of-place'. Our embodied emotions not only create a sense of being-in-place but also shape the ways that we may impulsively or decisively move our bodies within social situations (Sheets-Johnstone, 1999).

Embodied dimensions of emotion are experienced in relation to the socially constructed meanings of emotion within socio-cultural contexts. Hochschild (2003) shows how emotional repertoires are learned within social interactions situated within wider cultural and political contexts. She uses the term 'feeling rules' to describe the socially constructed parameters that guide how people learn to 'perform' emotion within particular situations. Her research revealed the ways that individuals working as flight attendants and bill collectors 'limit their emotional offerings to surface displays of the "right" feeling' (p. x). Hochschild's notion of emotional labour has since been extended to children; for example, Seymour's (2005) work explores children's emotional labour in family-owned hotels, pubs and boarding houses. In my work, I have considered how children work upon their emotions to both feel and express emotions in ways that align with the feeling rules that circulate within school contexts (Procter, 2014); children come to understand the socially constructed feeling rules at work within different contexts and utilise ways of performing emotions in their navigations and negotiations of their situated encounters with others. This chapter seeks to bridge the notions of 'embodied emotion' explored in the previous paragraph, with this understanding of 'constructed emotion' (Procter, 2015 forthcoming) to consider how both the constructed meanings and embodied practices of emotion are central to the production, reproduction and potential transformation of patterns of relating and identities between people and within groups.

Emplacement reflects the way that the constructed and embodied patternings of emotions in institutional spaces are developed over time. Ahmed (2004) suggests that these patterns produce 'affective economies', which Wetherell (2012), in drawing on this work, describes as how 'affective value [is] assigned to some figures and not others' (p. 16). Ahmed's work examines the cultural politics of emotions through considering the ways that affective economies are sustained and reproduced over time within and across institutions. These insights can be applied within school contexts, where children's emotional responses have a long history of being valued and categorised in positive and negative ways (Boler, 1999). Within these contexts children's emotions shape how they navigate the emotional landscapes of schooling. The paragraphs above provide a lens for thinking about the ways that children's emotional responses are framed by the school's feeling rules and also shaped by their embodied experiences. This can be linked to theories of affective practice, for example Stewart (2007) suggests that 'ordinary affects', the affective repertoires and choreographies of everyday life, encompass states of both resonance, as they connect with past events, and potentiality, as they direct and shape unfolding future events. It is possible therefore to see how emotional responses have a ritualistic dimension, given that they are intimately tied to past histories, but are also in flight and directed towards multiple possible futures.

The 'lines of flight' perspective (Deleuze and Guattari, 2004) from which Stewart's work draws, when combined with a conceptualisation of place as produced through 'the experiencing body' (Casey, 1996 as referenced in Pink, 2009, p. 30) suggests that place is never stable or fixed. Massey (2005) also contests the notion of place as 'settled', 'coherent' and 'pre-given'. Instead she argues in favour of the uniqueness of place, 'the unavoidable challenge of negotiating a here-and-now (itself drawing on a history and a geography of thens and theres)' (p. 140). This perspective highlights how place 'demands negotiation' (p. 141). These dynamic meetings between places and people demand inventiveness. Massey recognises the 'spatio-temporality' of place and argues that the production of place is a 'throwntogetherness' of both human and non-human entities (p. 140). Her definition of place accounts for the unpredictability of children's relational emplacement. While embodied patterns of relating within and with spaces and places may emerge over time, Massey's work shows how these can be unsettled by new entities and new situations. Recognising the interplay between the material/immaterial environment and human/non-human entities within the throwntogetherness of place has been shown to extend the analysis of children's emotional experiences. For example, Kraftl's (2013) research looking at alternative spaces of education reminds us of the importance of paying attention to the 'more-than-social' when analysing children's social interactions. He argues that the material and non-human, including objects, animals, plants and so on, have agency within children's interactions with peers and adults. In addition, Somerville (2014) draws on new materialities studies to analyse the constitutive role of the material world within children's social relationships. These studies reflect the liminality (Turner, 2008) of children's emplacement, through which children's relationships and identities can form and reform. Drawing on these theoretical intersections between constructed and embodied emotion and emplacement, the aim of the remainder of this chapter is to foreground the role that these dimensions of experience play in the ways that children build relationships with others within a school context.

Research context

The fieldwork from which this chapter draws took place in a junior school (for children aged 7–11) in Sheffield over an eight-month period. The school was one of the 'first wave' of primary schools in Sheffield to apply the Social and Emotional Aspects of Learning (SEAL) initiative. SEAL was established in 2005 under Labour, and funding was withdrawn under the formation of the coalition government in 2010. However, schools have continued to use the programme materials (Personal Social Health and Economics Education Association ND). A key aspect of the curriculum was for children to manage their own and others' emotional responses. An example of this within the research site was the implementation of a 'peer-mentoring' scheme, where year 5 children were taught counselling prose to facilitate conversations between younger children to support them in resolving playground conflicts. This context is important because it had a significant influence on children's understandings of emotion. The study focused on a class of year 5 children (aged 9–10) who had become familiar with the SEAL curriculum during their time at the school. The study was divided into two stages and focused on the role of emotion in the ways that children's relationships and identities were formed and reformed through their place-making practices within the SEAL school. The first stage, which lasted for two months, included participant observations with children in a wide range of school spaces, semi-structured interviews with one local authority representative and three members of school staff, and drawing elicitation workshops with the year 5 class. Observations continued through the second stage, in addition to participatory research over a six-month period with a core group of nine children from the year 5 class, self-named the 'SEAL Squad'. The 'SEAL Squad' created dens, short films, scrapbooks, plays and presentations about what it was like for them and other children to be part of a SEAL school.

This chapter draws on field notes from participant observations carried out in both stages of the research process. In total I wrote around 40 sets of field notes documenting the year 5 children's school lives (around 25 children), each set of notes represent a full-day or half-day spent with children at the school and/or on fieldtrips. For the purposes of this chapter I have selected field notes of children's interaction in 'informal' school spaces. I have chosen to focus on one boy, Justin, who was diagnosed with high-functioning autism and was a target of a range of SEAL interventions intended to support him in managing his emotions and build relationships with his peers. For example, Justin received one-to-one therapeutic support from the SEAL coordinator at the school. I observed one of these meetings in which Justin spoke about how things were going at school and relayed techniques he was using for dealing with conflict and disagreements. Other interventions were devised at a socio-spatial level. For instance, in the classroom the teacher had arranged the desks so that Justin did not sit directly next to his peers. In the analysis that follows I draw on extracts where Justin's interactions with peers are away from the gaze of teachers. The extracts prioritise an examination of children's emotion during their 'in-the-moment' acts of place-making.

Emotion, affect and children's relational emplacement

'No. You've done it once, now not again!'

The first encounter I will draw on is between Justin and a small group of boys and girls in the 'field', which is a grassed space bounded by trees and sits beside the tarmac playground. I draw on this vignette to show how new relational identities and shared places are produced through the emotional exchanges between Justin and the group. I consider how the material/immaterial dimensions of the space make such emotional exchanges possible. The children particularly value the field in part, it seems, because of its novelty; the field only opens on days when the weather is good and typically in the summer months. The field was opened during the lunchtime break on one of my research visits to the school on a sunny day in April. Most of the children had opted to spend their break in the field. As I enter the field I see Justin.

> *Justin is walking across the field where other children are playing football. He has a big bundle of grass. He shouts over to me. He says he is making a giant mound of grass, and asks if I want to come and see. I say OK. He says that it is going to be as big as the empire state building. I ask him how tall it is. He says he doesn't know, but he thinks about 100 foot . . . At first I thought that Justin was playing alone. However, he is building the tower with a group of boys. He places his clump of grass*

onto an existing mound of grass. He is building the tower with year 3 children, both boys and girls. One of these boys, Richard, has Down's syndrome and is placed in a mainstream class. Troy and Jack, twin brothers from the same year as Justin are also there. Troy and Jack are both listed as having special educational needs and receive additional learning support and are also in the mainstream classes. They are in separate year 5 classes; Troy is in the same class as Justin. As they are building the mound, Justin tells Richard, 'No. You've done it once, now not again!' I do not know exactly what Richard has done. However, Justin has the tone of an authority figure. I later hear him telling Troy that he can no longer help to build the mound. Justin's voice gets a little louder as he continues to speak. He looks cross. I start to feel a little anxious. I back away from the situation, hoping that I would not be expected by members of staff to intervene . . . Justin lies on top of Troy. Troy is smiling as Justin is on top of him. Justin appears playful yet it also seems that there is a serious undertone to how he is interacting with Troy, which I can't quite place.

The field was rarely accessed by the children and therefore didn't seem to afford the same geographical segregations, framed by age, gender and disability, visible in the more commonly used play spaces. Justin chose to play with a group of younger children and two boys from his year group. In the regular play spaces I would sometimes see Justin attempt to play with children from his own class and at times this would result in his rejection. Being able to participate in games was important to Justin; he stated that he was happiest when 'people let . . . [him] join in their games'. However, his peers at times perceived Justin's emotional responses to be unpredictable and inappropriate, as one boy explains: 'He gets angry just when you just say there are too many people playing the game, because I said that and he chased after me.' The same boy stated that Justin 'would attack people for no reason'. Ahmed (2004) argues that emotions 'stick' to some bodies and not others, whereby emotional identities are ascribed to certain people and tend to remain, and I have explored elsewhere how in Justin's case 'anger' seemed to stick (see Procter, 2013). His classroom peers might have perceived Justin's actions described in the vignette above, including when Justin responds to Richard assertively and then later lies on top of Troy, through the lens of his ascribed emotional identity as an angry boy and perhaps deemed them as aggressive and thus inappropriate. Indeed, as an onlooker I was aware that lunchtime supervisors would typically interrupt these kinds of interactions between children; I felt that as an adult I might be expected by teachers and supervisors to intervene. However, neither Richard nor Troy challenged Justin's behaviour; in fact, Troy's response was one of laughter. This encounter reflects the significant role of children's embodied emotion in the production of new places, which can afford new identities and ways of relating for children. It also shows the possible ways in which school spaces that are relatively unfamiliar to the children can unsettle ascribed emotional identities shaped by socially constructed understandings of emotion.

'Yeah right Troy'

While suggesting that the irregular use of the field afforded opportunities for Justin to play with children who seemed to perceive his emotional responses quite differently to some members of his class, my field notes also noted a serious undertone to Justin's play practices. I build on this here by examining how a place for exploring versions of masculinity was produced within another 'more-than-social' interaction between Justin and Troy. During a residential fieldtrip at an outdoor pursuits centre, Justin and Troy were tasked by a teacher with washing up and drying the plates and cutlery after all the children had eaten an evening meal. The two boys were chatting to each other. I was especially alert to the ways that Troy seemed to be trying to impress Justin, and in turn the ways that Justin seemed to try and get one-up on Troy by bringing me into the conversation.

Troy and Justin are washing up dishes at the sink in the kitchen. I am helping. Troy tells Justin that he once threw an apple so far that it hit someone on the head. Justin tells him, 'yeah right Troy'. Troy seems to try and qualify the distance, stating that he threw it one hundred yards. Justin still doesn't seem to believe him. During washing up Justin also tells me he isn't really into films like Shrek *(Shrek, a popular animated children's film, is going to be shown on the TV later in the evening, as the night-time activity). However, earlier Justin told me how many times he had seen the* Shrek *movies. He tells me now that he likes films like* Fast and Furious, *a 2001 american action film centred on illegal street racing aimed at young adults, explaining that they are funny too.*

He gives me an example, like when someone is left hanging out a car door held only by his ankles and he shouts, 'shit, shit, shit'. He tells me again, 'that was really funny'. I am laughing at his story.

Troy chose to share a story with Justin about throwing an apple. He claimed that he could throw it a great distance, perhaps trying to impress Justin. However, Justin quashed Troy's claim of being able to throw well. Justin then shared with me his preference for violent films featuring fast cars and swearwords, rather than films like *Shrek*. This contradicts Justin's favourable comments about *Shrek* films earlier in the day. This interaction between the boys while washing dishes appears to be imbued with competing discourses of masculinity. For both boys masculinity is demonstrated through the actions of the body ('threw an apple so far', 'hanging out of a car door held only by his ankles'). For Justin it is also embedded in speech ('shit, shit, shit'). This process of making meaning of their own identities in relation to one another and to me by drawing on discourses of masculinity, I suggest, unfolded because of the situation they were in. Being a 'pot-washer' can be viewed as a typical adult role. The boys were asked to take on this role temporarily, which seemed to afford a different way for the boys to speak about themselves; as Justin said to me while cleaning the pots, 'I like helping'. This role of helper seemed to temporarily position the boys, who were commonly viewed as less mature than their male peers, as 'mature men'. Adults at the school associate helping with maturity and both boys and girls are commonly rewarded for performing actions that are perceived by adults to be helpful. This can be understood as a socially constructed notion of emotional maturity. However, in this instance these constructions seemed to intersect with alternative versions of maturity, which reflected the boys' perceptions of how emotionalised masculinities are performed through the body. Within this short encounter between Justin and Troy particular versions of maturity were enacted between them. Here the boys presented themselves as both helpful and physically tough. Through their inhabitation of the space around the sink in their role as 'pot-washers' the two boys drew on personal meanings and embodied practices of emotion in relation to being a 'mature man' as they competed for status by making claims. In doing so they created a place together for exploring mature masculine identities.

You know I dumped you last night, well I didn't mean it

I have explored how children create places for producing and transforming relationships and identities through their emotional encounters. This is further reflected in an encounter between Justin, his peers and me around a square dining table in the school dining hall over lunch. This interaction reflects the ways that constructed and embodied emotions are entangled within children's relational emplacement. Cheryl, Justin's friend (and occasional girlfriend), instigated the conversation that unfolded between us, which is documented in an extract from my field notes below. This conversation began soon after Cheryl, described by her teacher as 'assertive', and her best friend Katie, described by her teacher as a 'quiet' girl, asked to sit beside me (I was already sitting with Justin and a group of boys from his class (Didier, Harry and Lionel) at the table eating my lunch). Didier, who was named by the year 5 classroom teacher as 'the most mature boy' in his class, gave up his seat so that they could both sit beside me. He found himself another seat at the same table.

The main topic of conversation is boyfriends and girlfriends. Cheryl is sitting opposite Justin and tells him, loud enough for everyone sat at the table to hear, that he is dumped. Justin moves from his seat and walks around the table to Cheryl. Her asks her 'what's up?' and then whispers, 'Cheryl, just pretend'. Cheryl ignores him and Justin returns to his seat at the table. He then asks Cheryl who the boy that she was going out with outside of school was. She doesn't answer. Some of the boys at the table ask her again. Justin tells the boys at his end of the table that she is just pretending and that there isn't anybody. Cheryl then starts listing the different people she has been out with; one boy, she tells me, she went out with for ten seconds. She tells me that she kissed one of the boys at the table. Justin tells me not to listen, that she is just making things up. Cheryl tells me that Justin is just embarrassed. Katie then starts to join in. She tells me the names of the boys that she has been out with and those she has kissed and that she is now going out with Justin. Justin shouts to Katie across the table, 'you know I dumped you last night, well I didn't mean it' ... Justin then asks the people on the table to put up their hands if they have kissed any of the girls on the table. Katie puts up her hand. She then says, 'oh, girls, oops, no I haven't done that'. She then raises her hand again and says, 'yes I have', and she kisses her own hand. She says 'I've kissed myself'. Then

Justin asks, 'who on this table has kissed a boy'. He doesn't really get much of a response. One of the lunchtime supervisors who is passing by remarks, 'you shouldn't really be talking about things like this at your age'. Didier gets up to leave the table; he tells me he didn't really like his food today.

Cheryl, supported by Katie, is directing the production of place, and in particular how her peers are placed within the social encounter, through stirring emotional responses in others. Justin is the only boy who participates vocally. Cheryl counters his provocations by ignoring him. Katie does respond to one of Justin's requests, but misinterprets what he has said. She then uses humour to stave off her embarrassment and regain a more powerful role within the encounter again. Thorne (1993) used the concept of 'borderwork' to describe the social construction of gender boundaries within children's play. She argues that these boundaries are 'episodic' and 'ambiguous' (p. 84) but that power is an important dimension of children's borderwork. She suggests that while girls start from a 'one-down position', they can adopt powerful roles, as can be seen in the vignette above. The children's borderwork occurs through their performances of emotion; for example, the girl's ways of being and relating allow them to dominate the conversation. This encounter – like the interaction between Justin and Troy over the sink – seems to draw on notions of gendered emotional maturity. Both Cheryl and Katie present themselves as actively interested in relationships of intimacy with boys. Justin's masculine identity is directly implicated in Cheryl's comments, and he seems to navigate the situation by attempting to re-ignite a relationship with Katie. Katie ignores this attempt. Not all of the children on the table engage in the production of these emotionalised perceptions of gender maturity. In fact, Didier verbally positions himself against them, stating assertively that he didn't like his food today. This reflects how children position themselves within or outside particular constructions of emotion, and how inner felt experiences can shape how children can choose to actively un-place themselves from social interactions, as in the case of Didier. This reflects Clark's (1990) view that emotions are integral to the ways that people come to know their 'place' within social relationships. It is possible to see how within the space of the dining table the children are engaged in place-making, producing and resisting narratives of gender through their words and gestures. These internal felt signals and external emotional communications of senses of place are central to the performative gender politics at work between Justin, Cheryl, Katie and Didier. This reflects the central role of emotion in shaping children's gendered relational emplacement.

Conclusion

This chapter has drawn on theories of emotion and emplacement in order to examine peer relations within a school context. I have suggested that as children inhabit spaces of schooling they engage personal meanings and feelings in the production of their peer relationships and identities. In this way I have argued that emotions are central to the production, reproduction and potential transformation of patterns of relating among children at school. These patterns of relating develop over time, and are in states of both resonance and potentiality. Children's emotional responses are entangled within past histories as well as potential futures. In recognising that children's emplacement is both dynamic and emergent, I have suggested that the spatio-temporal nature of place is an important analytical lens when researching children's experiences. To employ it requires recognising the interplay between the material/immaterial environment and human/non-human entities. Spatial theories offer a means of understanding the ways that children's patterns of relating and emerging identities are produced and also transformed throughout their school lives. Time and accident offer opportunities for consistency and rupture reflecting both the stability and potential instability of children's 'more-than-social' interactions. I drew on three encounters involving a boy called Justin to explore how these theoretical framings have offered new insights into children's experiences, with a specific focus on gender relations and identities. I reflected on the ways that Justin's aggressive (masculine) play in an unfamiliar space afforded new relational opportunities where his actions were not perceived through the emotional identity ascribed to him within the classroom context of an 'angry boy'. The second encounter showed how particular versions of masculinity, which seemed to centre on the performing male body, entered into Justin's conversation and became entangled within the situation he was in and the role he had undertaken. Finally, I considered how Justin's interaction with two girls reflected how emotions are embedded in the gender politics of children's relational emplacement. Looking at Justin's encounters with his peers through a spatial lens reflected how his emotional responses were enmeshed within wider social, spatial and cultural contexts. I have shown how both the material and immaterial dimensions of place directly influenced how Justin emotionally engaged with others. These dimensions offered insights into how gender is produced by children through their relational emplacement. I have explored how gendered patterns of relating and gender identities are formed in and across encounters with peers in many different school spaces. I have also shown how some children will resonate with these productions and others will resist them, showing how multiple places of meaning can co-evolve through children's inhabitation of space. These productions of place work to unite and divide children into different social groups. Children's emotional responses are central to the ways that they navigate these places and the types of social relationships they foster.

References

Ahmed, S. (2004) *The Cultural Politics of Emotion*, Edinburgh: Edinburgh University Press Ltd.

Boler, M. (1999) *Feeling Power: Emotions and Education*, Oxon: Routledge.

Christensen, P. M. and O'Brien, M. (eds) (2003) *Children in the City: Home, Neighbourhood and Community*, London and New York: Routledge.

Clark, C. (1990) 'Emotions and Micropolitics in Everyday Life: Some Patterns and Paradoxes of "Place" ', in T. Kemper (ed.) *Research Agendas in the Sociology of Emotions*, New York: State University of New York Press.

Cresswell, T. (1996) *In Place/Out of Place: Geography, Ideology and Transgression*. Minneapolis: University of Minnesota Press.

Deleuze, G. and Guattari, F. (2004) *A Thousand Plateaus: Capitalism and Schizophrenia*, London: Continuum.

Fog Olwig, K. and Gulløv, E. (2003) *Children's Places: Cross-Cultural Perspectives*, London: Routledge.

Hackett, A. (2014) 'Zigging and Zooming All Over the Place: Young Children's Meaning Making and Moving in the Museum', *Journal of Early Childhood Literacy*, 14 (1), 5–27.

Hammond, L. (2003) 'How will the children come home? Emplacement and the creation of the social body in an Ethiopian returnee settlement', in Fog Olwig, K., and Gulløv, E. (eds) *Children's Places: Cross-Cultural Perspectives*, London: Routledge, 77–96.

Hochschild, A. (2003) *The Managed Heart: Commercialisation of Human Feeling* 2nd edition, London: University of California Press.

Ingold, T. (2007) *Lines: A Brief History*, Oxon: Routledge.

Kraftl, P. (2013) 'Beyond "Voice", Beyond "Agency", Beyond "Politics"? Hybrid Childhoods and Some Critical Reflections on Children's Emotional geographies', *Emotion, Space and Society*, 9, 13–23.

James, A., Jenks, C. and Prout, A. (1998) *Theorizing Childhood*, London: Polity Press.

Lefebvre, H. (translated by Nicholson-Smith, D.) (1991) *The Production of Space*, Oxford: Blackwell Publishing Ltd.

Massey, D. (2005) *For Space*, London: Sage.

Pink, S. (2009) *Doing Sensory Ethnography*, London: SAGE Publication Ltd.

Procter, L. (2013) 'Emotions, Schooling and Power: The Socialisation of "Angry Boys"', *Journal of Political Power*, 6 (3), 495–510.

Procter, L. (2014) *Children, Schooling and Emotion: The Role of Emotion in Children's Socio-Spatial Practices at School*. PhD thesis, University of Sheffield (http://etheses.whiterose.ac.uk/6224/).

Procter, L. (2015 forthcoming) 'Exploring Emotions at School with Children: Reflections on the Role of the Visual and Performative in Engaging with Children's Constructed and Embodied Meanings of Emotion', in P. Shutz and M. Zembylas (eds) *Methodological Advances in Research on Emotion and Education*, Springer.

Personal Social Health and Economic Education (PSHE) Association. (ND). *Healthy Schools, Every Child Matters and Social and Emotional Aspects of Learning*. https://www.pshe-association.org.uk/content.aspx?CategoryID= 1176 (Accessed on 23.01.2015).

Seymour, J. (2005) 'Entertaining Guests or Entertaining the Guests: Children's Emotional Labour in Hotels, Pubs and Boarding Houses', in J. Goddard, S. McNamee, A. L. James and A. James (eds) *The Politics of Childhood: International Perspectives, Contemporary Developments*, Basingstoke: Palgrave Macmillan.

Sheets-Johnstone, M. (1999) Emotion and Movement: A Beginning Empirical-Phenomenological Analysis of Their Relationship. *Journal of Consciousness Studies*, 6, 11–12, 259–277.

Somerville, M. (2014) 'Entangled Objects in the Cultural Politics of Childhood and Nation', *Global Studies of Childhood*, 4 (3), 183–194.

Stewart, K. (2007) *Ordinary Affects*, London: Duke University Press.

Thorne, B. (1993) *Gender Play: Girls and Boys in School*, London: Open University Press.

Trigg, D. (2012) *The Memory of Place: A Phenomenology of the Uncanny*. Athens, OH: Ohio University Press.

Turner, V. (2008) *The Ritual Process: Structure and Anti-structure*, Rutgers, NJ: Aldine Transaction.

Youdell, D. and Armstrong, F. (2011) 'A Politics Beyond Subjects: The Affective Choreographies and Smooth Spaces of Schooling', *Emotion, Space and Society*, 4, 144–150.

Wetherell, M. (2012) *Affect and Emotion: A New Social Science Understanding*. London: SAGE Publications Ltd.

Part III
Spatial Agency

8
Approaches to Children's Spatial Agency: Reviewing Actors, Agents and Families

Julie Seymour

Introduction

This chapter will review the consideration of space as an element of children's agency within the social study of childhood and particularly the sociology of families. These two sub-disciplines may be seen as operating in parallel with each other but, as will be discussed, there have been calls to re-centre children within their families and other institutions as a recognition of the context in which they experience their everyday lives (Brannen and O'Brien, 1996; Jensen and McKee, 2003; Seymour and McNamee, 2012). The chapter will initially address the issue of children's agency, reiterating Mayall's (2002) distinction between social actors and agents. It will draw on this distinction to review studies which focus on children in spaces and children's spaces. It will particularly consider the concepts of the betweenness of space and spaces of betweenness as they relate to the exercise of children's agency and consider this at a variety of scales: domestic, public/local, international and global. The second part of the chapter will respond to the call to re-situate children into their family lives and discuss the role and study of space in family sociology; literally, to re-place them in family life. This will go some way to right Widerberg's (2010, p. 1182) contention that 'Within sociology ... the tradition has been to focus more on the social relations than on the material space of their context'.

Children as social actors or agents

By 2009, James could state 'the idea that children are social actors is a commonplace one' (p. 40). In her useful chapter on agency in *The Palgrave Handbook of Childhood Studies* she outlines the development of the theoretical view of children as active participants and contributors to their society rather than passive recipients of social structures. She considers in depth what it means to be an agent and points out the difference between the political use of child-as-agent to identify them as a subordinate group which is worthy of research, and the study of the reality of the agency of the individual child. She expands on Mayall's (2002) discussion of the role of the child as a social actor – that is, someone who participates in social life – and how this varies from the child as agent – that is, someone whose participation makes a difference to social life. This agency can occur through interaction where this difference can be 'to a relationship or to a decision, to the workings of a set of social assumptions or constraints' (Mayall, 2002, p. 21). As such, this participation makes a contribution to social and cultural reproduction, perhaps not via individual children but as a generational group. This latter distinction is important: while the child as social actor may amend their lifeworld through personal actions, it is the child as 'a member of the generational category of children' (James, 2009, p. 43) whose agency contributes to structural change. This distinction between actors and agents can be useful when explicitly applied to approaches to the study of space and children. It can highlight differences in situations when children are *involved* in changing spatialities and when they can be shown to have *constructed them*. By considering the extent to which children can exercise spatial agency and what resources allow this, child–adult and child–child relationships can be examined. This can make a contribution to childhood studies; perhaps surprisingly, *The Handbook of Childhood Studies* does not address space explicitly except in Zeiher's (2009) accounts of children's institutionalisation, which suggests a gap that the current volume can fill.

By differentiating between children as spatial social actors and having spatial agency, the ongoing debate as to whether children will always be constrained by structural, generational and contextual relationships (Qvortrup, 2009) can be interrogated. By examining studies of children's use of space and attempts by adults as parents, educators and policy makers to prevent or mould it to acceptable uses (as outlined in chapters 9 and 10), as well as children's resistance to these constructions, the extent of agency can be made clear. Indeed, the interpretation of the recognition and response to children's resistance can reveal whether children are viewed, by researchers as well as lay commentators, as social actors operating in an adult world who are finding niches or moments in which to contest adult spatialities or spatial innovators in a child-centred environment whose alternative interpretations and use of places are read through adult constructions of space as resistance.

Here the concept of betweenness can be illuminating. It can be used in two ways. First it can be used to consider 'spaces of betweenness' (Katz, 1994), that is the small gaps or interstices within power relations where subordinate groups can exercise resistance. Children, as such a group, may enter into negotiations with authority figures or carry out small forms of resistance such as responding slowly to parental requests (Seymour and McNamee, 2012). However, they could be viewed here more as social actors than agents. Alternatively, as mentioned in the introduction to this edited collection, it can refer to the betweenness of spatial experience, where children transfer their experiential knowledge between locations in an embodied and material manner. This can lead to the reproduction of behaviours and/or the movement of material objects between settings such as between the home and school (Corsaro, 1985) or the home and hospital (La Francois, 2007). Where these behaviours are acceptable, as in Connelly's (2004) study of middle-class boys reproducing well-surveilled home behaviours at school, they may be allowed to continue. Where, however, they are designated inappropriate, as when children in a hospital respond to the exhortations that this is a 'homely' environment by behaving as they would in their own homes, they will be discouraged and children will be labelled as having an incomplete understanding of the boundaries and divisions between places (La Francois, 2007). These examples highlight the marginalisation of children, both in relation to adults and, for some children, in relation to their peers, which Holt (2011) discusses and was also raised in Chapter 5.

As Aitken (2001) has pointed out, the child is neither an autonomous subject nor merely a node in a matrix of power and this can be shown by examining children's worlds through a spatial lens at a variety of scales – domestic, public/local, international and global. Zeiher et al. (2007, p. 1) remind us that 'Socially children's spaces are multi local. Culturally they are enlarged through mobility in the globalized and virtual spaces in the media-saturated world'.

Children as actors and agents: Spatial agency at multiple scales

Domestic spaces

To consider the spatial agency of children in the domestic sphere, we can compare those studies which present the household as an adult-controlled environment in which children exercise marginal decision-making or influence with those where children are co-constructors of their home.

Sibley's well-known 1995 study of families and domestic routines argues that parents establish boundaries within the domestic environment and children have only limited opportunities to carve out their own places of meaning. As a result, the home becomes a space of unavoidable 'tensions surrounding the use of domestic spaces' (p. 94). Sibley's study was used as a counterpoint by Seymour (2007) in her work on families growing up in Commercial Homes, such as hotels, pubs and boarding houses. Here the tension was exacerbated by the addition of members of the public in the form of guests also using the home. Here, while children were social actors in the home and business, their use of space (and time) could be prescribed by the work requirements of the Commercial Home. One interviewee remembered that family members:

> Couldn't use the bathroom just when you wanted to. You had to fit in and have it when the guests were having their meal.
>
> (Interview 5, male ex-hotel owner)

This can be compared with more recent studies of the use of domestic space, including bathroom facilities, where, for example, Lewis (2011, p. 78) considered that young people had considerable agency, which was respected by parents. In her study on 'shutting the bathroom door', she recognises this was aided both by architectural changes, such as the development of en-suite facilities, and changing attitudes towards bodily privacy emerging from the larger scale privatisation of bathrooms from public to private to en suite. Other changes in the material and attitudinal expectations of domestic space include the expectation that most children in the minority world will have a dedicated and personal bedroom space which will be multi-functional and with varying access to parents, adults and other children. McNamee (1998) has shown how, when this is the site of a computer, it can illustrate aged and gendered power relations between children. These structural constraints on agency are also discussed by Widerberg (2010) who posits that it is as a child, and when one visits the homes of others, that one learns about gender, class and ethnicity as well as variations on family life and the role of children within it.

Jacqui Gabb's work on intimacy in families (2008) resonates with Part II of this book, on space and emotion. She uses the literal mapping of emotions to show how intimate and emotional interactions are influenced by the household spaces in which they take place but also how those spaces become defined and marked by emotional practices. She uses the technique of emotion maps with her household interviewees, both adults and children, to identify key areas in the house which provoke a range of positive and negative emotions such as love, anger and sadness. Her research shows that kitchens are areas where a multitude of emotions are played out but often anger features highly, whereas bedrooms are often the site of love. Noticeably, boundary areas such as bedroom and fridge doors are frequently sites of negative emotions and tension between children and adult family members as children conflict with parents over privacy and eating practices. These sites of tension are spatial indications of where agency is being enacted, not always successfully.

Public/local places

Woolley (Chapter 9) outlines the issues that can arise when children use outdoor environments. She considers in depth the concepts of constructed space, where buildings or spaces are planned for a purpose, and found space, where the use is designated by those who appropriate it. The former can be seen as spaces in which the users are social actors in an architect's vision, whereas found spaces are those where children 'assert their agency in the urban environment and play in and use different open spaces' (Woolley, Chapter 9 this volume).

The arenas of public and private space are often conceptualised as separate areas but May (2011) has outlined the importance of public spaces for accomplishing relationality with intimates, acquaintances and strangers. As such, she confirms public spaces as key components in personal life. This is pertinent for children but may be reducing with the advent of social media. The relationship between domestic space and street space for children is illustrated by McNamee's (1998) study of computer use by children, where the use of computers in the home linked boys in social relationships beyond the house thus changing their spaces of sociability. The location of computers in the home showed a gendered pattern of placement in boy's 'spaces' and exacerbated differences in computer use-time between male and female siblings, as boys could exercise agentic power and deny their sisters entry to their bedroom. Thus before the advent of portable media, parental decisions on the placement of technology had an impact on children's technological development and social networks. The impact of social media has led to a focus on virtual spaces, particularly as an imaginary subspace (Lefebvre, 1991) in which children can exercise agency. This may be conceived as a response to the loss of public space for children (Mayall, 2001), which results in them turning to virtual spaces or heterotopias (Foucault, 1986; McNamee, 2000). Such imaginary spaces are not free of parental or adult control but given the technological abilities of many children compared with their parents, there is considerable scope for agency.

International spaces

To avoid a Eurocentric approach to this chapter the work of children's researchers in the majority world should also be acknowledged in this discussion of the role of space in the construction of children as actors or agents. Nieuwenhuys (2003) reminds us that the spatial segregation of children is a Western urban practice and does not occur in all societies. However, through examples from her work in Poomkara, South India and Addis Ababa, Ethiopia, she emphasises that 'spatial contiguity is matched by strong social distancing' (p. 100) and that, while present, children can still occupy a liminal position. There are, nevertheless opportunities for children to exercise agency. In Punch's work on rural Bolivia (2004), she shows how children subvert the exercise of domestic chores to create play spaces with friends or siblings or to pace their chores. This is aided by the fact many of these chores (which might involve searching for animals or wood, or collecting water) take place in public spaces and are not overseen by parents. Punch conceptualises this behaviour as a form of resistance to parental control. As such, the outdoor location of these tasks provides 'spaces of betweenness' for the children to exercise control over their time and activities.

An aspect of children's spatial agency which is increasingly focused on is that of international migration. Several researchers have written eloquently about the role of children in families separated by parental migration or the impact on children as contributors to and constructors of transnational families (Bryceson and Vuorela, 2002; Baldassar and Merla, 2013; Juozeliuniene and Seymour, 2015). Research studies vary in the extent to which they consider children to exercise agency in family decisions about migration (Huijsmans, 2011). Yet once family members are spatially separated from their children, whether it is parents separated from their children or nuclear families separated from their wider family group, children have been shown to be key players in maintaining transnational links. Walsh (2015) has shown how, through the use of social media, international visits and family display, children can actively contribute to the construction and reconstruction of a transnational family. She elucidates the 'enablers of display' which increase the agency of specific children in this activity, particularly age, language skills (both speech and knowledge of their home nation language) and technological ability, which allow them to communicate independently. Other children can more appropriately be seen as social actors in a family display which is facilitated by their parents. These children are often younger and speak only English. They may play a prominent role in the family display activities through their birth, naming or by being 'displayed' wearing culturally specific presents; but the child's personal agency is limited. While their presence results in the reconfiguring of family relations often through extra contact, they can be described as objects rather than agents of display (Seymour, 2011).

Global spaces

Children's awareness of global processes may be heightened through migratory practices but can also be present through their sense of themselves as actors in a global space. Hörschelmann and Schafer (2005) investigated the awareness and attitudes of young East

Germans to globalisation through their spatial practices. Using cognitive maps of urban spaces and interviews with teenage girls, they showed that while all the participants were conscious of the impact of globalisation on their local and urban areas, this was met with both positive and negative attitudes and spatial responses. For those who were negative, movement around the city was constrained and areas with 'foreigners' were responded to with avoidance and fear. For other interviewees, globalisation was seen as providing positive opportunities and the teenagers' spatial maps and embodied patterns of movement were wider and more diverse. As a result they developed more 'cosmopolitanism', which was considered to enhance their future life opportunities.

This examination of the extent of children's spatial agency has focused on studies which have taken children as their key participants in keeping with the basic tenet of the social study of childhood. As outlined in the introduction, however, more recent research has contested the extent to which children are able to exercise agency in their everyday lives and called for a re-centring of children in their relationships and the institutions in which they spend their day-to-day time (Brannen and O'Brien, 1996; Jensen and McKee, 2003; Seymour and McNamee, 2012). This is not to simply return children to the status of, for example, family members, but to re-site them in context while still focusing on their perspectives and experiences. For while the family may be considered the key 'place' for children in terms of belonging, as Fog Olwig and Gulløv (2003, p. 8) remind us 'analysing children's use of places gives insight into patterns of relations, social opportunities and varying forms of agency'. The next section of this chapter will interrogate children's spatial agency within research on families.

Children's spatial agency within family studies

It is noted that family studies show less awareness of space as a concept and children's space in particular than the work in childhood studies. In the recently published book *Key Concepts in Family Studies* (Ribbens McCarthy and Edwards, 2011), space is discussed in relation to children and their publically bounded space but much less so with regard to families. Similarly, and perhaps surprisingly, geographers have not looked at spatiality in relation to families much until recently. Holloway says (Holloway and Pimlott-Wilson in Holt, 2011) that the geographies of children and young people imbued the social studies of childhood with 'a sense of spatiality' (p. 13) but, as Holt says in the same volume (p. 2), geographers did not pay very much attention to children *in families*. Indeed she acknowledges a neglect of certain socio-spatial contexts for children, notably that of the family, and considers that geographers have generally neglected not only children in families but the familial sphere itself. The latter was partly for political reasons, with researchers in the social study of childhood feeling that children had been subsumed into the family, but also, more pragmatically, because there was a lack of research in this area; an omission that Holt's edited collection aims to remedy.

Recent work on relationality has emphasised the increasing fluidity and flexibility of contemporary personal life and drawn on this to develop earlier research which focused on the forms and functions of intimate life. In contrast to this well documented move from forms of relationships (particularly family forms) and concomitant functions, the *locational* fluidity of intimate relationships has been somewhat underexplored in the sociology of families. There is still a need to think more creatively about the spaces in which these relational practices occur. This can be done through the use of Keith and Pile's (1993) concept of spatiality; that is, the arena 'where the social and spatial are inextricably realized in one another' (p. 6). Spatiality as an intertwining of the social and spatial develops previously static constructions of the location in which family life takes place. It allows for ideas concerning fluidity, liminality and permeability to be applied to the spaces of relational life in the ways that they have earlier been applied to family forms and functions. It stresses that space is implicated in a process and can no longer be simply treated as a discrete or additional variable. It foregrounds the importance of space in the construction of relationships and the impact of relationality on the construction of space. It demands a focus which includes, but also moves beyond, the domestic dwelling but also emphasises that the home is a place where not only *private* activities take place (Seymour, 2007; McIntosh et al., 2011).

David Morgan in his recent book *Rethinking Family Practices* has argued eloquently for a greater focus on the interaction of space and family practices particularly for those who are reconstituting families. As he reminds us 'Family practices are conducted *within* time and space and involve the *use* of time and space' (Morgan, 2011, p. 80, original emphasis). The conceptually fluid nature of both spatiality and family practices results, he considers, in a 'close reflexive interplay between space and family practices' (2011, p. 88). Crucially, family practices combine everyday activities with ideological discourses of the family. Thus, through family activities, they provide the potential for the production of new discourses alongside the reproduction of existing ones. Interrogating spatial family practices, then, can reveal when – to draw on Mayall's earlier distinction between actors and agents – children's participation makes a structural difference. The following examples will use the same typology of increasing level of scales as used in the consideration of research on the social study of childhood to outline research on space and children within families.

Children's spatial agency within families: Examples from multiple scales

Domestic

Domestic locations reflect pragmatic and ideological familial decisions as this space is utilised, through activities and the use of material and symbolic boundaries, to achieve actual and expressed expectations of family life. However, while a number of studies show how family practices impact on domestic space, such as Gabb's work on emotions in families (2008) discussed earlier, others show how the nature of the space occupied by the household impacts on family members, such as Dowling (2008) who discusses the impact of open plan homes in Australia on children's play, tidying activities and movements.

In my own work on family hotels (Seymour, 2007), the negotiation of spatial family practices, such as the attempt to create private family space, is unusually transparent and as such highlights the frequently unrecognised significance of space in family lives and how family practices are expressed through spatial means. The outcomes for the families living in hospitality establishments are often an inversion of 'typical' spatial practices in the family. For example, the fact that homes rarely contain a door marked 'Private' to prevent the entry of strangers emphasises the usually unexamined conflation of domestic with private space. Such delimitations in hotels however can be fluid and permeable and they intersect with individuals, seasons, economic circumstances, parenting practices, state legislation, power and resource distributions within the home as well as historical time and global processes. Given this, the extent of children's spatial agency in such Commercial Homes is impacted on by significantly more factors than in a typical domestic home, yet they are still able to show resistance to the demands of the guests, staff and parents especially in the area of the emotional labour requirements of the business (Seymour, 2005). This latter finding suggests that the study of children, space and emotions (as outlined in Part II of this edited volume) could include, not only children's management of their own emotions in different spatial settings but their labour in managing the emotions of others, both children and adults.

Local

The focus on spatiality is contributing to the developing body of research which stresses the need to consider the social production of family life in arenas beyond the household and in conjunction with other practices. This is not, as Bailey (2000) suggests, to discard the spatial dimension of the private by reconfiguring what it means but just to explore more fully the non-domestic intersections between relationality and space, place and location. For, as Morgan reminds us, family practices are frequently 'moving practices' (2011, p. 88). The extent of these movements can vary considerably.

My study of the hospitality establishment as home (Seymour, 2007) showed how families made creative use of non-domestic space to conduct family practices such as meals together. In order to have a family gathering without interruptions they had to move beyond the family home and this relocation was valued by the children as it confirmed the adults' roles as those of parents rather than workers.

Valentine (1997) has shown how children act as agents to allay their parents' fears about public space. As a result, they are given more licence to control their own movements. Valentine considers that children and young people have a greater familiarity with their local spaces than do their parents. Children therefore see themselves as more competent in public space than their parents do and will, for example, simply not tell parents about events which might worry them in order to maintain their freedom outdoors. Here we can see children's involvement and negotiation with parenting practices.

While acknowledging the power relations involved in adult–child relations, such spatial examples show the agency of children in engaging with these practices.

International

Widmer and Jallinoja's (2008) edited collection on family assemblages stresses spatial configurations and provides a useful corollary to the micro-focus on contemporary domestic spaces in UK family studies through its historical focus, its aim to move beyond the nuclear family or household and its emphasis on migration. Hence it places the assembling of family lives in a globalised world and includes a chapter on transnational adoption. It also considers how family practices operate in scattered families (who do not share the same home or locale), whether this has been caused by migration, divorce or old age.

Research on leisure and hospitality studies has engaged with the social study of childhood and the re-centring of children within families to consider children's agency in movement, travel and leisure activities beyond the home. Studies have moved from a focus on children's roles in decision-making in holiday locations (where they may be social actors) to a whole family approach (Schanzel et al., 2012). This approach recognises children's more agentic position as co-producers of family life while at leisure (Schanzel, 2010; Carr, 2011) or in providing leisure for others (Lynch et al., 2009; Seymour, 2011).

Global

In transglobal migrations, spatiality, particularly that of place, is perhaps more intrinsically visible. Johnson's anthropological studies of diasporic Filipino migrant workers in the Middle East has challenged persistent stereotypes of migrant Filipinos as servile labour and docile bodies, disclosing how migrants 'creatively engage with the places and landscapes in which they live and labour' (Johnson and Werbner, 2010, p. 206). In contrast with the frequent perception that transglobal migration results in spatially separated family members, some of those involved in Johnson's research had moved with their families to the Middle East. The ability to do this was more available to those in a professional job and hence aspects of class intersect with space to result in particular diasporic spatialities (Johnson, 2010).

Such migrants would 'display' their families in public spaces as a way of affirming their professional and moral status, providing an example where the 'doing' of family in space is conducted for a wider audience. Again the issue of whether children were active agents in the display or being 'displayed' suggests a need for further research on migrant children and spatial agency.

Conclusion

The standpoint of this book is not to privilege or centre the role of space in understanding the perspectives and experiences of children above other social factors but to show that there could be greater emphasis on both the role and the utility of spatiality for researchers in the field of childhood studies and family sociology. As this chapter has shown, space can be used as a substantive topic to address the contested issue of the extent of children's agency. Conversely, childhood and family studies can contribute to the development of work on spatiality by recognising the active participation of children in its production and construction. In the contemporary environment, where some children remain static in the family home well into their adulthood and others are in positions of forced migration, a spatial focus provides an appropriate heuristic lens to interrogate further issues of children's contribution to family practices and the limits of their individual agency.

References

Aitken, S. (2001) *Geographies of Young People: The Morally Contested Spaces of Identity*, London: Routledge.

Bailey, J. (2000) 'Some Meanings of "the Private" in Sociological Thought', *Sociology*, 34 (3), 403–420.

Baldassar, L. and Merla, L. (2013) *Transnational Families, Migration and the Circulation of Care: Understanding Mobility and Absence in Family Life*, London: Taylor and Francis.

Brannen, J. and O' Brien, M. (1996) 'Introduction', in J. Brannen and M. O'Brien (eds) *Children in Families: Research and Policy*, London: Falmer Press, pp. 1–12.

Bryceson, D. F. and Vuorela, U. (2002) *The Transnational Family: New European Frontiers and Global Networks*, New York: Berg.

Carr, N. (2011) *Children's and Families' Holiday Experience*, London: Routledge.

Connolly, P. (2004) *Boys and Schooling in the Early Years*, London: RoutledgeFalmer.

Corsaro, B. (1985) *Friendship and Peer Culture in the Early Years*, Norwood, NJ: Ablex.

Dowling, R. (2008) 'Accommodating Open Plan: Children, Clutter and Containment in Suburban Houses in Sydney, Australia', *Environment and Planning A*, 40 (3), 536–549.

Fog Olwig, K. and Gulløv, E. (2003) *Children's Places. Cross-Cultural Perspectives*, London: Routledge.

Foucault, M. (1986) 'Of Other Spaces', (trans. J. Miskowiec), *Diacritics*, Spring, 22–27.

Gabb, J. (2008) *Researching Intimacy in Families*, Basingstoke: Palgrave Macmillan.

Holloway, S.L. and Pimlett-Wilson, H. (2011) 'Geographies of Children, Youth and Families: Defining Achievements, Debating the Agenda', in L. Holt (ed.) *Geographies of Children, Youth and Families. An International Perspective*, London: Routledge, pp. 9–24.

Holt, L. (ed.) (2011) *Geographies of Children, Youth and Families. An International Perspective*, London: Routledge.

Hörschelmann, K. and Schafer, N. (2005) 'Performing the Global Through the Local: Globalisation and Individualisation in the Spatial Practices of Young East Germans', *Children's Geographies*, 3 (2), 219–242.

Huijsmans, R.B.C. (2011) 'Child Migration and Questions of Agency', *Development and Change*, 42 (5), 1307–1321.

James, A. (2009) 'Agency', in J. Qvortrup, W. Corsaro and M-S. Honig (eds) *The Palgrave Handbook of Childhood Studies*, Basingstoke: Palgrave Macmillan, pp. 34–45.

Jensen, A. and McKee, L. (2003) 'Introduction: Theorizing Childhood and Family Change', in A. Jensen and L. McKee (eds) *Children and the Changing Family. Between Transformation and Negotiation*, London: RoutledgeFalmer, pp. 1–14.

Johnson, M. (2010) 'Diasporic Dreams, Middle-Class Moralities and Migrant Domestic Workers Among Muslim Filipinos in Saudi Arabia', *Asia Pacific Journal of Anthropology*, September–December, 11 (3 & 4), 428–448.

Johnson, M. and Werbner, P. (2010) 'Diasporic Encounters, Sacred Journeys: Ritual, Normativity and the Religious Imagination Among International Asia Migrant Women', *Asia Pacific Journal of Anthropology*, September–December, 11 (3 & 4), 205–218.

Juozeliuniene, I. and Seymour, J. (eds) (2015) *Family Change in Times of the De-Bordering of Europe and Global Mobility: Resources, Processes and Practices*, Vilnius, Lithuania: Vilnius University Press.

Katz, C. (1994) 'Playing the Field: Questions of Fieldwork in Geography', *Professional Geographer*, 46, 67–72.

Keith, M. and Pile, S. (eds) (1993) *Place and Politics of Identity*, London: Routledge.

La Francois, B. (2007) 'Children's Participation Rights: Voicing Opinions in Inpatient Care', *Child and Adolescent Mental Health*, 12 (2), 94–97.

Lefebvre, H. (1991) *The Production of Space* (translated by D. Nicholson-Smith), Malden: Blackwell Publishing.

Lewis, R. (2011) 'Shutting the Bathroom Door: Parents, Young Teenagers and the Negotiation of Bodily Boundaries at Home', in L. Holt (ed.) *Geographies, of Children, Youth and Families: An International Perspective*, London: Routledge, pp. 67–80.

Lynch, P. A., McIntosh, A. and Tucker, H. (eds) (2009) *Commercial Homes in Tourism. An International Perspective*, London: Routledge.

May, V. (2011) 'Personal Life in Public Spaces', in V. May (ed.) *Sociology of Personal Life*, Basingstoke: Palgrave Macmillan, pp. 109–120.

Mayall, B. (2001) 'Understanding Childhood: A London Study', in L. Alanen and B. Mayall (eds) *Conceptualizing Child–Adult Relations*, London: RoutledgeFalmer, pp. 114–128.

Mayall, B. (2002) *Towards a Sociology for Childhood. Thinking from Children's Lives*, Buckingham: Open University Press.

McIntosh, I., Dorrer, N., Punch, S. and Emond, R. (2011) ' "I Know We Can't Be a Family, but as Close as You Can Get": Displaying Families Within an Institutional Context', in E. Dermott and J. Seymour (eds) *Displaying Families: A New Concept for the Sociology of Family Life*, Basingstoke: Palgrave Macmillan, pp. 175–194.

McNamee, S. (1998) 'Youth, Gender and Video Games: Power and Control in the Home', in G. Valentine and T. Skelton (eds) *Cool Places: Geographies of Youth Cultures*, London: Routledge, pp. 195–206.

McNamee, S. (2000) 'Foucault's Heterotopia and Children's Everyday Lives', *Childhood: A Global Journal of Child Research*, 7 (4), 479–492.

Morgan, D. H. J. (2011) *Rethinking Family Practices*, Basingstoke: Palgrave Macmillan.

Nieuwenhuys, O. (2003) 'Growing Up Between Places of Work and Non-Places of Childhood: The Uneasy Relationship', in K. Fog Olwig and E. Gulløv (eds) *Children's Places. Cross-Cultural Perspectives*, London: Routledge, pp. 99–118.

Punch, S. (2004) 'Negotiating Autonomy: Children's Use of Time and Space in Rural Bolivia', in V. Lewis, M. Kellett, C. Robinson, S. Fraser and S. Ding (eds) *The Reality of Research with Children and Young People*, London: Sage, pp. 93–119.

Qvortrup, J. (2009) 'Children as a Structural Form', in J. Qvortrup, W. Corsaro and M-S. Honig (eds) *The Palgrave Handbook of Childhood Studies*, Basingstoke: Palgrave Macmillan, pp. 21–33.

Ribbens McCarthy, J. and Edwards, R. (2011) *Key Concepts in Family Studies*, London: Sage.

Schanzel, H. A. (2010) 'Whole-Family Research: Towards a Methodology in Tourism for Encompassing Generation, Gender and Group Dynamic Perspectives', *Tourism Analysis*, 15 (5), 555–569.

Schanzel, H. A., Yeoman, I. and Backer, E. (2012) *Family Tourism: Multidisciplinary Perspectives*, Bristol: Channel View Publications.

Seymour, J. (2005) 'Entertaining Guests or Entertaining the Guests: Children's Emotional Labour in Hotels, Pubs and Boarding Houses', in J. Goddard, S. McNamee, A. James and A. James (eds) *The Politics of Childhood: International Perspectives, Contemporary Developments*, Basingstoke: Palgrave Macmillan, pp. 90–106.

Seymour, J. (2007) 'Treating the Hotel Like a Home: The Contribution of Studying the Single Location Home/Workplace', *Sociology*, 41, 1097–1114.

Seymour, J. (2011) ' "Family Hold Back": Displaying Families in the Single-Location Home/Workplace, in E. Dermott and J. Seymour (eds) *Displaying Families: A New Concept for the Sociology of Family Life*, Basingstoke: Palgrave Macmillan, pp. 160–174.

Seymour, J. and McNamee, S. (2012) 'Being Parented? Children and Young People's Engagement With Parenting Activities', in J. Waldren and I. Kaminski (eds) *Learning From Children: Childhood, Culture and Identity in a Changing World*, Oxford: Berghahn, pp. 92–107.

Sibley, D. (1995) 'Families and Domestic Routines: Constructing the Boundaries of Childhood', in S. Pile and N. Thrift (eds) *Mapping the Subject: Geographies of Cultural Transformation*, London: Routledge, pp. 123–137.

Valentine, G. (1997) ' "Oh Yes I Can. Oh No You Can't". Children and Parents' Understandings of Kids' Competence to Negotiate Public Space Safely', *Antipode*, 29 (1), 65–89.

Walsh, J. (2015) 'Displaying Across Borders: The Role of Family Display in Maintaining Transnational Intergenerational Relations', in I. Juozeliuniene and J. Seymour (eds) *Family Change in Times of the De-Bordering of Europe and Global Mobility: Resources, Processes and Practices*, Vilnius, Lithuania: Vilnius University Press.

Widerberg, K. (2010) 'In the Homes of Others: Exploring New Sites and Methods When Investigating the Doings of Gender, Class and Ethnicity', *Sociology*, 44 (6), 1181–1196.

Widmer, E. and Jallinoja, R. (2008) *Beyond the Nuclear Family: Families in a Configurational Perspective*, Bern: Peter Lang.

Zeiher, H., Devine, D., Kjorholt, A. and Strandell, H. (2007) *Flexible Childhood? Exploring Children's Welfare in Time and Space*, Odense: University Press of Southern Denmark.

Zeiher, H. (2009) ' Institutionalization as a Secular Trend', in J. Qvortrup, W. Corsaro and M-S. Honig (eds) *The Palgrave Handbook of Childhood Studies*, Basingstoke: Palgrave Macmillan, pp. 127–140.

9
Children and Young People's Spatial Agency

Helen Woolley

Children's outdoor environments as expressions of social justice

This chapter will focus on outdoor environments and some of the issues to do with the use of those environments by children and young people. As a landscape architect the author's interest focuses on the planning, design and management of outdoor environments underpinned by an understanding that such outdoor environments are not primarily for those who plan, design or manage them. Neither should outdoor environments be considered as only provided for those who pay for them: the client. Outdoor environments are for those who do and who might use them. Indeed it has been suggested that many outdoor environments are at their best when used by people whose daily lives intertwine with them in necessary, optional and social activities (Gehl, 1996). So this chapter will focus on outdoor environments exploring concepts of constructed and found space and the relationship of these to children and young people's use and responses to them.

Types of open spaces

The fabric of urban settlements includes buildings and the outdoor environments in which buildings are set. Outdoor environments include a variety of open spaces which can be influenced in design, management and use by history, culture, climate and politics and understood from different professional and user perspectives. This influence might be from the knowledge base of planners who consider the bigger picture of a city or settlement; from the client who may be paying for an open space to be developed, enhanced or managed; or from the perspective of the people who are going to use the space and who arguably have a longer term interest in the nature and character of the space.

For example, one planning-led typology suggested a hierarchy of open spaces including linear open spaces and regional, metropolitan, district, local and small parks (Llewelyn-Davies Planning, 1992). More recently planning practice in England was framed by Planning Policy Guidance 17 (PPG 17) (ODPM, 2002), which categorised open spaces as parks and public gardens; natural and semi-natural spaces; green corridors; outdoor sports facilities; amenity green spaces; provision for children and young people; allotments and community gardens; cemeteries and churchyards; and civic spaces and accessible countryside in urban fringe areas. Another typology takes a user's perspective and addresses outdoor spaces in the context of proximity to home: domestic, neighbourhood and civic open spaces (Woolley, 2003). Domestic open spaces are those close to where people live and include spaces associated with housing, gardens, community gardens and allotments. Neighbourhood open spaces are physically a little further away and are more likely to be used by a larger number of people. These spaces include parks, playgrounds, playing fields and sports grounds, school playgrounds, streets, city farms and incidental natural green spaces. Civic open spaces include those in the city centre and those which people may have to travel to in another part of their habitation and where the potential community of users again may be bigger and more mixed than in domestic and neighbourhood spaces. These civic open spaces include commercial, health and educational, transport corridors and recreational spaces such as golf courses.

Differences in understandings of typologies of open spaces can also exist between countries, even within Western culture. For example, American typologies include regional parks, linear parks, squares, plazas, playgrounds and playing fields, adventure playgrounds, wasteland (Lynch, 1981), pedestrian malls, commons, corporate plazas, festival market places, town trails and vest pocket parks (Carr et al., 1992). Some of these are similar in name and even meaning as those in the English context mentioned above, while other types differ as a result of their historic, cultural and political influences.

Yet stating that an open space may be of a particular type does not give a full explanation of how it is designed to, or might, be used. Indeed Carr et al. (1992) discuss that some American public spaces are both designed and managed in ways that do not adequately meet the needs of people for 'comfort, relaxation and discovery' (Carr et al., 1992, p. 17) and that public spaces should be 'responsive, democratic and meaningful' (p. 19).

This brings us to consider open space in another way with respect to the user: *constructed* and *found* open spaces; these concepts will now be discussed before moving onto their application with respect to some of the outdoor environments of children and young people.

Planned and constructed space

Most of the different types of outdoor spaces already mentioned, from whichever perspective, can be understood to be *planned* spaces. Planned spaces are usually the result of a decision by someone or a group of people, often representing society rather than themselves, that a specific space should exist in a particular location and in a particular form. This may be associated with a building in the way that a courtyard may be surrounded by houses or a school playground adjacent to a school building. But planned spaces may also stand alone or as part of a network of open spaces in the way that many parks do, whether they are linear, regional or neighbourhood ones. During the 20th century these planned spaces were increasingly the result of regulations associated with land zoning and planning processes, often in a specific period of time such as school playing fields in England in the post-World War II period or plazas in America from the 1960s onwards (Carr et al., 1992).

Constructed space is another term which can be applied to spaces in urban settlements. The origins of this term appear to be from the architectural literature. In this context constructed space is used in opposition to and in conjunction with the terms plot, street and open space, where the different ratios of these elements make up the urban form or morphology of a city or settlement and have changed over time, particularly since the beginning of the 20th century (Levy, 1999). However, the term constructed space also holds a similar meaning to the term planned space, used by Carr et al. (1992). That is, constructed space may relate not only to buildings but also to open spaces which are built, or constructed, for a particular purpose.

Open spaces in the outdoor environment may change physically over time as a result of planning, design and management processes. Yet such spaces can also evolve in response to social action and the appropriation of such spaces by users or for uses which were not originally intended (Carr et al., 1992). *Appropriation* can be understood as one of the five dimensions of spatial rights identified by Lynch (1981) and seems to have a similar meaning to the term *claim* (Carr et al., 1992). These two terms have a shared understanding that an individual person or group of people might use a space in a way that was not the original intention. The latter authors relate this to the concepts of privacy and territoriality but both terms can be understood in the light of Gibson's (1979) theory of affordance, which provides a framework for understanding that people do use spaces for activities other than that for which they were originally intended. People use open spaces for the activities they choose as a result of the configuration of a space, a desire to use such space in a particular way and sometimes in light of, or despite, a management regime for a particular open space or group of open spaces.

Found space

In opposition to constructed space, that is space built for a specific purpose, is the concept of *found* space. An early explanation of found space was building-focused and related to the needs of higher education for expansion into additional accommodation (Kliment and Lord, 1974). This happened in the 1970s at a time when some higher educational institutions in parts of America, especially in cities, did not have enough and needed to expand into additional premises. The found space approach sought to prevent institutions from buying expensive land for new buildings, usually away from an existing campus. If existing older and unused buildings on campus did not exist then one way forward was to search for buildings elsewhere which were no longer in use for their original purpose: found space. This resulted in found space being buildings which could be used for the higher educational institution, sometimes providing innovative solutions to the problem of inadequate existing accommodation. Such found spaces included industrial buildings, office buildings, commercial buildings, department stores, public buildings, residential and agricultural buildings and former colleges. A series of nine criteria were identified for such found space: adequacy, suitability, safety, health, flexibility, accessibility, efficiency, expansibility and pleasantness (US Office of Education and Department of Defense Civil Preparedness Agency, 1973).

A few years later the concept of found space was used in relation to issues of accommodation but this time with respect to the use of space by homeless people (Rivlin and Imbimbo, 1989). The American housing crisis of the late 1980s provided the background to a series of housing types: larger scale congregate shelters, hotels and motels, small shelters, transitional housing, public housing, private rented housing and private housing. Accommodation provided in congregate shelters, temporary housing or private shelters usually had a time limitation. In addition there was often not enough accommodation for the numbers of people needing it. Many people were homeless both at night and in the daytime, when those who had overnight accommodation would also be out on the streets. Homeless people were found to spend much of their time in the day both searching for and using found spaces with such spaces suggested as being either visible or invisible. Visible spaces included fronts or lobbies of buildings while invisible spaces included transportation stations, alleys, and empty buildings and apartments. Found spaces may be used by individuals or groups of people. Some found spaces, such as libraries, cinemas, parks and benches, have a use which is socially understood as the norm but homeless people may use these found spaces in different ways. This alternative use of found space is sometimes deemed inappropriate by other users or managers of a space and thus sometimes results in attempts to move the homeless people on.

But in this way different spaces are shared in time with homeless people appropriating elements in the landscape such as benches or parks at times, in the day, that other users are not frequenting them. Appropriation of interior spaces such as cinemas also results in them being shared in time. For homeless people their found spaces support their daily lives and activities as long as others do not move them on or seek to control their activities, with the result that 'homeless people become expert at detecting the degree of tolerance of the people in the places they inhabit' (Rivlin and Imbimbo, 1989, p. 715).

The concept of found space in the outdoor environment has been further explored by Rivlin (2007), but this does not focus solely on children and young people and so having considered the origins of constructed and found space, the discussion in this chapter will move on to explore these with respect to children and young people.

Children, young people and constructed space

So what can be understood as constructed space for children in the outdoor environment of cities and settlements in contemporary society? Some of the typologies mentioned earlier indicate that certain open spaces are provided and built, or constructed, specifically for use by children and young people. Such outdoor spaces are variously called playgrounds, school playgrounds and *provision for children and young people*, a term used in England by the government when PPG17 was revised in 2002 (ODPM, 2002). There seem to be two underlying assumptions in these terms: that such spaces are the only spaces that children and young people should use, and that these spaces are good for children and young people. We will return to the former point in the section about children, young people and found space.

Reasons for the constructed spaces of playgrounds being considered as good spaces for children go back to the introduction of playgrounds in many countries, particularly as recorded for America and England. During the 19th century indoor gymnastic equipment was introduced to the outdoor environment, an approach that was possibly introduced from Germany, which was followed by the development of specific equipment (Frost, 1992), now called fixed play equipment. Different periods in the history of playgrounds have been described as the manufactured apparatus era, the novelty era and the modern era; all of which included varying types and forms of fixed play equipment (Frost, 1992). Most of these eras were accompanied by an emphasis on physical activity in the outdoor environment. As the number of cars increased on the roads so did concerns that children might be injured if they continued to play on streets. Thus playgrounds were increasingly provided in parks, schools, backyards, vacant spaces and housing areas (Stevens, 1926) and some streets were closed to cars to allow children to play (Jenkins, 1924). Apart from the adult concern of increasing vehicle traffic, playgrounds were also a response by social and moral reformers to get children away from bad influences (Hart, 2002). So, the increasing provision of playgrounds has been a result of both physical and social concerns in (parts of) society in some parts of the world.

The development of playgrounds in England followed a similar pattern to America with the first mention of the provision of outdoor spaces, 'playgrounds', being made in legislation in the mid-19th century. Playgrounds were developed in parks and on recreation grounds and play streets were facilitated after World War II (Heseltine and Holborn, 1987). Adventure playgrounds, which included a worker to support or facilitate children's play, were also introduced but these were not as frequent as playgrounds. As the 20th century progressed commentators in America and then Britain criticised the paucity of playgrounds with fixed play equipment (Holme and Massie, 1970; Moore, 1989; Cunningham and Jones, 1999; McKendrick, 1999). By the turn of the 21st century many playgrounds could be described as consisting of a kit, fence and carpet: a kit of fixed play equipment; a fence apparently increasingly to keep children in the space and a carpet of rubber surfacing (Woolley, 2007, 2008). The play value of this approach has been shown to be dominated by opportunities for physical play and social connections with fewer opportunities for fantasy, creative and fine motor functioning, sensory experiences, manipulation and interaction with the environment than play spaces which included more natural elements (Woolley and Lowe, 2013).

An older, very physically active group of young people (and adults) are skateboarders, who sometimes use their skateboards as sustainable transport (Borden, 2001). It is in connection with skateboarders that the term constructed space has been used for 40 years in a very direct way with respect to open spaces in the urban fabric. As seen above, the term constructed space derived from the field of architecture and it is the very architectural structures of skateparks which are the physically constructed spaces provided by society for skateboarders. Skateparks were first developed in the mid-1970s in California. In these early years of skateparks, concrete was used to exaggerate 'fragments of the city' (Borden, 2001, p. 57), mainly using a bowl format. This approach copied the overall form of swimming pools and provided the experience that skateboarders enjoy in their bodily relationship with the urban fabric. Designs changed and evolved in an attempt to replicate the experience of and physical details of the swimming pools and streets that skateboarders used (Borden,

2001). In the summer of 1976 skateboarding started to become popular in the United Kingdom and within a year over 80 purpose-built
skateboard facilities had been built. As in America, the quality of
these early constructed spaces was not ideal and commercial developments were initiated. By the end of the 1970s about 20 of the 100
constructed skateparks in the United Kingdom were still open. In different parts of the world, including Argentina, Canada, France, South
Africa, Japan and Peru concrete skateparks were developed in the late
1970s (Borden, 2001).

From the late 1970s the constructed spaces of skateparks were
sometimes supplemented by ramps which skaters would bring to the
location. In time ramps were also incorporated into the constructed
spaces and could be added or removed, showing a more responsive
approach to the early concrete skateparks. This evolution in provision resulted in indoor facilities being based around the inclusion of
ramps. In this way the constructed spaces of skateparks evolved from
being expensive, concrete provisions to being lower in cost with the
ability to change as ramps were added or removed (Borden, 2001).

The origins of skateparks are clearly embedded in the west coast of
America but there has also been another driver for these constructed
spaces. This driver is often associated with the re-development of
urban open spaces, particularly civic open spaces in town and city
centres and seems to be a response to physical concerns about
skateboarders using civic open spaces. This concern relates to the fact
that, when using found civic spaces, skateboarders can cause damage
to the urban fabric by waxing ledges, or damaging elements such as
handrails, steps and edges (Borden, 2001; Woolley and Johns, 2001;
Woolley et al., 2011). Associated with this concern about damage to
the physical environment is the cost of repairing such damage and a
desire to protect the investment of expensive regeneration projects.
In addition social drivers to control have also been identified, including the noise of the activity, conflict (often perceived) with other
users and an understanding by some that skateboarding is just not
an appropriate activity in some civic open spaces. In response to
these physical, economic and social drivers, policy and practice can
result in social, legal and physical controls of skateboarders' use of
civic open spaces. The physical controls can take the form of a design
philosophy, design response or design detail excluding skateboarders
from such civic open spaces or the construction of skateparks in
locations away from the civic open spaces. Social controls can take

the form of city centre wardens or ambassadors who, as part of their responsibilities, reinforce the legal control of byelaws prohibiting skateboarding in designated civic open spaces (Woolley et al., 2011).

So, constructed open spaces in the form of playgrounds and skateparks have been some of the dominant expressions that society has deemed acceptable in providing for children and young people to experience urban landscapes. This started in the 20th century and has continued into the 21st century in many parts of the world.

Children, young people and found space

If playgrounds and skateparks are some of the constructed spaces for children and young people, what are their found open spaces in the urban fabric? Despite the fact that in many cities society seems to consider that children should play only in the constructed spaces of playgrounds, children will assert their agency in the urban environment and play in and use different open spaces. This reflects the knowledge, accepted by many but not by all, that children will play anywhere (Opie and Opie, 1969) and that play is the nature of childhood (Prout and James, 1997).

Key explorations of children's outdoor environments, called children's geographies by some, resulted in a series of seminal texts: *The Child in the City* (Ward, 1978), *Children's Experience of Place* (Hart, 1979) and *Childhood's Domain* (Moore, 1986). Each of these texts in their own way provide an insight into the way that children used a multitude of different found open spaces during the 1970s and 1980s across a range of locations and contexts in the world. Despite the fact that different methods were used for gathering the data and information for the three texts they each reveal that children were using a rich palette of found spaces which were not constructed or designated as children's playgrounds or play spaces.

In asking where children play, Woolley (2007) highlighted other research that identified different found open spaces that children use. These open spaces include the *domestic* open spaces of individual gardens (Francis, 1995), communal gardens and courtyards (Rasmussen, 2004). In other domestic open spaces in housing areas, children were observed playing in roads and pavements, car parks, paved areas, public grass, gardens, wild areas, planted areas and access areas, as well as on walls, fences and the flat roofs of garages (Hole, 1996;

Department of Environment, 1973). More recently research identi-fied that the housing areas that better supported children's play were the ones which had traffic calming measures, street closures, walls and driveways, and grass areas set back from roads (Wheway and Millward, 1997). So children use many different found open spaces in these urban contexts, especially in domestic and neighbourhood open spaces (Woolley, 2003). In all these pieces of research, paths that connect the open spaces together within the housing areas are considered to be very important elements in the landscape because of the opportunities they afford for children's independent mobility and social connections.

The fact that children use found spaces in the urban environment has also been explored in different geographic locations and across time by research into children's use of outdoor environments across two or three generations in locations such as New York in America (Gaster, 1991), Newcastle in Australia (Tandy, 1999), Amsterdam in the Netherlands (Karsten, 2005), Brummundahl in Norway (Skar and Krogh, 2009), Tokyo in Japan (Kinoshita, 2009) and Sheffield in England (Woolley and Griffin, 2014). The found spaces of grandpar-ents and parents in the most recent of these studies included fields, streams, woods with bluebells, the housing estate where they lived, the middle school playground and the space outside the local shops (Woolley and Griffin, 2014).

Across these studies there was not only a reduction in the home range, that is the distance a child is allowed to go from home with-out an adult (see Hart, 1979), of children over the generations but also in the number and type of open spaces children were and are using: a reduction in the variety of found open spaces used over several generations. These reductions in both home range and use of found open spaces seem to be the result of a range of issues that include parents' and other adults' concerns, which predominantly relate to traffic and safety, including fear of strangers abducting children (Valentine and McKendrick, 1997; Outley and Floyd, 2002; Karsten, 2005; Skår and Krogh, 2009). Despite the reported evidence of reduced home range and found space, if one walks through a city it is possible to see children using found spaces in contemporary society and this will vary between cities, rural areas, cultures and countries. This raises questions such as: how prevalent children's use of found space is in different contexts, cultures and countries; how desirable such use is; and how such use is allowed or controlled in any democratic context.

One specific group of young people, skateboarders, use, if not delight in using, found spaces in urban areas. (At this point it is important to acknowledge that skateboarders are not only young people: many continue the activity beyond the age that might be considered young.) 'Adopting and exploiting a given physical terrain' (Borden, 2001, p. 29) is central to skateboarding and for many skateboarders skating the street is the essence of the activity and thus found rather than constructed spaces are their preference.

In the early years of skateboarding such found spaces were common in suburban areas of Los Angeles and other Californian coastal cities. Many skateboarders were initially surfers who turned to skating when the surf was flat and these Californian cities, 'allowed frustrated surfers to re-enact the sense of being on the sea, rolling down the tarmac drives and roads of its undulating residential sectors as if they were an ocean wave' (Borden, 2001, p. 29). These skateboarders used their bodies as a mechanism to relate to their urban environment in a way unknown and experienced by other users of open spaces in cities. These early skateboarders also found other elements in the urban landscape that satisfied their desire to explore the outdoor environment in a specific way and to this end they used schoolyards and particularly those with inclinations. In the 1970s additional found spaces were identified and used in Los Angeles. In particular, empty private swimming pools of large villas provided affordances for new and changing moves as skaters responded to the detailed design elements of differently designed pools in the urban fabric. Other found spaces were drainage ditches, water management projects and large concrete (drainage) pipes, many of which were in 'wastelands, deserts and forgotten spaces of the city' (Borden, 2001, p. 45).

The use of found spaces by skateboarders was also identified in England, particularly in London in the mid-1970s. The Boardwalk in Kensington Gardens, the island at the southern end of Wandsworth Bridge and the concrete elements beneath the Queen Elizabeth Hall/Haywood Gallery in the South Bank area by the River Thames were identified as places that skaters were using (Ward, 1978). The latter space, which became known as the Undercroft, in the South Bank has been continuously used by skateboarders since the 1970s and came under threat of a £120 million redevelopment to shops and restaurants in 2012. A long campaign entitled Long Live South Bank was initiated by the skaters; it used social media, an educational campaign and a presentation at a Royal Town Planning Institute conference in 2014, and raised a petition of 27,286 objectors and obtained the support of the Mayor of London (Long Live South Bank, 2015). This resulted in the Southbank Centre agreeing to save the area for skateboarders and other urban activities in September 2014 (Brown, 2014).

Skateboarders have sought to assert their agency in various parts of the world by using found open spaces such as the edge of city centres and car parks, similar to the wastelands of California. For some these found spaces have included civic open spaces in city centres (Woolley and Johns, 2001). However, the use of such open spaces has sometimes resulted in concerns about the social use of such spaces and potential physical damage that might result from skateboarding activities. A response to this has been expressed in the design and management of some city centres with the use of social, legal and physical controls as mentioned above (Woolley et al., 2011).

Concluding thoughts

It is clear that the origins of the concepts of both constructed and found space are in the literature and practice of architecture. Yet the use of these concepts has translated to other aspects of the built environment in urban settlements: namely to the outdoor environment and landscape of cities. These concepts can then also be applied specifically to the outdoor environments of some children and young people's activities of play and recreation in cities.

With this translation of concepts there has been a shared understanding that a constructed space is something made for a specific purpose whether it be a building for the purpose of higher education, a playground for children to play in or a skatepark for skateboarders to practice and share knowledge of their tricks. Similarly there is a shared understanding of found space which relates to the use, or appropriation, of something for a purpose for which it was not built. Examples of this include an office or retail building being used for higher education; car parks and paths being used for children's play in housing areas; and empty swimming pools, civic open spaces in city centres and open spaces on the edge of cities being used by skateboarders.

It appears that much of society, in some countries, expects that children and young people will and should only use constructed open spaces, such as playgrounds and skateparks. These constructed open spaces are an expression of the power of adults and society provided through the planning, design and management of cities and often do not meet the real needs of children and young people. In this way society, predominantly adults who construct society, seek to exert power and control children and young people in their use of the outdoor environment of cities.

Yet it is clear that such constructed open spaces do not (always) meet the needs of the users. Thus children and young people become actors in their daily lives and often respond by using found spaces for activities such as play and skateboarding, eschewing the constructed spaces and the power they represent. The challenge for society is to support and enable rather than suppress and control children and young people in the provision and use of outdoor environments in cities.

References

Borden, I. (2001) *Skateboarding, Space and the City: Architecture and the Body*, Oxford: Berg.

Brown, M. (2014) http://www.theguardian.com/uk-news/2014/sep/18/skaters-southbank-centre-undercroft-london-remains-open, accessed 20 October 2014.

Carr, S., Francis, M., Rivlin, L. G. and Stone, A. M. (1992) *Public Space*. New York: Cambridge University Press.

Cunningham, C. and Jones, M. (1999) 'The Playground: A Confession of Failure?', *Built Environment*, 25 (1), 11–17.

Department of the Environment (1973) *Children at Play*, London: Her Majesty's Stationery Office.

Francis, M. (1995) 'Childhood's Garden: Memory and Meaning of Gardens', *Children's Environments*, 12 (2), 1–16.

Frost, J. L. (1992) *Play and Playscapes*, New York: Delmar.

Gaster, S. (1991) 'Urban Children's Access to Their Neighbourhood: Changes Over Three Generations', *Environment and Behaviour*, 23 (1), 70–85. DOI: 10. 1177/0013916591231004.

Gehl, J. (1996) *Life Between Buildings: Using Public Space*, Copenhagen: Arkitektens Forlag.

Gibson, J. J. (1979) *The Ecological Approach to Visual Perception*, Boston: Houghton Mifflin.

Hart, R. (1979) *Children's Experience of Place*, New York: Irvington Press.

Hart, R. (2002) Containing Children: Some Lessons on Planning for Play From New York City. *Environment and Urbanization*, 14 (2), pp. 135–148.

Heseltine, P. and Holborn, J. (1987) *Playgrounds: The Planning, Design and Construction of Play Environments*, London: Mitchell.

Hole, V. (1996) *National Building Studies Research Paper 39: Children's Play on Housing Estates*, London: Her Majesty's Stationery Office.

Holme, A. and Massie, P. (1970) *Children's Play: A Study of Needs and Opportunities*, London: Michael Joseph.

Jenkins, A. L. (1924) 'Public Playgrounds Versus Highway Perils', *The Playground*, 18 (3), 155.

Karsten, L. (2005) 'It All Used to Be Better? Different Generations on Continuity and Change in Urban Children's Daily Use of Space', *Children's Geographies*, 3 (3), 275–290. DOI:10. 1080/14733280500352912.

Kinoshita, I. (2009) 'Charting Generational Differences in Conceptions and Opportunities for Play in a Japanese Neighborhood', *Journal of Intergenerational Relationships*, 7 (1), 53–77. DOI: doi.org/10.1080/15350770802629024.

Kliment, S. A. and Lord, J. (1974) 'Build If You Must but Consider Found Space', *Planning for Higher Education*, 3 (3), 1–6 (Society for College and University Planning, New York).

Levy, A. (1999) 'Urban Morphology and the Problems of the Modern Urban Fabric: Some Questions for Research', *Urban Morphology*, 3 (2), 79–85.

Llewelyn-Davies Planning (1992) *Open Spaces Planning in London*, London: London Planning Advisory Committee.

Long Live South Bank http://www.llsb.com/llsb-speaks-at-world-town-planning-day-2014-who-has-a-right-to-the-city/, accessed 31 March 2015.

Lynch, K. (1981) *A Theory of Good City Form*, Cambridge MA: MIT Press.

McKendrick, J. (1999) 'Playgrounds in the Built Environment', *Built Environment*, 25 (1), 5–10.

Moore, R. C. (1986) *Childhood's Domain: Play and Place in Child Development*, London: Croom Helm.

Moore, R. C. (1989) 'Playgrounds at the Crossroads', in I. Altman and E. Zube (eds) *Public Places and Spaces*, New York: Plenum, pp. 83–120.

Office of the Deputy Prime Minister (ODPM) (2002) *Planning Policy Guidance 17: Open Space, Sport and Recreation*. London: ODPM.

Opie, I. and Opie, P. (1969) *Children's Games in Street and Playground: Chasing, Catching, Seeking, Hunting, Racing, Duelling, Exerting, Daring, Guessing, Acting, Pretending*, Oxford, UK: Clarendon Press.

Outley, C. W. and M. F. Floyd. (2002) 'The Home They Live in: Inner City Children's Views on the Influence of Parenting Strategies on Their Leisure Behavior', *Leisure Sciences: An Interdisciplinary Journal*, 24 (2), 161–179. DOI: 10.1080/01490400252900130.

Prout, A. and James, A. (1997) *Constructing and Re-Constructing Childhood*, London: Falmer Press.

Rasmussen, K. (2004) 'Places for Children – Children's Places', *Childhood*, 11 (2), 155–173.

Rivlin, L. G. (2007) 'Found Spaces Freedom of Choice in Public Life', in K. Frank and Q. Stevens (eds) *Loose Space: Possibility and Diversity in Urban Life*, London and New York: Routledge, pp. 38–53.

Rivlin, L. G. and Imbimbo, J. E. (1989) 'Self-Help Efforts in a Squatter Community: Implications for Addressing Contemporary Homelessness', *American Journal of Community Psychology*, 17 (6), 705–728.

Skår, M. and Krogh, E. (2009) 'Changes in Children's Nature-Based Experiences Near Home: From Spontaneous Play to Adult-Controlled, Planned and Organised Activities', *Children's Geographies*, 7 (3), 339–354. DOI: 10.1080/14733280903024506.

Stevens, M. (1926) 'Play Streets', *The Playground*, 20 (4), 219.

Tandy, C. (1999) 'Children's Diminishing Play Space: A Study of Intergenerational Change in Children's Use of Their Neighbourhoods', *Australian Geographical Studies*, 37 (2), 154–164.

United Nations (1989) United Nations Convention on the Rights of the Child.

US Office of Education and Department of Defense Civil Preparedness Agency. (1973) *Protected Educational Facilities in Found Spaces*.

Valentine, G. and McKendrick, J. (1997) 'Outdoor Play: Exploring Parental Concerns About Children's Safety and the Changing Nature of Childhood Experience', *Environment and Behaviour*, 40 (1), 111–143.

Ward, C. (1978) *The Child in the City*. London: The Architectural Press.

Wheway, R. and Millward, A. (1997) *Child's Play: Facilitating Play on Housing Estates*. Coventry: Chartered Institute of Housing With Support From the Joseph Rowntree Foundation.

Woolley, H. (2003) *Urban Open Spaces*, London: Spon Press.

Woolley, H. (2007) 'Where Do the Children Play? How Policies Can Influence Practice', *Proceedings of the Institution of Civil Engineers Municipal Engineer*, 160 (ME2), 89–95 DOI: 10.1680/muen.2007.160.2.89.

Woolley, H. (2008) 'Watch This Space! Designing for Children's Play in Public Open Spaces', *Geography Compass*, 2/2, 495–512.

Woolley, H. and Griffin, E. (2014) 'Decreasing Experiences of Home Range, Outdoor Spaces, Activities and Companions: Changes Across Three Generations in Sheffield in North England', *Children's Geographies*, DOI: 10.1080/14733285.2014.952186.

Woolley, H. and Johns, R. (2001) 'Skateboarding: The City as a Playground', *Journal of Urban Design*, 6 (2), 211–230.

Woolley, H. and Lowe, A. (2013) 'Exploring the Relationship Between Design Approach and Play Value of Outdoor Play Spaces', *Landscape Research*, 38 (1), 53–74, DOI: 10.1080/01426397.2011.640432.

Woolley, H., Hazelwood, T. and Simkins, I. (2011) 'Don't Skate Here: Exclusion of Skateboarders From Urban Civic Spaces in Three Northern Cities in England', *Journal of Urban Design*, 16 (4), 471–487. DOI: doi.org/10.1080/13574809.2011.585867.

10
A Proper Place for a Proper Childhood? Children's Spatiality in a Play Centre

Caterina Satta

Introduction

In prosperous Western countries children's everyday urban experience is characterised by a general tendency towards a separation from adults' space and by a high degree of spatial and temporal differentiation functional to meeting the children's needs (Zeiher, 2003). Children fluctuate continuously between spatially demarcated places designed specifically for them and the wider adult space. In particular, we have recently witnessed the significant expansion of children's play centres (outdoor and indoor afterschool clubs, sport and leisure organisations and so on), planned and sponsored as safe sites for their play activities in recognition of their right to the city.

My aim in this chapter, which is written from the perspective of the new sociology of childhood (Jenks, 1982; James and Prout, 1990; Qvortrup, 1991; Corsaro, 1997; Alanen and Mayall, 2001) and which adopts the concept of *spatial justice* as an analytical tool (Soja, 2010; Philippoupolos, 2014), is to explore how children's spatiality is constructed within these 'play institutions'. To what extent do they meet children's desires and promote their agency?[1] To what extent do they establish the basis for constructing equal opportunities between adults and children in public space? Far from being a secondary detail, the fact that the mission of these places is to 'make' children play may have implications for the interpretation of the nature of child–adult relationships fostered in society.

The research was conducted in a neighbourhood play centre for four- to six-year-old children, in a medium sized city in the centre of Italy; this location was attended regularly in order to carry out participant observation during afternoon activities and to conduct formal and informal interviews with play-assistants, children and their parents.[2]

After an overview of the ambivalent relation between children and public space, I outline the structural space-time configurations of a free-entry play centre. I then focus on the child–adult relationships developed within the play frame and through play activities.

My argument is that, within play centres, traditional adult representations of the 'child in need' and of the 'adult in charge of his/her care' interfere in the planning and managing of these spaces as truly belonging to children. Through an in-depth analysis of the different meanings that play can assume in regulated places, I discuss whether play centres, despite being presented as gateways to public space, sustain generational spatial justice (Soja, 2010) or not. In Soja's words, spatial justice (and injustice) is something different from other 'related concepts [such] as territorial justice, environmental justice, the urbanisation of injustice, the reduction of regional inequalities, or even more broadly [from] the generic search for a just city and a just society' (2009, p. 1).[3] The difference lies in the adjective 'spatial'. In other words, for Soja, after the *spatial turn*, we can no longer avoid considering:

- the ontological spatiality of being (we are all spatial as well as social and temporal beings);
- the social production of spatiality (space is socially produced and can therefore be socially changed);
- the socio-spatial dialectic (the spatial shapes the social as much as the social shapes the spatial).

(ibid., p. 2)

Play and space are intimately related: whether practised in free external urban space or inside an organised centre, we cannot avoid thinking of play spatially. Children's play is progressively more and more organised under the rubric of various educational goals and is also structured following spatial rules and prohibitions. So children's *spatial agency* is also a question of spatial justice or injustice.

As stated by Soja:

> Locational discrimination, created through the biases imposed on certain populations because of their geographical location, is fundamental in the production of spatial injustice and the creation of lasting spatial structures of privilege and advantage. The three most familiar forces shaping locational and spatial discrimination are class, race, and gender, but their effects should not be reduced only to segregation.
>
> (Soja, 2009, p. 3)

The localisation of children in a place specifically *for* them, the fact that they are not free to move around the city, and not only for safety reasons, produces spatial injustice and the 'creation of lasting spatial structures of privilege and advantage', based mainly on their age difference.[4] Indeed, spatial injustice does not occur only through children's segregation (in school, in the play centre, at home and so on) but also through a set of spatial bans and prohibitions that influence their agency and substantive right to access to public space (Satta, 2014). Therefore, we cannot uncritically assert children's agency without 'putting it in place' and without taking into serious consideration the social and spatial contexts of childhood that can constrain or enable children's agency. The dominant concept of 'children's agency', theorised by the sociology of childhood, cannot be adopted in an abstract way but must always be constructed in context (James, 2009).

What follows is an account of fieldwork research inside a play centre aimed at unveiling, beyond its rhetorical celebration, the ways in which the ideal of a 'proper childhood' is emplaced producing forms of justice, or injustice, that need to be recognised.

The place *for* children in public space: An overview

The ambivalent relationship between childhood/youth and urban space has always characterised public debate as well as the literature of sociology of childhood and of children's geography (Holloway and Valentine, 2000; Christensen and O' Brien, 2003; Horton and Kraftl, 2006; Holt, 2011). Space is a central issue in understanding children's life because, as comprehensively explained by Ariès in his magisterial book *Centuries of Childhood* (1979), with the emerging consciousness of children as 'being different' from adults there arose the need to find a suitable space in which to locate them.

Although the relationship with space is a critical issue for everyone, because we are all exposed to more or less evident 'geographical and spatial prohibitions' (James et al., 1998, p. 37), for children this becomes a substantive constraint because it is not always possible for them to circumscribe and independently determine the borders of their spatial agency. In this sense, we could also assert that the process of the progressive recognition of childhood as a 'structural social phenomenon' (Qvortrup, 1991) had to go through the construction of spaces 'for children', shaped on adult ideals of childhood.

In Western countries children's identity (as different from that of adults) and their place in society have been constructed through their bodies and the different meanings attached to them. From the beginning of the 16th century control over children was exerted through a strict disciplining of their bodies, which were mainly represented in two opposing ways: as the embodiment of purity or of wickedness (Hörschelmann and Colls, 2010). These two images had, and continue to have, a strong impact on children's spatial everyday life. Whether considered as 'angelical creatures' in need of protection, or as 'unruly evils' requiring discipline, these dominant representations have both led to the exclusion of children from public space and to the modern institutionalisation of childhood (Jenks, 1996). Children and teens are in fact subjected to space restrictions, justified for reasons of care and safeguarding, and regulated in their access to public space more than other groups of people.

Zeiher, in describing the spatial and temporal configuration of children's everyday life, talks of 'insularisation', addressing the 'process where children growing up in an urban context tend to be ferried between dislocated "islands" of activity' (Christensen and O'Brien, 2003, p. 7). As Zeiher states 'places geared toward children's needs, often toward the needs of children of a particular age, are scattered like islands on the map of the city at greater or lesser distances from one another' (2003, p. 66).

This separation/insularisation is never neutral or abstract but is inscribed in bodies which can be female or male, very young, ill, healthy or with somatic attributes which symbolise their difference. Difference is inscribed in bodies and troubles once it becomes visible in public space. There are some bodies which are silently designed as 'natural' occupants of specific positions within the city and other bodies, deemed symbolically and physically 'out of place' (Cresswell, 1996), which appear as 'space invaders' (Puwar, 2004). According to Puwar (2004), the first group of bodies occupy metaphorically and politically the centre of the public space and have the power to define the urban socio-spatial order; the second group lives at the margin of the city but these bodies can rupture this order and generate social change when they enter a space which was not defined for them. This is the case of children (one need only think of the alarmist discourses in many of our cities surrounding the presence of unsupervised groups of children who do not conform to adult definitions of appropriate behaviour in a public space or even simply of all those urban signs which rule against or ban many forms of children's use of space, including play). Children are often considered as 'out of place' (James et al., 1998) and as space invaders when they are not inside those places that adults project for them.

Indeed, these places for children are often constructed following the adults' rather than the children's way of seeing things: the adults are the ones who construct the 'interaction order' (Goffman, 1967) as a generational order in which children, 'as juniors, are incorporated into the society under the guidance of various senior carers or educators' (Olwig and Gulløv, 2003, p. 2). However, the places designated *for* children are not always children's places; that is, informal, meaningful to them and places that they would choose for their activities (Rasmussen, 2004). The distinction between places for children and children's places opens up the path to a critical vision of spaces and to the acknowledgment of a generational perspective within space not only in the planning but also in the daily management of a play centre.

Organised play contexts are primarily places and fields of leisure, but also sites constituted through a series of recurring contradictions between the adults' views and aspirations and those of the children. On the one hand, such contexts promote children's fundamental right to play and to have fun, through the combination of individual development, group spirit and entertainment; but on the other, these activities are often controlled in a way that seems to leave little room for the child's subjectivity and free expression (Moss and Petrie, 2002). The risk is that the play component is erased.

The presence of a place such as a play centre – specifically planned, that is, as a site for children's play – reveals the idea of childhood upheld in a specific society and the space 'left' for children's agency. One of the conditions generally shared by children in Western countries is that 'more than other social groups, they are regulated by places and spaces' (Jenks, 2005, p. 419) in which, until they reach the age of legal majority (generally 18), they spend most of their time separated from adults. If, in accordance with Tuan (1974), the concept of place can be regarded both as index of social position and as expression of physical location, children's places 'become [...] a matter of their relative status in the generational order of socio-cultural transmission' (Olwig and Gulløv, 2003, p. 2).

Therefore, the study of children's spatialities in a play centre can become an analytic lens through which to explore children's social position in society at large. As stated by Simmel, space is not something that exists beyond social relations, 'spatial relations not only are determining conditions of relationships among men, but are also symbolic of those relationship' (1971, p. 143). Thus, following this line of theorisation, the spaces targeted at children express an idea of the child and of accepted modalities of child–adult relations; they are, on the one hand, a symbol of inter-generational relationships and, on the other, the precondition for these relationships to exist.

Thus, a place such as a play centre is the expression of a representation of childhood that in Italy, as in other Western countries, has undergone over the last two centuries a process of 'domestication'.

> This process is not simply a material one, in the sense that children are spending increasing amounts of time in the home, but is also ideological, in that there is a sense in which this is where children should spend their time.
>
> (Holloway and Valentine, 2000, p. 15)

This vision of domesticated places as safe and caring places strengthens, and is in turn strengthened by, the recent trend which affirms that public spaces belong to adults and that children should be removed from the urban street if their presence there is out of the control and the protection of adults (Valentine, 2004).

The play centre: To play 'around the corner'

According to Perrot (2011) the need for a separate children's room arose with the adults' problem of spatially and temporally organising children's play; this was primarily a problem of maintaining order within the domestic sphere. Toys and play activities created mess inside the house, and the toys' room – or the space devoted to this function and to its users (the children) – was created to this end, following a rationalistic vision of space. On a larger scale, the play centre can be seen as a room entirely dedicated to play and to its young users within an otherwise adult-centred society (McKendrick et al., 2000).

Though there exist several types of play centres, I am referring here to a space, run by an independent organisation, mostly funded by public money, whose aim it is to improve the living conditions and the environmental, social and cultural development of children and young people. This type of play centre requires a membership card, which costs around ten euros a year per child and covers insurance expenses, thus making admission virtually free. Inside the play centre there are various kinds of toys and play-assistants are present to 'facilitate' play activities. Parents are allowed to enter and indeed cannot leave their children alone during the opening times. Unlike baby parking (commercial playspaces/playgrounds aimed at young children where parents can leave them alone for few hours under a surveillance of one or two play-assistants), in the play centre parents are warmly *requested* to 'play with their children' as an expression of good parenthood.

The play centre where I carried out my research was depicted as a place 'for' children where, as soon as they entered, they could find that freedom of bodily movement and self-expression which was unavailable to them in the outside urban environment. What follows is the presentation of a specific space in the play centre – called the soft space because of the presence of a ball pool – that the director, Marina (all names are pseudonyms), gave me on the first day:

> *This is a space for the children's bodily activities, where they can 'use' their body because, you see, very often children outside are told 'don't do that', 'be careful', 'don't behave like that', 'do not touch that' etc. while here it is different. They can run, they can jump, they can do everything*

with their body. They have to take their shoes off while they are here. They come in, they take off their shoes and put them in the shoe rack. They can come in here only when only when the educator decides so. They can't spend all afternoon here, it's the educator who tells them that it is time to go in and opens the door for them.

(Excerpt from an interview with the play centre director)

This was my first encounter with the play centre. I remember that, as she was closing the door of the soft space, my eye caught some writing on a sheet of white paper attached to the door at the children's eye level. It said: 'Rules of the soft space'. Though I couldn't stop to read it all because of my ongoing conversation with the director, I could distinctly make out, in capital letters: 'IT IS FORBIDDEN TO ENTER WITH SHOES', 'IT IS NOT ALLOWED TO THROW THE SMALL BALLS', 'SHOUTING IS FORBIDDEN' and below 'IT IS NOT...' and so on. All the while the director carried on in her description of the play/toys room:

[Describing the play centre corners] *Here they have several areas in which to play: here they have the symbolic corner – pointing at a small child-size kitchen – here the costume corner – showing me an area of wall where a mask was hanging – and all around here the children can move freely, indicating the rest of the little room.* [As she was concluding, she said] *Here it's not like out there: this is a child-sized place. Out there children always have to adapt to the adult world, here it is the contrary.*

(Excerpt from an interview with the play centre director)

The other areas, called 'the play centre corners', also seemed to express an educative geometry based on the principle that every game has to achieve specific educational purposes. These corners direct the child's play from above in accordance with a vision of childhood still related to the traditional models of developmental psychology and pedagogy. Through the director's words the play centre appeared as a 'space of representation' (Lefebvre, 1991) of the child as he or she might be. That is, a place planned for the development of the good citizen of the future, built on that rhetoric which promotes children's well-being but that risks losing contact with the real child and his/her experience of everyday life (Lee, 2001).

The play centre is ambiguously placed in an imaginary temporal line between present and future because, despite operating daily with children, it is projected forward towards the achievement of future results. The transition to adulthood is the framework within which play-assistants rank their actions and while working with the children 'here and now', they in fact project the final objective of their work into the metaphorical and idealised space of the 'adult that will be'.

In her presentation Marina regularly put forward a dichotomous vision between bad external space and good internal space (the play centre), following the idea that 'outside' children's spatial agency is restricted by rules and prohibitions, while 'inside' the 'child can', 'the furniture is for them', 'everything is different' and so on. However, comparing Marina's representations of the play centre with what I observed day after day, I could not entirely understand the distinction between outside/inside that she had initially described to me. On the contrary, this space seemed to reproduce the same features and dynamics attributed to the public space – as a space both dangerous and proscribed for children – and appeared to follow the same script of the adults encroaching on the children's space.

On the basis of my fieldwork research, play-assistants recognise that the urban environment is not child friendly or easily accessible for children, so they reproduce for the child a space specifically devoted to the development of his/her bodily activities, which otherwise would be neglected. However, play-assistants retain power within this space. They are in charge of what to do and when to do it, as for example in the case of the 'soft space' where they decide when children can go in; they are the only ones allowed to open the door and to lay down the rules of behaviour.

Looking at the internal settings of the play centre I was able to observe how the play assistants were engaged for most of their time in the promethean task of guiding something that is, precisely in terms of how it is composed, unmanageable: the activity of play. Indeed, the fact that this place was designed for playing complicated their efforts to foster a static and realistic vision of reality. In play activities the point in question is not the appearance of reality but the distance from reality because 'there is a limit to be kept and to protect, and a rather complex balance to set up and maintain, if we want to stay inside the play, between normal reality and the distancing reality'

(Dal Lago and Rovatti, 1993, p. 17).[5] Even in child–adult relations it seems that the correct distance between children and adults is never kept because it is often occupied by the constant interference of the adult in the child's life (Aitken, 2001).

> *When Ilene, the play-assistant, said: 'Now we are going into the soft space'. Some girls jumped up and down screaming with joy. Ilene stood in front of the closed door, lined up the small number of children into queue and then opened the door. As soon as the children entered she shouted: 'Children you can't scream in here, or we'll get a headache'. The little girls initially behaved acceptably but soon began screaming and then Ilene repeated in a higher tone: 'Girls, what did I say? You must not shout in here'.*

(Excerpt from field notes)

It also often happened that the parents would intervene to reprimand their children for playing in ways they did not judge appropriate for the place. Nevertheless, for them the play centre is a great space: it is as safe as a domestic space, it is 'family style' – as many mothers told me in describing it – children have their snack 'like they do at home' and there are many adults around to keep things safe, even if it is 'outside home'. Moreover, it gives parents the opportunity 'to see how their children play with other children', as one mother told me during an interview. In this sense, we can propose that if public space is rhetorically constructed as unsafe and dangerous compared to private space, play centres are constructed following the ideal representation of the child's room as the safest place for a growing child. It is in this mixture of security, children's right to play, family atmosphere, control and protection, that spatial justice and indeed spatial injustice, from the children's point of view, is expressed through the medium of the play centre: a place designed for children but also functional in satisfying the adults' need to control them.

We should, however, spend a few more words on the characteristics of these adults. Since, as already stated, two types of adults exist in the play centre – the play-assistants and the parents – it is interesting to point out how this space is not just about child–adult relations, but also about adult–adult relations.[6] The children's experience must therefore be placed within a more heterogeneous framework of adult figures, which influence the interactions that take place within it. On the basis of the ethnographic observation carried out, it seems that the 'order of discourse', to use Foucault's words (1972), is established by the play-assistants not only with regard to the children, but also to the parents, who themselves need to be educated in their role as parents. For their part, the parents often appear to autonomously take on a subaltern position during their time at the play centre, granting, as it were, the play-assistants' greater capacity to play with their children. And it is through the meaning attributed to play within this space that the implicit visions of the adults and the potential spaces of conflict between these figures may be discovered. While to the parents play seems an activity which concerns children and in which, therefore, precisely because it is placed within a didactic horizon, it is preferable that they should be accompanied by expert adult figures; for the educators play has instead a 'total' educational function. They feel that each parent, in order to be adequate, should carry out the activity of play with his/her child and, given the absence of the parents, themselves perform it in an almost subsidiary manner. Play is therefore constantly suspended between a position of major or minor interest depending on the educational importance which is accorded to it.

What is at stake, therefore, is the adult's 'face', by which I mean his/her success in performing his/her role within an implicit contest with the other adult figure over who holds the most legitimate knowledge of childhood (Oakley, 1994). All this often happens to the detriment of the meaning children themselves attribute to play and, it must be noted, to his/her own 'face' in a play situation with his/her peers. To summarise, in the case observed, the heterogeneity of the adult group contains a potential conflict when play is considered as an activity of 'greater interest' inasmuch as its end is to develop specific competences in the child; on the other hand, this heterogeneity lessens when the children's activities are considered (and managed) as activities of 'minor interest', when, that is, they are self-managed by the children.

In this case we may state that a perspective that pays due attention to the generational dimension in reading a space such as the play centre constitutes a valid interpretative lens. It highlights, through a relational approach, the role and the agency of the subjects, but especially, through a categorical approach, it reveals the dimensions of social stratification and the power disparities related to generational status in the use of a specific space (Wyness, 2015).

Questioning children's play and place in space

Today Eleonora and Giada went into the play room called 'soft space'. They started to play pretending that the big pool was the sea, or a place full of water, where in turn they each pretended they were drowning. They placed themselves at the corner of the pool submerged by the small balls and stretching out their hands towards their playmate, shouted 'Sister, help me!'. This was done four, five times. Then they took some little puppets and asked me to guard them while they ran around the room and jumped inside the pool. In particular, there was a dog puppet that Giada used, as I observed many times, like a real dog and other times, as if it were a rope to give to her friend as she was drowning.

At one point Giada turned to me and said 'You keep it, mummy', leaving the little dog to me. I nodded as a sign of agreement, perceiving the game she wanted to play. After a while she turned to Myriam (the play-assistant) and said to her 'Mummy, keep it'. Myriam replied 'yes' in a low voice, but when Giada called her 'Mum' twice, she asked Giada very seriously 'Why are you calling me Mummy?' And Giada immediately answered 'It's only pretend!'

(Excerpt from field notes)

If, as maintained by Bateson (1972), games are to be played accepting the uncertainty of crossing the borders of reality and moving into another field where different rules hold, it could be asserted that the play-assistants actually display an attitude of *not* wanting to play or even an inability to play another role with other rules. When one plays, all the participants assume they are sharing the illusion produced by play, which can only be confirmed by joining it. In my fieldwork experience, the two girls, after having introduced me into the frame of play, also tried to include the play-assistant, Myriam, telling her 'Mummy, you keep it'; however, the second time she was called 'Mummy', she broke the illusion by asking 'Why are you calling me Mummy?'.

'Play creates a framework for behaviours' and every framework implies a certain 'style of behaviour' (Bateson, 1972 p. 36). Giada's ready response, 'It's only pretend', reveals not only her knowledge of the framework but also her capacity to take on one role and then return to her original one, creating and recreating new meanings for the interaction. Myriam, on the contrary, in showing her inability to disengage from her main role as educator, behaves as an agent of a fixed culture that she has to *transmit* to the children; a culture where 'the adults must act as an adult' and where it is not educative if a child calls you 'Mummy' if you are not his/her mother (the reality principal). Redl, analysing the ways in which play 'can be spoiled', claims that an 'activity can lose its traits of play both for an excessive degree of proximity to the real world as well as for an excessive distance' (in Bateson, 1956, p. 143). In the case observed, the play-assistant 'spoiled' the play not only by not being able to keep her distance from the reality but also by wanting to reaffirm it.

Play overturns the adult–child generational order, it creates disorder in this order. 'To play the game' means precisely this: accepting the loss of certainty that your own mask gives you, with all the guarantees and the status linked to it, and adopting a new, completely unknown mask. By not playing with the children, the play-assistant refused the creative value and the potential of play to change the generational order internal to the play centre. As stated by Bateson 'almost every activity people do can be play. It is the attitude they adopt that denotes it as a play' (1956, p. 142).

During my fieldwork I rarely saw the play-assistants playing with the children, most of the time they were concerned with designing the space for children to play but they never really entered into the play-frame created by the children. It is not a question of 'not being an adult' but of playing your own adulthood differently, paying attention to 'the relational processes whereby people come to be known as children, and whereby children and childhood acquire certain characteristics' (Mayall, 2002, p. 27) and, we might add, whereby other people come to be known as adults.

During play the risk is that of questioning adult features and the position of power linked to adult roles. This is the reason why assistants adopt an 'educated play' with children, whose risks have already been assessed and whose objectives are pre-determined. However, if play continues to be educative and to be interpreted only as an educative tool, the risk is that we may lose the potential to construct a different generational order, one which may guarantee greater fairness and equality for children.

Today, the experience of playing is spatially and temporally fixed within special places designed for leisure time, and it is misrepresented in adult life and even more so in the child's world when, as emerges from the arguments of 'professional carers', it is linked to ideologies which interpret play as a means of anticipating adult roles and capacities. Ironically, play is mystified precisely in those places which have been designed for play because it is here that such a significant attempt is made to force it into one single concept or dimension that can never fully represent its multiple facets. This is the same process to which childhood itself seems to be subjected, progressively controlled as it is by training curricula designed to create and care for the citizen of the future. Thus a space *for* children seems to express in spatial terms the denial of childhood because it confines the child to a restrained and functional world, in preparation for his/her future and not simply in order to experience the present in itself, here and now. While often presented as services of promotion and expression of children's right to the city, I wonder whose rights exactly these regulated spatial segments of city are promoting. What space is left for children growing up in a risk society – one which has projected onto them all its anxieties and social phobias – to run the risk of doing something unexpected?

According to Fink (2008) to play is a 'fundamental existential phenomenon'. Unlike 'the other existential facts of our life, [play] is not directed toward a final aim, on the contrary it contrasts with the aspirations of the future that press on and afflict our very life' (Rovatti, 2008, p. xi).[7] Play has an aim, but this aim is internal to itself, it doesn't refer to other things and 'when we play "with the aim" of reinforcing our body, [...], or of reaching a state of good health, the play is immediately misrepresented and transformed into an exercise of something else' (Fink, 2008, p. 18). So, we could say that structured play is no longer play because it eradicates play from this dimension of eternal present and drives it into the instrumental flow of everyday life.

Children's play is not only, as is commonly affirmed, a way of attaining and experimenting with adult competences, but it is rather a resource to be used by children in their everyday life activities in the peer culture (Corsaro, 2009). Therefore play is not a fiction that children display for other reasons but it is a *way of being* and a way of constructing their unique culture.

An example of an adult attempt to translate children's activities into a language adults themselves are familiar with is the interpretation of role play as a 'means' for the social and emotional development of children. Kids do not, however, simply imitate adult models in their role play; rather, they continually elaborate and embellish adult models in order to address their own concerns (Corsaro, 1992). Engaging in role play is for children one of the routines within which they live and construct their peer cultures, which are not separate from the adult world. Whether taking on imaginary or real roles (teachers, mothers, cash clerks, etc.) playing is for children a way of enacting one of the many *selves* they can play; selves that are no less artificial than the ones taken on as sons and daughters, siblings or students in everyday life.

To conclude, in the play centre children's spatial agency exists but it is limited by the adults' concern to maintain this place in such a way as they imagine and assume is for the children's good.

Conclusion

The question we should ask ourselves is therefore what kind of play are these 'institutions for playing' promoting? Are they promoting children's play, where the children are the only ones who can infuse sense into their actions, or the play designed by adults as an educative experience, a play deriving from a modern ideology that divides the world into play and work, and limits children's experiences to the play-side of life alone?

This subdivision also mystifies children's experience through a constant devaluation of the very activity of playing (Goffman, 1961), commonly represented as something of low importance and insignificant compared with other activities (Thorne, 1993). Play is 'sociability' (Simmel, 1949) but it is also a very serious activity where power and recognition are themselves *at play*. However, when this activity is developed under the supervision, and sometimes with the participation, of adults, the play patterns change on account of the inter-generational dynamics between children and adults.

In particular, through the significant development of after-school clubs, leisure clubs, play centres, sport clubs and similar environments, we are facing a profound change in play configuration because we have moved from play as a child's form of appropriation of the urban space to play centres as a way of *expropriating* children's spatial freedom, even if discursively sustained as places designed *for* children. The play centre thus conceived runs the risk of promoting a merely fictional idea of play and of childhood. This fiction is functional to the detachment of adult space from children's spaces but, above all, to keeping children in a subordinate position, not only in terms of their diminished spatial power but also in terms of political and economical power. In other words, children's spatiality is interstitial, something that just 'happens' when caregivers turn away momentarily and do not stand in front of the child closely watching what she/he is doing. A different space can therefore happen if adults change their idea of children, and learn to consider them not only as young people 'in need' but as active agents capable of expressing their views and even of contributing to a change in their own and in the adults' world. Or even better, a different space can happen if adults change their views about themselves and their role with respect to children; if they recognise, in other words, not only the heterogeneity of adults (parents, and within this group, fathers and mothers, caregivers, play-assistants, teachers and so on) but also of the ways in which an adult may be a parent or, as in this case, a child-assistant. Children's spatiality is not therefore simply tied to the presence/absence of adults but rather to the way in which the adults themselves perceive their adulthood based on their vision of what constitutes a 'proper adulthood', a 'proper childhood' and a proper 'adult–child relationship'.

Only a change in perspective may produce a new way of framing children's activities, which, instead of affirming what children should be or do, should question our much too solid convictions about and conceptions of children. It is these convictions and conceptions that give rise to social inequalities and produce patterns of inter-generational injustice between children and adults.

Notes

1. I decide here not to speak about children's needs but about what I think are more properly termed children's desires as a way to draw attention to an issue that is often forgotten in adults' agendas: children are not only people 'in need' but possessed of wishes independent of their condition of necessity (see also Moss et al., 2000).

2. The research project was first presented to and discussed with the director of the play centre and the team of play-assistants who, after approving it with no substantial changes, submitted the proposal to the parents as an additional activity that the association wished to host, given its scientific relevance and the authorisation granted by the University of Padua for this part of my doctoral research. The second step was to present the research to the group of parents, though it was clear that their consent had already been given to the play centre team. During the meeting I explained the aim of the research and my way of participating in it, distributed a schematic leaflet outlining the process, and answered their questions, mostly of a pragmatic nature (duration of the project, number of hours I would be present and possible usefulness of the research for dealing with educational 'problems' in their relationship with their children). The children, with their parents' consent, received a brief oral presentation of the research. I was first introduced by the play-assistants as a 'researcher', and I then explained, in very basic terms given their young age, who I was, what a researcher does, why I was there and what I would be doing with them, that is 'spending time with them' and 'joining in with all the activities'. No video recording took place during the participant observation and this aspect reduced the level of formality in gaining access to the field, and indeed facilitated it. There is no room here for a discussion of field access procedures with children in the Italian context; without wishing to generalise, one might state that, compared to the British context there is a prevalence of trust between the researcher and his/her interlocutors over the procedural aspect played out at the institutional level. The procedure is less rigidly codified, with each field of research dictating its formal and informal rules for field access, especially when the research is ethnographic. In this specific case the play centre acted as guarantor both in the initial phase and throughout the research period, with all the opportunities but also the constraints that this may naturally engender.

3. Available at http://www.jssj.org/article/la-ville-et-la-justice-spatiale/. Accessed 11 December 2014.

4. I am aware of the intersectionality approach (Crenshaw, 1989) and of all the differences (of gender, class, race, ethnicity, religion and so on) among children that intersect with the age difference (see also Thorne, 2004), but here I wish rather to stress the age difference as a marker of distinction which can create disadvantages for younger people compared to adults.

5. This is my translation from Italian to English.

6. It would also be worthwhile to reflect on how this is an essentially female space, of mothers and female play-assistants. This confirms what has already been stated in the literature (Alanen, 1994, 1998; Mayall, 2002), that women continue to be the depositories of the care and education of children even outside the domestic and familiar space, and that play itself, we might say, is a 'female question'. Leisure, women and children share the same stigma of minority or of being of minor interest. A male-connoted gender configuration of adults emerges, at least in the Italian

context, when we move into the field of children's sport, where the object
is no longer leisure but rather embryonic forms of agonism guided by predominantly male trainers (e.g. in Italian the English word 'mister' is often
used when referring to the trainer).
7. My translation from an essay written in Italian.

References

Aitken, C. S. (2001) *Geography of Young People. The Morally Contested Spaces of Identity*, London: Routledge.
Alanen, L. (1994) 'Gender and Generation. Feminism and the "Child Question" ', in J. Qvortrup et al. (eds) *Childhood Matters. Social Theory, Practice and Politics*, Averbury: Aldershot, pp. 27–42.
Alanen, L. (1998) 'Children and the Family Order: Constraints and Competencies', in I. Hutchby and J. Moran-Ellis (eds) *Children and Social Competence. Arenas of Action*, London: Falmer, pp. 29–45.
Alanen, L. and Mayall, B. (eds) (2001) *Conceptualizing Child–Adult Relations*, London: RoutledgeFalmer.
Ariès, P. (1979) *Centuries of Childhood*, London: Penguin.
Bateson, G. (1956) 'The Message "This Is Play" ', in B. Schaffner (ed.) *Group Processes: Transactions of the Second Conference*, New York: Josiah Macy, Jr. Foundation, pp. 145–242.
Bateson, G. (1972) *Steps to an Ecology of Mind*, Chicago: The University of Chicago Press.
Christensen, P. and O' Brien, M. (eds) (2003) *Children in the City. Home, Neighborhood and Community*, London and New York: RoutledgeFalmer.
Corsaro, W. A. (1992) 'Interpretive Reproduction in Children's Peer Cultures', *Social Psychology Quarterly*, 55, 160–172.
Corsaro, W. A. (1997) *The Sociology of Childhood*, Thousand Oaks: Pine Press.
Corsaro, W. A. (2009) 'Peer Culture', in J. Qvortrup, W. A. Corsaro and M.-S. Honig (eds) *The Palgrave Handbook of Childhood Studies*, Basingstoke: Palgrave Macmillan.
Crenshaw, K. (1989) 'Demarginalizing the Intersection of Race and Sex', in *University of Chicago Legal Forum*, pp. 139–167.
Cresswell, K. (1996) *In Place/Out of Place. Geography, Ideology and Transgression*, Minneapolis: University of Minnesota Press.
Dal Lago, A. and Rovatti, P. P. (1993) *Per gioco. Piccolo manuale dell'esperienza ludica*, Milano: Raffaello Cortina Editore.
Fink, E. (2008) *Oasi del gioco*, Milano: Raffaello Cortina Editore.
Foucault, M. (1972) *The Archaeology of Knowledge*, New York: Pantheon Books.
Goffman, E. (1961) *Encounters: Two Studies in the Sociology of Interaction. Fun in Games and Role Distance*, Indianapolis: Bobbs-Merrill.
Goffman, E. (1967), *Interaction Ritual: Essays on Face to Face Behaviour*, New York: Anchor Books.
Holloway, S. L. and Valentine, G. (eds) (2000) *Children's Geographies. Playing, Living, Learning*, London and New York: Routledge.

Holt, L. (2011) *Geographies of Children, Youth and Families. An International Perspective*, New York: Routledge.

Hörschelmann, K. and Colls, R. (2010) *Contested Bodies of Childhood and Youth*, Basingstoke and New York: Palgrave Macmillan.

Horton, J. and Kraftl, P. (2006) 'Not Just Growing Up, but Going On: Materials, Spacings, Bodies, Situations', *Children Geographies*, 4 (3), 259–276.

James, A. (2009) 'Agency', in J. Qvortrup, W. A. Corsaro and M. S. Honig (eds) *The Palgrave Handbook of Childhood Studies*, Basingstoke: Palgrave Macmillan, pp. 34–45.

James, A. and Prout, A. (eds) (1990) *Constructing and Reconstructing Childhood*, Basingstoke: Falmer Press.

James, A., Jenks, C. and Prout, A. (1998) *Theorizing Childhood*, Oxford: Polity Press.

Jenks, C. (ed.) (1982) *The Sociology of Childhood. Essential Readings*, London: Batsford.

Jenks, C. (1996), *Childhood*, London: Routledge.

Jenks, C. (2005) 'Journey Into Spaces', *Childhood*, 12 (4), 419–424.

Lee, N. (2001) *Childhood and Society: Growing Up in an Age of Uncertainty*, Milton Keynes: Open University Press.

Lefebvre, H. (1991) *The Production of Space*, Oxford: Blackwell.

Mayall, B. (2002) *Towards a Sociology for Childhood: Thinking From Children's Lives*, Maidenhead: Open University Press.

McKendrick, J. H., Bradford, M. G. and Fielder, A. V. (2000) 'Time for a Party! Making Sense of the Commercialization of Leisure Space for Children', in S. L. Holloway and G. Valentine (eds) *Children's Geographies: Playing, Living, Learning*, London and New York: Routledge, pp. 100–116.

Moss, P., Dillon, J. and Statham, J. (2000) ' "The Child in Need" and "the Rich Child": Discourses, Constructions and Practice', *Critical Social Policy*, 20 (2), 233–254.

Moss, P. and Petrie, P. (2002) *From Children's Services to Children's Spaces: Public Policy, Children and Childhood*, London: Routledge-Falmer.

Oakley, A. (1994) 'Women and Children First and Last. Parallels and Differences between Children's and Women's Studies', in B. Mayall (ed.) *Children's Childhoods: Observed and Experienced*, London: Falmer Press, pp. 13–32.

Olwig, K. F. and Gulløv, E. (eds) (2003) *Children's Places: Cross-Cultural Perspective*, London: Routledge.

Perrot, M. (2011) *Storia delle camere*, Palermo: Sellerio.

Philippoupolos, A. (2014) 'The Movement of Spatial Justice', *Mondi Migranti*, 1, 7–19.

Puwar, N. (2004) *Space Invaders. Race, Gender and Bodies Out of Place*, Oxford and New York: Berg.

Qvortrup, J. (1991) *Childhood as a Social Phenomenon. An Introduction to a Series of National Reports*, Vienna: European Centre for Social Welfare Policy and Research.

Rasmussen, K. (2004) 'Places for Children – Children's Places', *Childhood*, 11 (2), 156–173.

Rovatti, P. P. (2008) 'Prefazione', in E. Fink (ed.) *Oasi del gioco*, Milano: Raffaello Cortina.

Satta, C. (2014) 'Una città giusta è una città a misura di bambini? Note critiche su un immaginario urbano', in *Mondi Migranti*, 1, 83–99.

Simmel, G. (1949) 'The Sociology of Sociability', *American Journal of Sociology*, 55 (3), 254–261.

Simmel, G. (1971) 'The Stranger', in G. Simmel (ed.) *On Individuality and Social Forms*, Chicago and London: University of Chicago Press.

Soja, E. W. (2009) *The City and Spatial Justice*. September 2009. Available at http://www.jssj.org/article/la-ville-et-la-justice-spatiale/ accessed 11 December 2014.

Soja, E. W. (2010) *Seeking Spatial Justice*, London: University of Minnesota press.

Thorne, B. (1993) *Gender Play: Girls and Boys in School*, Buckingham: Rutgers University Press.

Thorne, B. (2004) 'Editorial: Theorizing Age and Other Differences', *Childhood*, 11 (4), 403–408.

Tuan, Y. F. (1974) 'Space and Place. Humanistic Perspectives', *Progress in Geography*, 6, 211–252.

Valentine, G. (2004) *Public Space and the Culture of Childhood*, Hants: Ashgate.

Wyness, M. (2015) *Childhood*, Cambridge: Polity Press.

Zeiher, H. (2003) 'Shaping Daily Life in Urban Environments', in P. Christensen and M. O' Brien (eds) *Children in the City*, pp. 66–81.

Author Index

Subject Index

Printed and bound by CPI Group (UK) Ltd, Croydon, CR0 4YY